THE
UNITY OF MANKIND IN
GREEK THOUGHT

THE
UNITY OF MANKIND
IN
GREEK THOUGHT

BY

H. C. BALDRY

Professor of Classics in the University of Southampton

CAMBRIDGE
AT THE UNIVERSITY PRESS
1965

CAMBRIDGE UNIVERSITY PRESS
Cambridge, New York, Melbourne, Madrid, Cape Town, Singapore, São Paulo, Delhi

Cambridge University Press
The Edinburgh Building, Cambridge CB2 8RU, UK

Published in the United States of America by Cambridge University Press, New York

www.cambridge.org
Information on this title: www.cambridge.org/9780521118118

First published 1965
This digitally printed version 2009

A catalogue record for this publication is available from the British Library

Library of Congress Catalogue Card Number: 65–14356

ISBN 978-0-521-04091-4 hardback
ISBN 978-0-521-11811-8 paperback

China's just on the edge of Cookham

STANLEY SPENCER

CONTENTS

vii

CHAPTER I

INTRODUCTION

MAN, *anthrōpos*, was the centre of the world for the Greeks, and a review of all they thought about him would involve discussion of most of their literature and art. This book has no such wide scope or ambitious aim. Its theme is not the whole Hellenic conception of man, but the development among the Greeks of ideas about one aspect of humanity—the unity of mankind; an aspect which never had more than a minor place in their thought, although it may seem all-important in the twentieth century A.D.

In our own day human unity is generally seen as a practical problem. We take as a self-evident fact the existence of the human race as a distinct species, an aggregate made up of individuals whose present numbers are approximately known; and with almost equal readiness most of us draw the inference that between all these representatives of *homo sapiens* there is some sort of kinship or fellowship which should influence their behaviour towards each other. 'One world', 'the human community', 'the brotherhood of man', are phrases on everybody's lips, and their theoretical validity is hardly called in question. The crucial issue, as we see it, is the gap between theory and practice: the paradox of a human race acknowledged in theory to be a single family, yet split by divisions of creed and colour which threaten its destruction. The solution is commonly sought not in reconsideration of the basic theory, but in the practical field of organisation, and attempts at practical world co-operation become more and more a characteristic feature of our time.

The Greeks, of course, knew nothing of all this. The conception of human fellowship as a practical problem scarcely entered their thoughts; still less, any organisational means of solving it.

Although modern civilisation owes them much, the United Nations Assembly and the disarmament conference are not part of the debt. In their thought the unity of mankind had quite another place, and my main concern in this book is not with any practical conclusions which they drew from it, but with the development of the notion itself and the changes of mental outlook which that development involved; to some extent, with the movement of their minds towards a position which we—partly thanks to them—take for granted.

My subject, in short, is the emergence of an idea—or rather, perhaps, of an attitude of mind. It is not a matter of tracing the changing use of any one Greek term, although a number of words —homonoia, philanthrōpia and others—play their part in the story. The process with which we are concerned was a far more complex and gradual one than has sometimes been supposed. The concept of the unity of mankind has been treated as a doctrine 'discovered' by a single individual, and variously attributed to Antiphon, Alexander, Zeno, and other rival claimants. But the history of thought is not so simple. The true picture is a long and complicated chain of development to which many individuals contributed, including some—Plato and Aristotle, for example— who are often denied a place in this company. Apart from those who made contributions of reasoned and stated doctrine, there were many others whose beliefs had implications, important though only half realised, for the growth of the same theme; while behind and beneath the movement of conscious thought lay the background of unconscious assumptions, already in existence when our evidence begins, and continually changing as the new ideas of one generation were absorbed into the accepted mental outlook of the next. After all, the very use of the word 'man' implies some underlying notion, however unrealised, of a unified type to which the word refers; and the whole process with which we are dealing may be seen not as the building of a doctrine, but as the ever-changing elaboration and enrichment of the content of a concept which was in existence from the first.

The evidence for this theme is as complex as the development of the theme itself, and is to be found at many points in our whole knowledge of the Greek world. Much might be inferred from Greek institutions and the events of Greek history, just as today conclusions about the real strength of our belief in human fellowship might well be drawn from the successes and failures of the United Nations. A study of slavery from this point of view would be fruitful, or a survey of the relations between outlying Greek communities and their 'barbarian' neighbours, or of the various attempts at combination between the Greek states themselves. However, in the present book the limitations of the author and the extent of the subject have combined to prevent such a wide range of view: I have confined myself to the literary evidence, bringing in some slight account of institutions or events only where it seemed essential for the understanding of the documents I wanted to cite. It is significant that no single Greek work deals specifically with the subject of human unity or mankind as a whole, and authors' opinions on the matter have to be sought out in writings on other themes. The principal source, of course, is the philosophers; but from Homer onwards there is relevant material in all sections of Greek literature. Poets, orators, historians, pamphleteers, medical writers—all in one passage or another throw some light on the development of the idea of the unity of man. A great deal of the evidence, unfortunately, is fragmentary, or available only at second hand or worse; and inevitably some pages here and there have been given up to discussion of the reliability and the interpretation of the evidence itself.

Hellenic civilisation in its early days provided far from fertile soil for the growth of the concept of the unity of mankind. In spite of the Greeks' deep concern with man and his destiny, they knew less than a modern schoolchild about the material facts of the human situation. They had comparatively little knowledge of the physical make-up of man or the other animal species. They knew almost nothing of his history—very little even of that brief segment of it which constituted their own past. From the small area of land and sea familiar to them they looked out upon a largely unknown world. Their chief guide to man's nature was observation of him as they saw him within the narrow limits of their own environment; and although this brought them profound understanding of some aspects of life, it was not likely to lead them towards the idea of human unity. On the contrary, the pattern of living which geography and history gave them was a natural breeding-ground for prejudice and division, and its fruit was an outlook which put far more emphasis on the differences than on the kinship between men.

Two modern curses they were spared—violent nationalism and colour prejudice. But hostility towards the outsider was one of the most marked features of Greek life, whether it was felt by the citizens of one city against all other Greeks, or by Ionian against Dorian, or by all those who spoke Greek against 'barbarians' who babbled in unintelligible tongues. Within the unity of the city-state there was again division. The natural difference between the sexes was widened by the inferior status and the seclusion of women. Between slave and free lay a gulf which most Greeks accepted as a fact of life just as unchangeable as sex or race. Less sharply defined, but little less widespread or persistent, was the antithesis within the citizen body itself between high and low, 'good' and 'bad' (as the 'good' called it); a distinction based first on birth and later on wealth, which affected the life of society in many ways besides the constant political conflict which was characteristic of the city-state.

Among these unpromising circumstances it may well seem unlikely that any realisation of the concept of universal human unity or fellowship would emerge. But time brought changes, and the keen Greek intellect was not slow to move towards fresh theoretical conclusions. The human species became more clearly distinguished from gods on the one hand and animals on the other. Growing geographical knowledge, which at first only emphasised the diversity of mankind, led in the course of the years to the idea of a total human population of the habitable world, though this remained a far more hazy notion than in these days of the camera and the aeroplane. Most important of all, the movement of history brought modification, sometimes even a breakdown, of the accepted prejudices and discriminations—a process which necessarily has a large place in this book, for it is complementary to the growth of the idea of unity, and the acid test of the strength of its impact on the mind. The extent of the change must not be exaggerated. To a large degree it consisted in a shifting of the dividing lines: the antithesis between Greek and 'barbarian' gave way to the distinction between the possessors of Hellenic culture and those who remained outside it; in the eyes of a minority at any rate, wisdom took the place of birth or wealth as the mark of the 'good' members of society in comparison with the 'bad'. All the modifications that came about were primarily adjustments of mental attitude, and had no great practical result. Yet with all these limitations it remains remarkable that even on a theoretical level the divided and conflict-ridden Greeks moved so far in the direction of the idea of a common fellowship linking all mankind.

All this, of course, is only part of a much longer story. Thought about man did not begin with the Greeks, and if I have taken Homer as my starting-point and said nothing of Eastern ideas which may have had some influence in Greece, I do not imply that no such ideas or influence existed; my only claim is that it is possible to treat the development of the concept of human unity among the Greeks as a single connected process, understandable in itself, and this is what I have made my theme.

More difficult was the choice of a place to stop, for it is obvious that the development of ideas which I am tracing continues without interruption through the Roman period, and has a sequel in more modern times which is still working itself out today. That I should include Cicero within the scope of the book, but not discuss Philo or St Augustine, may seem like the result of tossing a coin or mere inability to go further. In this last explanation there is indeed some truth, but I believe a rational case of sorts can be put forward for making Cicero the end of the section of the story with which I have tried to deal. He comes into the picture not so much in his own right, but rather as our chief witness for views of mankind common among educated people in his own and earlier generations, and in particular for the doctrines of Panaetius, Posidonius and Antiochus; and these thinkers, though greatly influenced by the new situation which Roman domination had brought into being, nevertheless belong to the same essentially Greek line of thought which goes back to Homer. The line, of course, does not end there; but after this point it becomes interwoven with strands from other sources—Hebraic and Christian, for example—which in their turn need to be traced back to non-Greek beginnings.

It will be evident that my aim in this book has been limited to a review of the Greek prelude to Roman and Christian ideas of the unity of man. I hope that this may seem to have sufficient relevance to the modern situation to be of some interest to others besides classical scholars, and for this reason I have tried to avoid anything that might make my account unintelligible to those who cannot read Greek or are unfamiliar with the details of Greek history. All quotations are given in translation (except where otherwise stated, my own) and Greek words are mentioned only here and there, where their use seemed necessary.

At the same time, I have for the most part resisted the temptation to apply modern terminology to ancient theories or to suggest modern parallels. In treating a subject which is so alive today nothing is easier than to read back twentieth-century ideas into documents which in reality have quite another meaning, or to seek views comparable with our own in situations where they did not, and probably could not, arise—to make a Sophist of the fifth century B.C. anticipate modern internationalism, or see Alexander as the first champion of the idea of world government. Some sort of equivalents can no doubt be found in antiquity for 'Western civilisation', 'international brotherhood', 'co-existence' and many of the other stock phrases of contemporary political argument, and the ancient world may appear in a more vivid light if we see it as anticipation of our own. But the modern terms do not really fit, the parallels are never completely comparable, and the usual result of both is to blur, rather than to illuminate, the historical facts. In some discussions of Greek thought about mankind I believe this line of approach has already led to a good deal of distortion, and my aim has been to discuss the ancient evidence in its ancient context, leaving to the reader the question of its relation to the modern world.

CHAPTER II

FROM HOMER TO HIPPOCRATES

THE HOMERIC PATTERN

THE *Iliad* and *Odyssey* are still our earliest sources of information on Greek thought about man. It is true that archaeological discoveries and the decipherment of Linear B tablets have now enabled us to form an increasingly detailed picture of Minoan and Mycenaean civilisation, including some conception of the actual relationships and divisions which existed within society perhaps as early as 1500 B.C. But so far nothing has come to light from which we can discover what ideas these pre-Homeric Greeks held on the human race and its place in the scheme of things. This can be learned only from literature, and therefore—until some fresh discovery changes the situation—from the rich store of evidence that the *Iliad* and *Odyssey* contain.

A remarkable feature of the Homeric picture of mankind is its uniformity. I do not mean, of course, that there is any lack of individual variety among the people of the two epics, or that everyone is on the same level in the society which they portray. The picture is uniform—more so, indeed, than most that we find in later Greek literature—in the sense that it depicts a single pattern within which all, or almost all, human beings have a place. There is no explicit statement of this unity in either poem; but as an unconscious assumption it is present throughout both, and provides a basis for that deep understanding of the common human lot which gives them much of their greatness.

In Homer's world there are many cities and many peoples, but nowhere is it suggested that any group which can rightly be called human lies outside the common pattern. There is no contrast between foreign goats and Achaean sheep. The pattern applies equally to both sides in the Trojan War: the Trojans, who in later literature became the prototype of the 'barbarian' enemies of Greece, are seen here with the same eyes as the attacking Achaeans.[1] Hector is no less a hero than Achilles, Priam fully as noble as Agamemnon. Difference of speech does not form the sharp dividing line which it later became, although there are a number of references to it in the poems. Troy has many allies with different tongues, so that while the Achaeans move into battle in silence the Trojans are like a great flock of bleating sheep: 'for they did not all have the same way of speech or a single tongue, but their language was mixed, and they were brought from many lands' (IV. 437–8).* Odysseus describes Crete as an island of countless men, with ninety cities: 'and they have a medley of different tongues' (19. 175). The adjective *allothroos*, 'speaking a strange language', is a regular epithet of foreigners in the *Odyssey*. Yet there is no suggestion in Homer of the deep gulf which later centuries created between Greek-speaking peoples and users of 'barbarian' ways of speech. The word *barbaros* does not occur in these epics except in the compound adjective *barbarophōnoi* applied to the Carians in the *Iliad*, where it probably refers to the way in which they spoke Greek.[2] It is significant that Homer does not appear to distinguish between differences of language and differences of dialect.

Even peoples who lie further afield and come incidentally into the story are cast in the same mould as the rest of humanity. Although the Egyptians are *allothrooi* (3. 302), neither this nor any consideration of race or colour causes any special antagonism to them in Odysseus' story of his visit to Egypt (14. 257 ff.). The Phoenicians receive harsher treatment, behind which may lie antipathies roused by trade rivalry between them and the Greeks. In two passages of the *Odyssey* they are greedy tricksters, using theft and kidnapping and slave-dealing as means to wealth; but

* Roman figures for book-numbers refer to the *Iliad*, Arabic numerals to the *Odyssey*.

in another Odysseus tells a story in which they deal fairly by him and refrain from stealing his goods when they leave him on shore.3 Although Homer comes nearer to prejudice against another people here than anywhere else, even the Phoenicians' villainy is an aspect of the one human pattern, and their commercial methods do not put them beyond the pale. Yet more remote from the centre of the Homeric world, but still part of the same picture, are distant peoples like the Abii of the extreme north, 'the most well-ordered' (or 'civilised'?) of men, and the 'blameless' Ethiopians, 'Burnt-Faced-Men', of the far south, whose colour does not prevent them from being favourites of the gods.4

It is true that in the regions described by Odysseus in his story of his travels, which later Greek writers and some modern scholars have sought to identify with places in the eastern or central Mediterranean, but which really belong to folk-lore or fiction, there are monsters and other strange beings with some human characteristics whose conduct *does* place them beyond the pale, outside the general pattern of humanity just as they are outside normal geography. But these are exceptions that prove the rule, since for the most part they are described as not human at all. The huge Laestrygones are 'not like men, but like giants' (10. 120). The land of the Cyclops is 'bereft of men' and feeds innumerable wild goats, 'for the tread of men does not scare them away'. Polyphemus is 'a mighty monster, not like a man that eats bread'.5 These passages are the first expression of a conception which recurs in one form or another at many points in the development of Greek thought about mankind: the idea that only those who conform to certain standards can properly be called men or included within the unity of the human race.

The problem of the causes of the uniformity of the Homeric picture is one to which we are not likely to find a complete answer. It is not a reflection of the general contemporary situation in the eastern Mediterranean area: the period in which the *Iliad* and *Odyssey* are commonly supposed to have reached their present form seems to have been a time of growing differentiation rather than uniformity. If there were more certainty about the environment in which the poems took shape, study of the circumstances of that particular place and time might indicate historical reasons for such an outlook—conditions, for example, in which contact with foreigners was limited to neighbouring peoples who did not differ greatly from the Greeks. Another line of thought is that the poems still preserve some memory of the wider and more 'international' Mycenaean world; but the gulf between their picture of society and the bureaucratic organisation implied by the Linear B tablets leads one to doubt whether on a wider scale they echo the relationships of Mycenaean times. Whatever the contribution of historical origins or traditions, the reader of the *Iliad* and the *Odyssey* cannot escape the conclusion that primarily their unified picture of man is a product of the poetic imagination, working all the more freely because it is unhampered by geographical or anthropological or historical knowledge. What we have here is not an intellectual concept of human unity such as that towards which later Greek thought groped its way, and which our own century tries to realise in organisation, but rather the fruit of the poetic vision of the composer or composers of these epics, naïve in its assumption that as men live in one place, so will they live elsewhere, yet profound in its awareness of the network of circumstance and destiny in which all human beings are caught, in spite of the differences between them.

The main elements in the Homeric pattern are of two kinds. Some are characteristics common to all human beings. Others are divisions, not geographical or racial but social, which recur in all communities and so also maintain uniformity between them. Both call for some attention at this point, if only because we find here in simple form most of the chief features which marked the Greek picture of the human race in later centuries. No doubt this continuity was partly due to the influence of the Homeric poems themselves; but even so it is remarkable how far the development of Greek thought about mankind, for all its originality, kept within the general framework of habits of mind already taken for granted in the *Iliad* and the *Odyssey*.

The features common to all men are indicated in the epithets which Homer constantly applies to them. His normal word for a human being is not *anthrōpos*, but 'mortal', *brotos* or *thnētos*: the chief characteristic which all men share, even an Achilles or an Odysseus, is that they must die. In many ways Homer's heroes are close to the gods. Zeus is 'father of men and gods'—a phrase pregnant with the two ideas, kinship with the divine and the brotherhood of man, which emerge to maturity in later centuries. But men are marked off from gods by the fact of death. 'Mortals' is their label not only in early epic, but in most Greek poetry, and it sets a stamp on them which persists throughout classical literature.

While their mortality distinguishes men from gods, other regular Homeric epithets separate them from the beasts. They are 'men that eat bread' (*siton edontes*): not eaters of grass, like grazing animals, nor of raw meat, like the Cyclops, but beings skilled in the growing and use of grain. In this phrase again there is a latent thought of great significance—that man is different from the animal world because he can develop the arts (*technai*), of which agriculture is one. Still more important is the thought implied in the adjective *audēentes*, which means 'using articulate speech'.[6] Men may speak different languages or dialects, but human speech, as opposed to mere animal noises, is common to them all. In view of the close link in the Greek mind between the spoken word and reasoning, both denoted by the one term *logos*, this epithet also points forward to one of the main elements in later Greek thinking about the nature of mankind: man is a talker, a creature that uses words.

No less frequent are adjectives which describe our common lot. Achaeans and Trojans alike are all wretched, pitiable beings (*deiloi*, *oizuroi*) in that the course of life is uncertain and death is inevitable. Besides constant use of these epithets and others with similar meaning, there are many places where Homer expresses the thought at greater length. Nothing is gained by lamenting our sorrows, says Achaean Achilles to Trojan Priam: 'This is the pattern the gods have woven for wretched mortals, to live in pain; but the gods themselves are free from troubles' (xxiv. 525–6). All men are at the mercy of the whims of heaven, Odysseus tells one of the wooers:

Of all the creatures that breathe and move upon the Earth, none that she rears is more feeble than man. He never thinks hard times will come later, as long as the gods give him prosperity and his limbs are nimble; yet when the blessed gods bring him sorrow, this too he bears, hard though he finds it, with long-suffering heart. Men's view of life on earth varies with the kind of day the father of men and gods sends them. (18. 129–37)

The thought that mankind are united at any rate in feebleness and misery haunts not only the *Iliad* and *Odyssey*, but all Greek poetry.

These are the main features of the Homeric picture that are shared by all members of the human race. Against them must be set the divisions within the pattern, common to all human societies and even reflected on Olympus. One dividing line, of course, is sex. Although there are noble portraits of women in the two poems—Andromache, Penelope, Alcinous' wife Arete, Nausicaa—it is assumed throughout that women are inferior to men and have a completely different station. 'Go to your part of the house', says the young Telemachus to his mother, 'and see to your own work, the loom and the distaff, and tell your maids to be busy with theirs. The bow shall be the men's concern, and especially mine. For I am the master in the house' (21. 350–3). Penelope obeys without question. 'Denied the right to a heroic way of life, to feats of prowess, competitive games, and leadership in organised activity of any kind, women worked, regardless of class', writes Mr M. I. Finley in *The World of Odysseus* (p. 78). The only exceptions are among the immortals: Athene, for example, has independence and initiative to which no mortal woman pretends.

More prominent in the poems, and equally taken for granted, is class division. To quote Finley again:

A deep horizontal cleavage marked the world of the Homeric poems. Above the line were the *aristoi*, literally the 'best people', the hereditary nobles who held most of the wealth and all the power, in peace as in war. Below were all the others, for whom there was no collective technical term, the multitude. The gap between the two was rarely crossed, except by the inevitable accidents of wars and raids.   (p. 56)

Distinctions between the groups on either side of this clear line are often blurred and may differ from place to place. The *aristoi* include both the kings and their nobles, but their relationship to each other is variable and often obscure. Among the multitude below the line are independent peasants, craftsmen, free servants of the nobles, hired labourers, and slaves; but the slave, usually called *dmōs*, not *doulos*, is not sharply distinguished from the rest as he is in later times, and on the whole his lot is better than that of the propertyless man who works for hire. Other groupings, such as the household, cut across the main division between the few and the many, the lords and the commons, but it is this that dominates the Homeric scene. It is this that gives such force to Achilles' description of the misery of life in Hades: 'Do not speak lightly to me of death, renowned Odysseus. Could I be on earth I would rather be another man's serf, in the house of a poor man with little to live on, than be king over all the dead.'[7] Better to 'cross the line' and become a mere labourer than to be even a royal ghost! When the suitor Eurymachus wants to insult the stranger who later proves to be Odysseus, he offers him work as a 'hired man' (18. 357 ff.); and later, when Penelope has promised to go with whichever of the wooers can string Odysseus' great bow and shoot through the twelve axes, she takes it for granted that the beggarly stranger cannot think of having her, even though he performs the feat (21. 316–22).

The most striking illustration of the gulf between high and low is Odysseus' behaviour in the *Iliad* when the Achaeans come near to sailing for home. He checks the nobles and men of note with a mild protest. 'But whenever he saw a man of the people and caught him shouting, he would strike him with his staff and rate him soundly. "You there," he would say, "sit still and listen to the words of others who are your betters. You have no courage for battle, no strength; you count for nothing in war or in council. We Achaeans cannot all be kings here"' (II. 198-203). When the commoner, Thersites, dares to take the floor, he is beaten for his insolence. He is a ludicrous figure: 'He was the ugliest man who had come to Troy. Bandy-legged he was, and lame in one foot. His shoulders were hunched round on his chest. His head narrowed to a point at the top, and the hair on it was thin' (II. 216-19). This is caricature. But Homer regularly assumes that there is a hereditary physical difference between the nobles and the multitude, a *natural* division separating them in bodily physique as well as in spirit and way of life. When Odysseus finds his father, Laertes, he is old and in rags, but still bears the stamp of his class. 'There is nothing of the slave to be seen', says his son, 'in your build or stature. You look like a king' (24. 252-3).

Here, as in other ways, the Homeric epics are only the first expression of an attitude which continues through most classical literature. The distinction between high and low, good and bad, worthy and unworthy, was given new meanings by later authors, but in one sense or another it was maintained by all, and had a profound effect on their thought about mankind.

Homer, then, sees the life of all men according to a single pattern. Human beings have in common the articulate speech and the skill which separate them from the beasts, and the inevitability of death and pitiable uncertainty of life that distinguish them from the gods. They are divided by differences of sex and of class; above all, by the cleavage between the 'best people' and the multitude. This Homeric picture reappears in the works of Hesiod, although it is seen from a different point of view. There are two points, however, at which the *Works and Days* goes beyond the *Iliad* and *Odyssey*. One is the idea that another, and a better, pattern is *possible*. There are glimpses of this conception in the *Odyssey*, but now it is elaborated in the story of the five races of man, five different versions of mankind: the present 'iron' race lives in conflict and hardship, but was there not once a time, in the days of the race of gold, when all men enjoyed ease and peace and happiness?

The other advance in thought by Hesiod relevant to our theme lies in what he has to say of *dikē*, conveniently translated 'justice', but perhaps nearer to 'the right' or 'good order'. Several passages in Homer imply that *dikē* is a characteristic of civilised man. Hesiod regards it as a quality shared by all humanity, a gift of Zeus which distinguishes men from beasts and enables them alone to live in peace and unity with one another: 'For the son of Kronos fixed this law for men, that fish and beasts and birds should devour one another, since there is no *dikē* in them; but to men he gave *dikē*, which is far the best' (276–80). Elsewhere, again carrying further a thought that makes a brief appearance in the *Odyssey*, he tells how the city of the just flourishes in a state of peace and prosperity reminiscent of the golden race.[8] *Dikē* is the way to unity and a better pattern of life, although Hesiod's vision of it does not extend beyond one imaginary city. We have here the germ of the idea that human nature is capable of a way of life which can end conflict and bring universal peace.

EXPANSION OF THE KNOWN WORLD

Recent views on the date of the poems ascribed to Homer and Hesiod have tended to narrow the time gap separating them from the next literature that survives in more than fragmentary form—the drama and choral lyric of the early fifth century B.C. But there is a wide difference between fifth-century writers and early epic in their conception of mankind. Their works reflect the results of a striking growth of geographical and anthropological knowledge, which had an impact on the Greek mind comparable with the effect of exploration on the Elizabethans. The known, or half-known, world has expanded far beyond its Homeric limits. Greek settlements have been established wherever a habitable and not too hostile coast is accessible to shipping: on the furthest shores of the Black Sea, in North Africa, at the mouth of the Rhone, on the eastern coast of Spain. Trade has carried Greek merchants and travellers far into lands of which Homer knows little or nothing. With the development of the Persian Empire, the Greek trader has made his way into Asia, at any rate as far as Susa. The foundation of Naucratis in the Nile Delta has provided a base for commercial intercourse with Egypt. Many of the new settlements round the fringes of the Mediterranean and the Black Sea have built up a flourishing trade with the hinterland, and made contact with peoples previously unheard of, and very different from themselves. In the remoter areas travellers' stories have told of peoples stranger still.

The natural result is a greatly increased awareness of the diversity of human life. No doubt there were many Greeks—probably the majority—whose knowledge of the world beyond the mountains or sea on their own horizon remained as limited as Hesiod's. Those affected by the new development, however, no longer saw mankind on a single pattern, but as a complex collection of different peoples, different in appearance, in language, in laws and customs. A striking illustration of the change is the philosopher-poet Xenophanes' assertion, in the latter part of the sixth century B.C., that each race has its own conception of the gods, modelled on its own appearance: 'The Ethiopians', he writes, 'think their gods have snub noses and black hair; the Thracians' gods are grey-eyed and red-haired' (fr. 16).*

The fifth century brought many expressions of the new knowledge and the new outlook in literary form. The earliest of which we know is the *Description of the World* by Hecataeus of Miletus: a kind of travel book, as far as we can judge from the many short

---

* Fragments from the Pre-Socratics are numbered as in Diels–Kranz, *Die Fragmente der Vorsokratiker* (6th ed., 1951). Other Pre-Socratic references are to the A sections of Diels–Kranz.

fragments, in which he set down all that he had seen or heard of foreign lands—their cities and peoples, their religion, their customs, their animal life. It may have been from Hecataeus that Aeschylus derived much of the miscellaneous information on these subjects which he brings into his plays; certainly the variety and strangeness of the remoter parts of the world and their inhabitants seem to have had a fascination for him, which must have been shared to some extent by his Athenian audience. The themes and settings of three of the seven surviving dramas take the minds of the spectators beyond the limits of Greece. The *Persians* carries us to the alien splendours of the Persian court; the *Prometheus*, to the wilds of Scythia; while the *Suppliants* presents at Argos the fifty daughters of Danaus in flight from Egypt, un-Hellenic in dress and language, yet seeking asylum on the ground of kinship with the Greeks. The contrast is accentuated by their dark skins: 'You are more like women of Libya,' says the king of Argos, 'not at all like those of our country' (279–80); and their pursuers, when they arrive, are several times described as black. But it is notable that here, as elsewhere in ancient literature, there is no suggestion of antipathy based specifically on colour: darkness of skin is only one of the elements in the strangeness of the picture as a whole.

As well as these three extant plays, a number of those now lost are shown by the fragments to have portrayed foreigners or described them. There is no reason to suppose that Aeschylus preferred myths involving the non-Greek world; but when his themes did take him to foreign lands, his vision of them was varied and particularised—far from the Homeric conception of humanity on a single pattern, and from the generalised 'barbarians' of later thought. 'His foreigners', writes Miss Helen Bacon, 'belong in a fully imagined world of many nations that extends in space from Colchis to the Pillars of Heracles, in time from Io to the present.'9 The same intense interest in other countries and their peoples, shared no doubt by many of the audience, is reflected in Aeschylus' use of foreign words and in many passages of the plays. He rarely misses an opportunity to

roll out a list of unfamiliar names, and sometimes may be sus-
pected of creating such opportunities where they are scarcely
justified by the needs of the play. Io is by no means irrelevant to
the plot of the *Prometheus* trilogy, but one of the poet's motives
for giving her such prominence was the chance to devote three
speeches to description of her remote wanderings, both those to
come and those already past. She must cross from Europe into
Asia, Prometheus tells her, and finally

> Afterwards you will arrive
> in a far land, among black people, those who dwell
> by the Aithiops and by the fountains of the sun.
> Go on along that river's bank until you come
> to a wanderfall, where from the Bibline mountains down
> the Nile lets loose his holy and his pleasant stream.
> This stream will guide you to the triangular country
> of Nile-land. And here, Io, at last you are fated,
> you and your children, to found your far-off settlement.[10]

Some of the fragments of the sequel, *The Release of Prometheus*, are
evidently drawn from passages of the same kind, carrying the
audience to lands on the distant fringes of the known world.

Knowledge of many different peoples, each with their own ways
and customs (*nomoi*), led naturally to the conclusion that custom,
regarded in each locality as fixed and absolute, is in fact variable
from place to place. The thought is expressed several times by
Pindar: 'Custom is king of all', he says, and 'Different peoples
have different customs, and each praise what is right (*dikē*) as they
see it.'[11] But it was Herodotus who, following the precedent set
by Hecataeus, gave the fifth-century Greeks the fullest picture of
the diversity of human ways. As he passes from Lydia to Persia,
Egypt, the rest of North Africa, India, and Scythia and describes
their many peoples, differing in physique, dress, habits, methods
of warfare, crafts, and ritual, he presents a kaleidoscopic succession
in complete contrast with the single human pattern which we
found in Homer. One of his best-known stories illustrates both
the strength of local tradition and the variety of such traditions

that man produces and upholds. After saying that the Persian king, Cambyses, must have been mad to make a mock of established custom, he goes on:

If one were to put before all men the suggestion that out of all customs they should choose the best, each people would examine them and then pick their own; so accustomed are they to think that their own customs are far the best. So no one except a lunatic is likely to make fun of such things. There are many proofs to show that all men customarily hold this attitude towards customs. The following incident is a remarkable example. Darius, when he was in power, summoned such Greeks as were at the court and asked for what price they would be willing to eat the corpses of their fathers. They declared there was no sum for which they would do it. Then Darius sent for the Indians called Callatians, who eat their parents. While the Greeks stood by and with the help of an interpreter listened to all that was said, he asked the Callatians for what reward they would agree to burn their fathers when they died. They protested loudly and asked him not to speak of such things. Such are the views that men have become accustomed to hold, and I think Pindar was right when he said that custom was king over all. (III. 38)

GREEKS AND BARBARIANS

Increasing knowledge of foreign peoples through colonisation and trade does not seem at first to have carried with it any feeling of enmity towards them. The attitude of the Greeks towards their neighbours varied according to local conditions, but in the history of the seventh and sixth centuries hostility between Greek and Greek, whether between rival cities or conflicting classes, figures more prominently than antagonism towards the non-Greek; there is little or no sign of antipathy against foreigners as such. The Greeks were eager to acquire knowledge and techniques from the East and from Egypt. Asiatic rulers, like the Greek states, sent gifts to enrich Apollo's shrine at Delphi. Our fragmentary remains of the lyric poetry of these centuries give us glimpses of wonder at the power and wealth and material civilisation of Lydia, but no sign of the adoption of a special attitude towards

Lydians because they are not Greeks. Alcman speaks of birth in the Lydian capital, Sardis, as a guarantee of good breeding proving that a man was no clumsy boor or mere keeper of sheep. Sappho's beloved Anactoria goes there, and shines among the Lydian women like the moon among the stars: she excels them all in beauty, but there is no suggestion that she stands out from them because she is Greek; Alcaeus does not hesitate at the thought of taking Lydian money in order to get back from exile to Mytilene.[12]

Much of Herodotus' work, written some time in the middle of the fifth century B.C., is infused with the same spirit of lively interest in the foreigner and admiration for his achievements. He pays some foreign peoples an almost exaggerated respect, and sometimes makes comparisons to the disadvantage of the Greeks. He recognises that the language line can be drawn in more ways than one: 'The Egyptians', he says, 'call all who do not speak their language barbarians' (II. 158). Nevertheless, the very first sentence of his history shows that the division between Greek and barbarian has now become a deep line bisecting the Greek picture of humanity. The difference of language, which to Homer meant so little that he did not distinguish it from variations of dialect, has now been chosen by the Greeks for emphasis as the one feature clearly separating them from the rest of mankind; and the common gift of articulate speech receives little attention compared with the consideration that some talk Greek but others make only an unintelligible noise.

While *barbaros* came to be the normal word for a foreigner, *Hellēnes*, which in Homer was the name of the people of a particular district, was now the common label of all who used Greek, and 'Hellenes and barbarians' was a regular way of referring to the whole of mankind. In spite of hostility between individual city-states and divisions into racial groups like Ionian and Dorian, a common outlook developed which involved on the one hand consciousness of membership of a single body of Hellenes, with certain common traditions and institutions, and, on the other, awareness of the contrast between Hellenes and all the rest of the human race.

The word *Panhellēnes*, which implies some realisation of such an outlook and later became the term regularly associated with it, occurs even in the *Iliad* (II. 530), but in lines which have long been regarded as a later interpolation. A more certain early example of it is in Hesiod, who uses it in a contrast with the people—presumably, of Africa—whom the sun visits in the winter:

Then the sun goes to and fro over the land and city of dark-skinned men, and shines more sluggishly on all the race of the Hellenes.

(*Works and Days*, 527–8)

The Olympic Games, at which all Hellenes could take part but barbarians were excluded, were founded as early as 776 B.C., and from the beginning of the sixth century there were four such 'Panhellenic' festivals. From equally early times the Delphic Oracle provided a common meeting-place and source of advice for the Greeks. In a sense these developments were steps towards realisation of unity, but their effect on the Greek view of mankind as a whole was to deepen a dichotomy which retained some effect throughout antiquity.

No precise date can be fixed for the beginning of antipathy between Hellene and barbarian. The close association in the Greek mind between intelligible speech and reason made it easy to take the view that *barbaroi* who lacked *logos* in the one sense were also devoid of it in the other, and the transition from wonder at foreigners for their strange speech to contempt for their lack of good order or political sense may well have been gradual. But there can be no doubt that it was given a great impetus by the Persian Wars, which forced upon the Greeks the conception of all the peoples under the Great King as a barbarian host threatening Hellas. It was the horrors and triumphs of the struggle against Persia and the continued fear of the Persian menace that gave the antithesis its emotional force. *The* barbarians were the Persians, who are constantly described in this way in Aeschylus' *Persians* (472 B.C.) and in Herodotus; and although neither Aeschylus nor

Herodotus sees all foreigners as naturally inferior to the Greeks, the racial hatred and pride in racial superiority engendered by the victorious struggle against the Persian invaders were turned in time against barbarians in general.

How deeply the antithesis was felt, how near it came to being universally accepted among the Greeks, are also questions which we cannot answer with any certainty for this early period, or indeed for later times. All through Greek history there are incidents which suggest that for some individuals or some groups hostility towards foreigners could easily be overcome where other more material motives were at work. The importance of the division seems to have varied from one area to another, depending on local circumstances and especially on the proximity of barbarian peoples. Even within one community attitudes may have differed according to class or other groupings.

Most Greeks, of course, did not have Herodotus' opportunities of seeing foreigners in their own lands. They knew the barbarian best as a servant in the home or on the farm, for their chief contact with him was through slavery, which had now spread through most parts of Greece as a normal feature of life. It is not surprising that the growth of the Greek-barbarian antithesis was strengthened by an equation which is often implied by writers of the fifth century B.C., although it receives clear and definite statement, and its full implications are realised, only in the fourth: Greek is to barbarian as free man is to slave. The majority of slaves, though by no means all, were non-Greeks—Asiatics, Thracians, Scythians; and the idea that this was their natural lot was encouraged by the belief that they lived in political slavery at home. This thought, which becomes a commonplace in Euripides, is already present in some lines of dialogue in the *Persians* (241-4), in which Queen Atossa questions the chorus leader about the Greeks:

Queen: Who is lord and master over their host?
Leader: They are no man's slaves or subjects .
Queen: How can they withstand those who come against them in war?
Leader: Well enough to destroy the fine great force of Darius.

One free Greek is worth half a dozen slavish Persians: we can hardly doubt that the lines reflect the views of the Athenian audience eight years after Salamis.

FIRST THEORIES OF UNITY

Awareness of the diversity of mankind and the growth of the divisions and prejudices I have described provide the background against which the development must be seen that is our main concern: the partial and tentative emergence here and there of a different attitude. It was only a small minority—perhaps only a few outstanding intellects—who moved by various paths in the opposite direction to the mainstream of contemporary opinion, towards the idea of the human race as a unity. For them this was no longer the result of an unconscious assumption or the poetical imagination, as the unified Homeric picture had been, but the fruit of rational abstract thought, now in its early stages.

There were two routes by which the idea could be reached, distinguishable from each other, though both leading to the same result. One was awareness of the human race as an aggregate, the sum total of all individual men; a notion which we may perhaps call human geography, a commonplace in our thinking today. Such an approach is clearly implied in the map-making of Anaximander of Miletus, on the eastern coast of the Aegean, about the middle of the sixth century B.C. Miletus was a commercial centre, a place to which many traders' and travellers' reports would come; and Anaximander probably used the knowledge gathered from these sources in constructing the first Greek map of the world. It is the function of a map to show the different sections of mankind, a purpose no doubt fulfilled more accurately by Hecataeus' improved version a few decades later; but a map unites as well as divides, and its maker must have seen the inhabited world as a single entity. The same assumption underlies the work of Herodotus, though it is difficult to know how definitely it took shape in his mind.

This line of thought figures more prominently in the evidence for our theme at a later stage. In the period down to the end of the fifth century B.C. it is easier to find indications of what may be called a biological approach, involving the conception of man as a *specific* being, a distinct type with certain typical characteristics that mark him off from gods on the one hand and from animals on the other. In a sense, of course, this idea of humanity had existed from the earliest times: it is implied, as has been said, in the use of the word *anthrōpos*, and taken for granted in the Homeric picture of human life. But it is only after Homer that we can trace conscious formulation of the notion of the species man, although some of the main features ascribed to him are those we have already noted in the *Iliad* and the *Odyssey*.

The first signs of this trend of thought are found, as we might expect, among our scanty evidence for the philosophers, whose varied speculations about human life were part of their wider efforts to explain the cosmos as a whole. If Anaximander's map involves the idea of mankind as an aggregate, the notion of the human race as a single species is equally involved in his remarkable picture of our beginnings, constructed to fit the stage in his cosmogony at which the earth, first covered by 'the moist element', emerges as dry land when the liquid is evaporated by the sun:

Anaximander of Miletus held the view that from water and earth, when they had become hot, there arose fish or creatures very like fish. In these human beings took shape, and the embryos were retained inside the creatures until puberty. Only then did the creatures burst open and men and women already able to feed themselves came out.   (A 30)

Or again:

Moreover he says that in the beginning man was born from creatures of another kind; for whereas other creatures soon become self-supporting, man alone needs prolonged nursing. Therefore, he argues, he could not have survived in the beginning in this form.   (A 10)

In spite of the claims sometimes made that Anaximander anticipated Darwin, it is clear that the underlying belief here is not evolutionary, but the concept of the species man, differing from other species in a physical characteristic—its early helplessness: 'other creatures are soon self-supporting, but man alone needs prolonged nursing'. Crude and fantastic though the theory is, it constitutes a first step away from traditional legend and prejudice in the direction of the biological study of mankind.

Xenophanes, probably a little later than Anaximander, has already been mentioned as attributing to each race the creation of gods in its own image. The idea of humanity as only one among a number of animal species comes to the fore in our fragments of his work, too, when he extends the same thought to them: 'If cattle and horses or lions had hands, or could draw with their hands and create works of art as men can, horses would draw forms of the gods like horses, and cattle like cattle, and they would make their bodies such as they each had themselves' (fr. 15). Still more remarkable and more significant for the later development of Greek thinking about mankind are the views of Heraclitus of Ephesus, who was in his prime about the end of the sixth century B.C. He was known in antiquity as 'the dark one', and the obscurity—probably intentional—of most of the extant fragments, together with the distorted interpretations of ancient commentators, makes his real meaning difficult to find and often open to dispute. But there can be no doubt that his view of man, also, can be understood only in the wider context of his doctrine as a whole. We have seen that one of the distinctive features of man implied in Homeric epithets is his power of articulate speech, and that in the Greek mind the spoken word and reason were so closely linked that one term, *logos*, came to do duty for them both. For Heraclitus the *Logos*—both a universal rational principle or Law, and at the same time the word, the message which the philosopher presents—is the key to all things. Wisdom consists in understanding the *Logos*: 'Wisdom is one thing: to understand the principle which steers all things through all.'[13] Because the *Logos* is 'common', thought also is common to all; and the universality of the *Logos* lies behind all human laws or customs (*nomoi*): 'Those who speak with understanding must rely on

what is common to all, as a city relies on its law, and with far
greater reliance. For all human laws are nourished by one law,
the divine law, which has all the power it desires and is enough,
and more than enough, for all.'[14] Yet it is an essential part of
Heraclitus' doctrine that all unity is made up of different and conflicting elements; and so within the unity of rational beings there
must be division and variety: 'Conflict is father of all and king of
all. Some it presents as gods, others as men; some it makes slaves,
others free.'[15] According to Aristotle: 'Heraclitus criticises the
author [Homer] of the words "May strife disappear from among
gods and men". For, he says, there would be no musical scale
without high or low, nor living creatures without male and
female, which are opposites' (A 22). The antithesis 'Greek and
barbarian' does not occur alongside 'free and slave', 'male and
female' in the extant fragments, although we shall see that they
do contain the word *barbaros*; we cannot tell whether Heraclitus,
writing before the Persian Wars, would have regarded this as
another natural and necessary division of mankind.

In these sentences we catch a glimpse of a picture far in advance
of the ideas of Heraclitus' time: the unity of humanity within a
wider unity, bound together by reason; a unity, however, which
is not homogeneous, but complex, comprehending within itself
the different sexes, classes, and races. But there was another side
to his outlook, equally prophetic of the later development of
thought about the nature of man. He was far from regarding
human unity as fully realised, or from supposing that all existing
human laws do in fact accord with the divine law. Men have the
power of reason, and so are one; but they fail to exercise it, and so
are divided against each other. Only God is completely wise.
'Although the *Logos* is common, most men live as though their
understanding were only their own' (fr. 2): they 'are unaware of
what they do after waking up, just as they forget what they do
when asleep' (fr. 1). 'For to those who are really awake, there is
one well-ordered universe common to all, whereas in sleep each
man turns away to a world of his own' (fr. 89). 'Eyes and ears

are bad witnesses for men', says another fragment, 'if they have barbarian souls' (fr. 107)—the first occurrence of the word *barbaros* in Greek prose: the minds of most men, Heraclitus means, do not understand the language of the senses, fail to comprehend the *Logos* which sense observation, correctly interpreted, would convey to them. Few writers have been so contemptuous of fools as Heraclitus, or so condemnatory of those normally praised as wise: 'What intelligence or sense have they? They trust the people's singers and use the mob as their teacher, not knowing that "most men are bad, and few good"' (fr. 104). Homer, Hesiod and Archilochus, Pythagoras, Xenophanes and Hecataeus are all included in Heraclitus' list of fools. The thought that man is a rational animal, yet not rational, that human beings should be brought together by this common gift but actually go their own disastrous ways, is as important as any aspect of Heraclitus' philosophy, and may lie behind the deliberate obscurity of his style, intended to appeal only to the few. It is a thought that often arises again in later Greek discussions of man and his problems, as indeed it still does today.

In our information about the thinkers of the fifth century B.C. prior to the Peloponnesian War there are further isolated glimpses of different moves in the direction of the idea of human unity. Alcmaeon, the earliest Greek writer we know of with a primarily medical approach to experience, declared that man differed from other animals in that 'only he understands, while the rest perceive but do not understand' (A 5). Empedocles (who, incidentally, shared Heraclitus' contempt for fools who fail to comprehend the laws of nature) proclaimed in his *Purifications* the transmigration of souls and railed against the slaughter of animals and the eating of meat, and therefore emphasised the kinship of man and beasts rather than the difference between them; but the poem included two striking lines on the universal validity of true law: 'That which is lawful for all stretches without a break through the wide-ruling air and through the boundless light' (fr. 135).

Diogenes Laertius records an anecdote about Anaxagoras, the philosopher friend of Pericles, which goes still further towards anticipating the Cynic and Stoic views of later times: 'When someone asked, "Have you no concern for your fatherland?", "Be silent", he replied; "I am greatly concerned with my fatherland", and pointed to the sky' (A 1). The truth of the story is open to question, like that of other tales in Diogenes. It bears no clear relation to the rest of our fragmentary evidence about Anaxagoras' views of mankind, some outline of which, fortunately, can be reasonably reconstructed without going into the difficult problem of his cosmology as a whole. For Anaxagoras, man is superior to the animals and learns to make use of them through his exercise of his experience, memory, wisdom and skill, although weaker in strength and speed; but this mental superiority is not due to possession of intelligence as a unique gift, for mind (*nous*) is present not only in man but in all living things, including plants. Man is the wisest of living creatures 'because he has hands'.[16] This remarkable statement, quoted with aversion by Aristotle, implies a conception of the grading of intelligence according to physical structure which is very different from the belief of so many Greek poets and philosophers, that mind is a divine property shared by gods and men alone. Anaxagoras' approach, as other fragments would lead us to expect, is physiological, akin to that of Anaximander and—as we shall see—the medical writers. We do not know how far he developed its implications, but in embryo at any rate there is here the notion of man as a tool-using animal, whose superior achievement, built up through the memory of repeated experience, consists in what we now call 'technical development'.

When we turn to the poets of this period we find evidence of the extent to which interest in *homo sapiens* and his achievements and his place in the scheme of things has developed, even outside the ranks of the philosophers; although here, of course, its expression may be mythical, not thought out in rational terms.

'One is the race of men, one the race of gods', proclaims Pindar at the beginning of an ode dated about 463 B.C. (*Nem.* VI); and in lines very different in spirit from the outlook of Anaxagoras he goes on to develop the double theme of man's kinship with the immortals, based partly on his 'power of mind', and on the other hand the gulf between human feebleness and uncertainty and the unchanging eternity of heaven. Aeschylus' *Prometheus*, on the contrary, probably written about the same time, portrays the present state of mankind as an achievement reached in spite of the hostility of a tyrannical Zeus. I have already used this play as evidence of the intense interest of Aeschylus and his audience in the variety of the world around them: it is equally notable for its picture of human civilisation as a single growth, in which the power of reason has played the key part. Prometheus, pinned to his Scythian rock, tells the daughters of Oceanus how he helped mankind:

Hearken to the plight
Of man, in whom, born witless as a babe,
I planted mind and the gift of understanding.
I speak of men with no intent to blame
But to expound my gracious services:
Who first, with eyes to see, did see in vain,
With ears to hear, did hear not, but as shapes
Figured in dreams throughout their mortal span
Confounded all things, knew not how to raise
Brick-woven walls sun-warmed, nor build in wood,
But had their dwelling, like the restless ant,
In sunless nooks of subterranean caves.
No token sure they had of winter's cold,
No herald of the flowery spring or season
Of ripening fruit, but laboured without wit
In all their works, till I revealed the obscure
Risings and settings of the stars of heaven.
Yea, and the art of number, arch-device,
I founded, and the craft of written words,
The world's recorder, mother of the Muse.[17]

Further items in Prometheus' story are the training of horses, the invention of ships, the arts of medicine and divination, the discovery of metals. In brief, he concludes, 'Prometheus founded all the arts of man'.

If we interpret the tale in non-mythical terms (as Aeschylus probably never did) and remember that for the Greeks the name Prometheus, whatever its real origin, meant 'Forethinker', the central place of reason in the picture is confirmed, and we have here an account of the onward march of the human race through the exercise of its own intelligence.

About twenty years later, in 441 B.C., Sophocles in the well-known chorus from the *Antigone* does describe the achievement as man's own:

> Wonders are many on earth, and the greatest of these
> Is man, who rides the ocean and takes his way
> Through the deeps, through wind-swept valleys of perilous seas
> That surge and sway.

> He is master of ageless Earth, to his own will bending
> The immortal mother of gods by the sweat of his brow,
> As year succeeds to year, with toil unending
> Of mule and plough.

> He is lord of all things living; birds of the air,
> Beasts of the field, all creatures of sea and land
> He taketh, cunning to capture and ensnare
> With sleight of hand;

> Hunting the savage beast from the upland rocks,
> Taming the mountain monarch in his lair,
> Teaching the wild horse and the roaming ox
> His yoke to bear.

> The use of language, the wind-swift motion of brain
> He learnt; found out the laws of living together
> In cities, building him shelter against the rain
> And wintry weather.

> There is nothing beyond his power. His subtlety
> Meeteth all chance, all danger conquereth.
> For every ill he hath found its remedy,
> Save only death.[18]

These lines show how the concept of mankind as a species with its own characteristics and its own triumphs has developed beyond anything to be found in early epic. Yet the main features of the Homeric picture are still there: man is still a 'bread-eater', a creature who controls and uses nature by his skill; speech and the reasoned thought that goes with it remain one of his greatest gifts; amid all his successes there is one failing, mortality, which he cannot overcome, and sure and lasting happiness continues to be beyond his reach.

As even this ode demonstrates, Sophocles does not readily lay aside tradition, but he is no mere exponent of accepted ideas. When Antigone upholds the unwritten laws of heaven against Creon's local edict, she is championing a wider view of human rights and duties than the city-bound outlook of the day. And in the *Ajax* there is a similar implied protest against the crude prejudice of the current attitude towards non-Greeks. Agamemnon abuses Teucer, son of the Greek Telamon by a foreign slave mother, in a style which must echo much contemporary talk against 'barbarians':

> Remember who you are
> And bring some other man, a free man, here
> To plead your cause instead of you before us.
> I cannot understand you when you speak:
> Barbarian chatter has no meaning for me. (1259–63)

Yes, replies Teucer, I am indeed 'the slave-son of a barbarian mother'; but was not your own grandfather that Phrygian barbarian, Pelops?[19] As Herodotus recognised and as we shall find Thucydides declaring more clearly, the Greek-barbarian division is not so absolute as it seems. It is Teucer who wins the argument.

LATE FIFTH-CENTURY CHANGES

Until late in the fifth century B.C. the development of the ideas I have described in the last few pages was slow, and they probably made little impact on the mind of the majority, even in enlightened

Athens. To the man in the street the notion of *homo sapiens* as a single species remained unfamiliar, if not unknown: he thought in terms of the particular Greek cities and their rivalries, the contrast between Ionian and Dorian, the superiority of men over women, the division into free men and slaves, the traditional cleavage between high and low (now dependent on wealth at least as much as on birth) and the newer, but now generally accepted, antithesis between Greek and barbarian. In the last decades of the century, however, largely under the stress of the Peloponnesian War, traditional beliefs began to lose their hold: a ferment of ideas and questions arose which inevitably affected the prevailing conceptions of human society.

One source of evidence of the extent of this mental upheaval, at any rate at Athens, is Dr Ehrenberg's survey of the life and outlook of the Athenian public as they are revealed in the extant comedies of Aristophanes, the earliest of which was presented in 425 B.C. Ehrenberg notes a decrease of political enthusiasm towards the end of the century, reflected 'in the first, as yet vague, signs of Cosmopolitanism, or at least in the clear signs of that Panhellenism which was trying to break down the barriers between the Greek States and to secure universal peace'.[20] The cosmopolitan trend was encouraged by the presence at this time of large numbers of non-Greeks, including (for example) dark-skinned Egyptians, as permanent residents at Athens, and the consequent decline in antagonism towards such 'barbarians'; although the treatment of a Persian in the *Acharnians* and a Scythian in the *Women at the Thesmophoria* shows that for Aristophanes—and, presumably, for his audience—they could still be contemptible figures of fun. Slaves, who were mostly non-Greek, were treated with more consideration after the outbreak of the war, if only because of the fear that they would run away to the enemy.

Another aspect of the time which Aristophanes' plays reflect, if only to ridicule it, is the talk of change in the status of women. But most important of all was the breakdown of the traditional respect for the aristocracy and the rejection of the division of society, which we first saw in Homer, into a well-born upper class and a humble mass of common folk. This distinction between high and low had, of course, already been modified and lost some of its rigidity in Athens and elsewhere, chiefly through the rise of a moneyed middle class. Late in the sixth century B.C. the disgruntled aristocrat Theognis, of Megara, had complained to his squire, Cyrnus:

> Cyrnus, our city is a city still.
> Its folk are changed. Who once outside our walls
> Pastured like deer, with goatskins round their sides,
> And knew not laws or judgments, these today
> Are good men, Cyrnus; and those high before
> Are now sunk low. Who can endure the sight? (53–8)

Or again:

> 'Tis wealth they honour. Good is wed to bad
> And bad to good. Money has mixed the stocks. (189–90)

Now, however, Athens saw a sharp acceleration of the process. In the last decades of the fifth century, writes Ehrenberg, the aristocratic mode of life underwent a critical change:

For a long time the Athenian aristocracy had been, politically, socially and intellectually, the ruling class, also in the democratic State. Gradually they lost their position and the upper classes changed in character. Much more fatal than the partial intrusion by the more wealthy among the middle classes was the change the nobility underwent in itself. This was even more devastating in its effect than the war casualties which had fallen most heavily on the upper classes. The nobles were rapidly moving towards self-destruction. . . .

At the time of the performance of the *Knights*, the old aristocratic ideal was still fully alive, but the threatening signs of change were also visible. Twenty years later the process was more or less complete. The attempts to restore, once again, the political rule of the upper classes . . . continued the decline of the aristocracy. The revolution of the Four Hundred in 411, and even more the rule of the Thirty in 403, failed, not so much because of the resistance of the democrats as through the weakness and corruption of the oligarchs. . . . The political leaders and events finally crushed the fading ideal of aristocracy. (pp. 111–12)

This picture is confirmed not only by the efforts of the more extreme aristocrats to resist the trend, but also by the bitter comments of one of their spokesmen. The 'Old Oligarch', to whom the *Constitution of the Athenians* handed down among the works or Xenophon is now ascribed, wrote his ironical defence of Athenian democracy as early in the disintegrating process as 425 or 424 B.C. His language is proof of the strength which belief in the upper class still retained in some circles: they are 'the noble', 'the good', 'the cleverest', 'the best', and 'there is no state in which the best section is well-disposed towards the people' (3. 10). And although his complaints may, as Ehrenberg thinks, be exaggerated, there must be some truth in his account of conditions at Athens, which he compares unfavourably with Sparta and other cities as the centre of decline from the good old days. Among the Athenians, he says, 'the vulgar and the poor and the common folk are everywhere given greater consideration than the good' (1. 4). 'The slaves and resident foreigners live without restraint at Athens. . . . The people there is no better clothed than the slaves and foreigners, nor any better in appearance' (1. 10). Whereas other Greeks have their own manner of speaking and way of life and dress, that of the Athenians is a mixture drawn 'from all the Greeks and barbarians' (2. 8). The decline of standards, as the 'Old Oligarch' sees it, is blurring the distinction between Greek and non-Greek as well as between the classes.

A less one-sided version of the clash between old and new ideas can be gained from Euripides, who is not a propagandist for any one point of view, nor a philosopher with a doctrine of his own, but a dramatist drawing material from the whole field of contemporary controversy and putting it, often with violent anachronism, into the mouths of his legendary characters. On the subject of man we find in the extant plays and fragments neither complete acceptance of tradition nor consistent opposition to it, but echoes of the various conflicting arguments which must have been heard in the streets of Athens at the time. Thus the old belief that the nobly born have a distinctive physique is repeated by Ion: 'You can usually tell by the look of them whether people are of noble birth.'²¹ Yet a speaker in the *Aeolus* debunks 'nobility' as merely a matter of hard cash: 'That man is noble, in whose house wealth stays the longest time' (fr. 22).* No Greek writer launches more attacks on women as morally and socially inferior to man; nevertheless, some of Euripides' portraits of women characters show a sympathy which clearly implies criticism of contemporary prejudices against them. Local patriotism, again, is blatantly proclaimed in some of the plays, and there is crude propaganda against the Spartan enemy; but among the fragments there are memorable lines which anticipate later ideas by speaking of wider horizons beyond the narrow limits of the *polis*, for those whose minds are capable of such breadth of outlook: 'Every quarter of the sky is open to the eagle's flight: every country is fatherland for a man of noble mind' (fr. 1047). Those who share the common world-fatherland have a certain kinship with each other: 'Though a wise man live far from my own land, though I never set eyes upon him, I count him as a friend' (fr. 902). The superiority of Greek over barbarian is usually accepted in the plays. Euripides tends to see foreigners not with all the variety of knowledge or imagination shown by Aeschylus, but as a generalised mass whose intrinsic inferiority to the Greeks is often asserted with brutal vigour. Iphigenia says to Clytemnestra: 'It is right for Greeks to rule over barbarians, mother, but not barbarians over Greeks. For they are slaves, but Greeks are free.'²² Yet the royal women of defeated Troy—regarded by this time as the prototype of barbarism—are depicted in the *Trojan Women* with understanding and sympathy. When Spartan Hermione rails at the captive Trojan Andromache as a barbarian slave, wildly accusing 'all the barbarian race' of incest, not to mention sexual promiscuity, Euripides makes Andromache answer her with crushing force and dignity; and to Hermione's cry that 'We do not govern *our* city by barbarians' laws' she replies, 'There, just as here,

* Numbers for fragments from tragedy refer to the second edition of Nauck's *Tragicorum Graecorum Fragmenta*.

infamous action leads to infamy.'[23] Although the cleavage between slave and free is normally taken for granted, often along with the slave-barbarian equation expressed in Iphigenia's words to her mother, some passages openly recognise that there are exceptions to the rule: 'For many slaves the name is their only disgrace; in spirit they are more free than men who are not slaves' (fr. 831). Or again: 'One thing alone dishonours slaves—the name. In all else a slave is no worse than free men, if he is honest.'[24] We are not far here from the thought that slavery is an artificial institution and creates no real division between men.

In many of these quotations the thought of human unity is implied. It is explicitly stated in a choral fragment from the *Alexander*, first performed along with the *Trojan Women* in 415 B.C., which develops denial of the importance of birth into one of the most striking assertions in the documents of the time of the single origin and nature of mankind:

We waste our words, if we praise high birth among mortal men. For when first of old we came into being, and Earth, the mother of mortals, gave them life of their own, she created the same form for all. No separate stamp divides us. High-born and low-born are a single stock. It is time, through custom [*nomos*], that brings pride of birth. (Fr. 52)

A parallel passage survives from the *Tereus* of Sophocles, which may have been produced about the same time. Although the play's theme seems to have set Greek civilisation and savagery in strong contrast with each other, the chorus, probably Bacchic worshippers from Thrace, express the egalitarian and unifying spirit which seems to have characterised the worship of their god. Derivation from common ancestors—probably father Heaven and mother Earth—makes all men one: 'There is one human race. A single day brought us all forth from our father and mother. No man is born superior to another. But one man's fare is a doom of unhappy days, another's is success; and on others the yoke of slavery's hardship falls' (fr. 532).

When knowledge of the diversity of human life had grown so far, and on the other hand the various forms of discrimination and prejudice which coloured men's attitude towards their fellow-men were being called in question, it is not surprising that more minds than before turned to deliberate consideration of the true nature of man. No doubt these were still only a minority, but that discussion of the subject was now widespread, if not popular, is shown by the opening paragraphs of the compilation included in the Hippocratic Collection under the title *Nature of Man*. The date of this part of the treatise is towards the end of the fifth century B.C.; and in pouring scorn on rival theorists the author shows incidentally that his subject is a regular topic for public debate:

Anyone accustomed to hear speakers discuss the nature of man beyond its connection with medicine will find no interest in following the present account. . . . When they adopt the same principle yet disagree in their statements, it is clear that their knowledge of the facts is also deficient—a point which one can realise best by attending their discussions. For though debaters and audience are the same, never does the same man win the argument three times in succession, but now one is victorious, now another, now he who happens to have the most glib tongue in speaking to the crowd.

The views which this writer mentions are concerned, it is true, with man's physical composition, but there can be no doubt that the question of man's real nature was also discussed in a wider sense. In our scanty evidence—probably only a fraction, be it remembered, of what was written on such matters during this period—there are several examples of new approaches to the subject, made from different angles and for different purposes, but with certain common features: they all involve consideration of humanity and human relationships as a specific problem, not merely an aspect of cosmology; and they all tend towards abandonment of divisions within humanity and acceptance of a single 'nature of man'. The extent of their advance on previous ideas must not be exaggerated: even the most enlightened of the Greeks were still far from complete grasp of the notion of the unity of mankind, and further from full understanding of its implications; and the new conceptions put forward by a few are no proof of any radical break by the majority from the old limitations and prejudices. But at any rate there were some thinkers at this time whose views on the subject were more advanced than were those of most Greeks for generations to come.

THE SOPHISTS

The place where one would expect to find such advanced ideas, even before they spread in other circles, is among the Sophists, especially as most of them seem to have travelled widely and must have gained a far more comprehensive view of the world than the average citizen. The portrait of several of them in Plato's *Protagoras*, written early in the fourth century, contains some valuable evidence for our theme. The occasion which the dialogue presents is a gathering probably supposed to have occurred about 433 B.C. But the views expressed, in so far as they are historical at all, presumably reflect the general attitude known to have been held by the speakers and cannot be given a precise date.

The most important figure for our purpose is Protagoras himself, who was one of the earliest and most famous of the Sophists. The few surviving remnants of Protagoras' own writings contain little that throws light on his conception of mankind, but Plato puts into his mouth a long speech which is certainly relevant.[25] Whether the speech is a Platonic fiction or the Sophist's own, as recent opinion has tended to suppose, is a point on which we cannot hope for a final decision. The question is not vital for our purpose, since Plato must at least be attributing to Protagoras the kind of attitude which he actually held. Whether the Athenians of the time would have accepted the speech as a defence of their point of view is another matter; Plato's implication that it is so shows what he believed to be the trend of popular ideas.[26]

Protagoras begins his speech with a story about the beginnings of life on earth. When the various mortal creatures had been fashioned by the gods, Prometheus and his brother Epimetheus—the foolish 'Afterthinker'—were given the task of assigning suitable powers to each species, and Epimetheus persuaded the Forethinker to let him do the distribution. He gave strength to one, speed to another, size to another, and so on, but in his folly used up all the available powers on the *aloga*, the unreasoning animals, leaving man unprotected. So Prometheus stole from Athena and Hephaestus the gift of skill in the crafts, together with fire, and by giving these to man equipped him with the resources he needed to keep himself alive.

Because men alone among living creatures were akin to the divine, they established worship of the gods; and by their skill they created articulate speech, and houses and clothing and cultivated crops. But because they lived in scattered groups, not in cities, they were helpless in the struggle against the beasts. When they did try to form communities, they injured each other because they lacked the art of living in cities, the art of politics. So Zeus sent Hermes to bring men respect for others (*aidōs*) and justice (*dikē*), so that there might be order in their cities and the bonds that lead to friendship; and he told Hermes that whereas the several crafts had been allotted to different groups, on the principle of specialization, in these qualities all must have a share. Any man who was incapable of respect for others and justice must be put to death, as a plague to the city. This, says Protagoras, is the reason why the Athenians expect all their fellow-citizens to be able to give counsel on political questions, but not on matters that involve technical skill.

If we strip off the mythical form, which we can legitimately do for Protagoras' story though not for Aeschylus' play, we have an account here of how the animal world is marked off into separate species with different faculties, and of the qualities common to the human species which distinguish it from the rest. It is taken for granted that man alone possesses reason (*logos*) as opposed to the *aloga*, and Protagoras would probably have agreed that his other distinctive powers flow from this. Worship of the gods, articulate speech, and the ability to create material civilisation by technical skill are attributes which all men share. But with regard to the social virtues, respect for others and justice and political wisdom, the position is more complicated, and there has been much dispute whether Protagoras' own thought, as represented by Plato, is clear.

The chief difficulty is caused by the apparently paradoxical position reached later in Protagoras' speech, where in spite of his earlier claim that all men have a share of these qualities, he asserts that they possess them not by nature, but by teaching. Probably the implications of this are not fully thought out; but the explanation which seems best suited to Protagoras' words is that while all men are capable in varying degrees of acquiring these virtues, they need instruction and practice to make this latent ability bear fruit and actually become politically wise to the extent of their natural aptitude. They possess these qualities, in fact, in the same way as they possess the crafts, except that the potentiality for political wisdom is shared by all, whereas the ability to become a doctor or a flute-player is limited to certain individuals. This interpretation seems to be confirmed by one of our brief fragments of Protagoras' works: 'Teaching needs nature and practice.'27

The phrase 'all men', however, also requires qualification. There are some—evidently a minority—whose nature does *not* include any potentiality for justice or for respect for others. They have no place in cities, in community life. Protagoras sometimes speaks—though here he is certainly not consistent—as though they, like Homer's Cyclops, are not to be regarded as really men at all. Everyone must have some sense of justice, or 'not exist among men' (323c). Even the most unjust of those brought up 'among laws and men' would prove to be an expert in justice compared with the savages, the 'misanthropes' put on the stage in a recent play.

We conclude that for Protagoras, if this speech in Plato's dialogue represents him correctly, man is a reasoning animal, and all members of the human species include among their common attributes worship of the gods, the gift of speech, and the power to acquire one or other form of technical skill. The great majority have also some ability to learn justice and respect for others and political wisdom, and they come together in civilised communities. Hence among civilised human beings, who alone fully deserve to be called 'men', differences in the qualities that make for unity are a matter of degree, not of kind. We cannot carry Protagoras beyond this, nor can we be certain how far his ideas went outside the confines of Greece; but his line of thought, taken further, would lead to a remarkable conception of the unity of the civilised world.

Another well-known Sophist who appears in the *Protagoras* is Hippias, who makes a short speech—this time, obviously Plato's own composition—caricaturing his constant reiteration of the contrast between 'nature and convention'. Hippias begins:

Gentlemen, I regard all of you as kinsmen and members of one family and fellow-citizens—by nature, not by custom (*nomos*). For by nature like is akin to like, but custom, the tyrannical ruler of mankind, does much violence to nature. So for us who know the nature of things and are the wisest of the Greeks and just for that reason have now assembled in this city, the central home of Greek wisdom, and in the largest and finest of the city's houses, it would be a disgrace if we produced nothing worthy of our reputation but wrangled with each other like the lowest of men.   (337c–e)

How wide is the 'one family' of which Hippias speaks? Is cosmopolitanism part of the outlook which Plato caricatures? Although the audience is said to contain many 'strangers' (315a), it is true that all are Greeks, and there is nothing in the speech itself that goes explicitly beyond Greece. But what we know of Hippias from elsewhere suggests a wider interpretation. He was remarkable even among the Sophists for the number of cities he visited and the extraordinary range of his knowledge. His writings included a work entitled *The Nomenclature of Peoples* (fr. 2); and on the famous occasion when he appeared at Olympia wearing clothes and ornaments entirely of his own manufacture, the chief object of admiration was a copy of a Persian girdle (A 12). In one fragment (6) he mentions among his many sources of information 'prose works, both Greek and barbarian'—a claim which seems to imply some knowledge of non-Greek languages. Finally, in Xenophon's *Memoirs of Socrates* (IV. 4. 19) he is represented as taking a view which certainly looks beyond Greece. Whereas in the *Protagoras* he is made to condemn *nomos* as dividing men against each other, here Socrates elicits from him the statement that there are certain unwritten laws (*nomoi*) which the gods must have laid down for men, since men, who 'could not have all come together and do not speak the same language', could not have made them. By itself, such a passage might carry little weight as proof of what the historical Hippias believed; but in conjunction with the rest of the evidence it points to a conception of mankind, not merely the Greeks, as a single human family united by nature and by a basic moral code, in spite of its division into peoples and its use of different tongues.

It must not be supposed that all the Sophists of this period entertained any such view of mankind: on this, as on other matters, there was no single 'Sophistic' doctrine. Our remains of the speeches of Gorgias emphasise the cleavage between Greeks and barbarians (of whom the Trojans are taken as prototypes) and between free men and slaves: in his oration at Olympia he called for concord between the Greek states, extending to relations between cities the use of the word *homonoia*, 'being of one mind', 'unity of outlook', which was then normally applied only within the family or the *polis*. But the only purpose of his Panhellenism was to achieve a united front in the struggle against barbarian Persia. Similarly a fragment of Thrasymachus (2) asks: 'Shall we Greeks be the slaves of barbarian Archelaus?' We do possess, however, one striking piece of evidence for a different attitude towards the Greek-barbarian division: the long papyrus fragment (44) which we now have from the work of Antiphon, who, unlike most Sophists, was a native of Athens. The fragment is a portion of his book entitled *Truth*, probably written late in the fifth century B.C. In it, as the title would suggest, he expounds what he believes to be reality as opposed to mere appearances, exploiting once again the familiar contrast between nature and law or convention and emphasising, like Hippias in the *Protagoras*, the natural kinship between like and like. The most relevant passage for our theme is the following, the immediate context of which has disappeared:

We respect and honour those born of noble fathers, but those not from a noble house we neither respect nor honour. In this we have become like barbarians in our relations with each other, whereas by nature we are all constituted alike in all things, both barbarians and Greeks. This can be seen by consideration of those things which are essential by nature to all men. . . . In these things no barbarian is set apart from us, nor any Greek. For we all breathe into the air through mouth and nostrils, and (we all eat with our hands?). . . .

The sentence I have omitted is so mutilated that it cannot be either restored or interpreted with any certainty, and the last words, which I have put in brackets, are still more doubtful. The thought of the whole passage is compressed, but it clearly contains a double attack on the accepted divisions of mankind, which may be put into more modern terms and set out more fully as follows:

Our prevailing class distinction between those of high and low birth, which goes back to Homer and is still with us, has created within our society a division like that conventionally drawn between Greeks and barbarians, so that this gulf which we imagine separates us from foreigners exists in our own midst, and the two sections of our community do not understand each other, any more than we Greeks understand the Egyptians.

Such a cleavage is wrong, whether in our own society or in the wider world. For by nature Greeks and barbarians are all alike, as a study of their essential attributes will show. After all, the operation of breathing, like all our necessary physical processes, is common to the entire human race.

It is significant that in this emphasis on common physical characteristics Antiphon adopts the same line of thought which we have already seen in Anaximander and Anaxagoras, carrying the biological notion of the species man to a logical conclusion which must have shocked his contemporaries.

Antiphon also wrote a book *On Concord* (*Homonoia*), of which, unfortunately, only a few scraps remain.[28] We have seen that Gorgias advocated *homonoia* between Greeks, and the occurrence of the word in Antiphon's title is another indication of its increasing use in intellectual discussion at this time. There has been much difference of opinion about the possible contents of Antiphon's work, and it has been questioned whether the book was his at all. Where the evidence is so slight there can be no certainty, but it is notable that of the eleven fragments definitely attributed to this work, two—words meaning 'shadowfeet' and 'longheads' —refer to strange peoples distinguished by some physical characteristic, and a third—'dwellers underground'—describes another by its way of life; while a fourth differentiates man from other animals: 'man, who claims to be the most godlike of all animals'. (Did the sentence continue, 'but fights his fellow-men like the beasts'?) These again are traces of a biological and anthropological approach, and it seems a reasonable inference that in part of the book, at any rate, *homonoia* was discussed as an ideal affecting all mankind.

THUCYDIDES AND THE MEDICAL WRITERS

So far our review of ideas about mankind in the last decades of the fifth century B.C. has been confined to Sophists, from whom one would expect such speculations. That thought on the subject was more widespread can be seen from the history of Thucydides and from the medical writers, to whom he is in some ways akin.

Thucydides' historical thinking, writes Jaeger, 'is founded on the assumption that there is such a thing as "human nature", always and everywhere the same'.[29] His purpose is to provide 'a clear understanding of events which have happened in the past, and of those which are likely at some time in the future to follow the same or a similar pattern, *in the course of human things*' (I. 22. 4).

He describes the great plague of 430 B.C. in detail, so that 'anyone with knowledge of the symptoms may not fail to recognise it if it should ever break out again' (II. 48. 3). His comment on the class-struggle at Corcyra three years later involves the conception, which we shall find elaborated in the medical writers, of a 'nature of man' constant in essentials, but variable according to the influences of time and place: 'As a result of civil conflict many calamities came upon the cities, such as do occur and always will, as long as human nature remains the same, though they vary in intensity and differ in form according to the particular circumstances of each case' (III. 82. 2). It may be added that Thucydides' opinion of human nature is low, and he certainly does not envisage any future peace or harmony or brotherhood among men: 'might is right' is the rule mankind obeys, ambition, fear and interest its motive forces.

How did this general concept affect Thucydides' attitude towards the current divisions within humanity? In most of his narrative he writes as though he accepted them without demur. Women are virtually left out of the picture, as if in accordance with the principles which the historian puts into the mouth of Pericles:

If I must now also speak of the duty of women for the benefit of those who will now live in widowhood, one brief piece of advice will cover all I have to say: great is your glory if you do not fall short of the character nature has given you; and greatest is hers who is least talked of among men, whether for praise or for blame.   (II. 45. 2)

'Barbarians' are frequently mentioned in contrast to Greeks, and the second Persian invasion is 'the return of the barbarian with his armada for the enslavement of Hellas' (I. 18. 2). In his opening pages, however, where in more philosophical mood he states the results of his meditations on early Greek history, his account is in agreement with the idea of a single permanent 'nature of man' of which such groupings as 'Greek' and 'barbarian' are only transient variations. He recognises that in the earliest times, as reflected in Homer, these categories had not yet come into existence. The history of those days cut across such divisions: 'In ancient times both the Greeks and those of the barbarians who inhabited the mainland coasts and the islands turned to plundering, as it became easier to make raids on each other across the sea' (I. 5. I). The early Greeks were like the present barbarians, carrying weapons and wearing belts when they boxed or wrestled: 'and it could be shown that in many other ways the Hellenic world of ancient times lived as the barbarians do today' (I. 6. 5). This is, of course, another way of asserting the superiority of contemporary Greece over non-Greeks. Thucydides is no pro-barbarian, *philobarbaros*, as Herodotus was later accused of being. But whatever his emotional attitude, his intellectual analysis carries him beyond mere acceptance of the prevailing cleavage as part of the nature of things.

One quarter from which both Thucydides and Antiphon drew their ideas was the experience and outlook of the medical profession, whose writings contain evidence on this, as on other subjects, which has not received the attention it deserves. The importance and wide influence at this time of medical men and their doctrines, which is obvious from Plato's frequent references to them, is reflected in the large number of treatises which has come down to us under the name of the great doctor Hippocrates. It is now generally agreed that this Hippocratic Collection is in fact a library, probably that of the medical school of Hippocrates on the island of Cos. It includes works by various authors writing at various times—some much later than the fifth century B.C.— and from various points of view. Those most relevant for our purpose, however, are among the treatises most likely to come from Hippocrates himself, or at any rate from an author before the close of the fifth century.

Medical work keeps its practitioners too close to the facts of the human body for easy acceptance of divisions and prejudices which those facts do not support, whether doctrines of Nordic superiority or theoretical justifications of the colour bar. The doctor is concerned with the physical nature of man, to which distinctions of language, status and class are largely irrelevant:

47

smallpox kills on either side of the class or race or colour line. How far was this true of Hippocrates and his fellow-practitioners? An interesting passage in Plato's *Laws* (720), written about the middle of the fourth century, shows that at that time in some places, at any rate, the dichotomy of free man and slave had its effect even on the treatment of the sick. The speaker distinguishes between the freeborn doctor, who has real knowledge of his art, and his assistant, who may be a slave, and who has only empirical skill. 'You are aware', he says, 'that as sick people in the cities include both slaves and free men, the slaves are usually treated by slaves ... but the freeborn doctor for the most part observes and attends to the ailments of free men.'

We have no means of knowing how common this division was. In the Hippocratic writings there is no sign of it, or of any discrimination in attitude. The Hippocratic *Oath* promised abstention from improper treatment of all patients, female and male, free and slave. The notes on particular cases given in *Epidemics* illustrate the catholic variety of the doctor's work, stating the symptoms and effects of disease without distinction of persons: 'Cases of dysentery were also common during the summer, and some also of those that had fallen ill, who suffered from haemorrhage, finally turned to dysentery: for example, the slaves of Erato and Myllus, after serious haemorrhage, were afflicted with dysentery. They recovered' (I. 15). 'The patients', says Dr W. H. S. Jones, 'are sometimes householders, sometimes members of their families, sometimes slaves. Several seem to have been lodgers.'[30] Unlike most Greek literature, these medical works are concerned with all classes of men. The doctors' opportunities for observation were increased by travelling from town to town, a custom often mentioned in the treatises. Presumably their journeys were normally confined to the Greek-speaking world, but this did not mean that they saw only Greeks: many of the slaves they treated would be barbarians.

The conclusions which the medical writers drew from their experience certainly do not seem to have been affected by distinction of persons: a broad view of humanity, undivided by artificial barriers, is implied in some of their comments on their work and the diseases they had to treat. The writer of *Prognostic*, probably Hippocrates himself, points out that the same symptoms have the same meaning everywhere: 'It must be clearly realised with regard to symptoms, certain and otherwise, that in every year and every region bad signs have a bad significance and good ones a favourable implication; for the symptoms mentioned above prove valid in Libya, in Delos, and in Scythia' (25). The author of *The Sacred Disease* makes the same assumption that the reactions of barbarian bodies do not differ from those of Greeks. He is deriding the idea that epilepsy could be caused by eating goats' meat or wearing or lying on goat-skin: 'I suppose that none of the inhabitants of the interior of Libya can be healthy, for they lie on goat-skins and eat goats' flesh. They possess no coverlet or cloak or footwear which is not from goats, indeed they have no other cattle besides goats and oxen' (2). The writer of the Sophistic essay *On Breaths*, probably produced near the end of the fifth century, sees epidemic disease as common to the human species, while other animal species have their own different reactions. His account of the matter shows how close we are to Antiphon:

Epidemic fever is of this character because *all men inhale the same wind*, and when a similar wind has mingled with the body in a similar way, similar fevers result. ... So whenever the air is infected with pollutions inimical to the human constitution, men become sick; but when the air becomes ill-suited to some other species of animals, these fall sick. (6)

In the realm of theory the result of this outlook was a doctrine of the 'nature of man'—a phrase frequently used in some of the Hippocratic treatises, as it is by Thucydides. The human species was divided into male and female, and into the healthy and the sick; but nowhere in the Hippocratic Collection, as far as I know, is it stated or implied that man's basic nature differs according to whether he is of noble or humble birth, rich or poor, Greek or barbarian, free or slave.[31] When the writers turned to the question, what *is* the nature of man, some borrowed an answer from the philosophers—the author of *Regimen*, for example, who asserts that we are composed of the elements fire and water, and builds up a whole system of belief on the subject by putting together ideas taken from various early thinkers. Hippocrates and his associates, however, insisted on a more down-to-earth approach, deriving theory from medical experience, rather than deducing the treatment of patients from theory:

Some physicians and sophists assert that it is impossible to know the art of medicine without knowing what man is: anyone, they say, must learn this who intends to give men correct medical treatment. . . . My view, however, is that the only source from which clear knowledge of nature can be gained is medicine. This knowledge can be won when the art of medicine itself has been correctly grasped, but prior to this it is far from possible—I mean the possession of accurate understanding of man's nature, the causes of his being, and so on.[32]

An example of such a theory of the nature of man is the remarkable treatise *On Airs, Waters, Places*, probably by Hippocrates himself, which is primarily based on the doctors' own experience but uses a wide range of information from other sources as well, bringing within its scope Asiatics and North Africans and peoples on the fringe of the known world. Like Thucydides, the writer believes in a single basic human *physis*, which takes on varying characteristics according to the environment in which it is placed. Differences in physical condition and proneness to disease are due to climatic causes—different winds, waters, and seasonal changes, so that the student of medicine must consider, for example, 'the hot winds and the cold, especially those that are common to all men, but also those that are local in each region' (1). Differences in the character of the various peoples are the result of either the climate or the institutions under which they live, and this principle is equally valid everywhere. After describing Asiatics, the author goes on: 'In Europe also there are peoples differing from each other in stature, in physique, and in courage; and the causes that differentiate them are the same as in the cases I mentioned earlier' (24). Sometimes a defect in 'nature' due to the climate can be corrected by 'law' or 'custom' (*nomos*). Where men live in enclosed regions, with hot winds and warm water, 'courage and endurance are not implanted in their character by nature, but the imposition of *nomos* can produce them' (24).

Without stating the point in so many words, the author makes it clear that where the division of mankind on these rational lines cuts across the categories of current prejudice, the latter are to be thrust aside. Thus the region of Asia (later Asia Minor) which lies 'midway between the heat and the cold' has many good qualities, but 'courage, endurance, industry and spirit could not be produced under such conditions *in either the local population or immigrants*, but pleasure inevitably takes first place' (12): Asiatic 'barbarians' and Greek colonists become alike in the same environment. The further cause of this feebleness, subjection to autocratic government, also operates without distinguishing between Greek and foreigner: 'All inhabitants of Asia, Greek or barbarian, who are not under despotic rule but are independent and enjoy the fruits of their own labours, are the most warlike of all men' (16). A similar rejection of the belief that class distinctions involve any natural difference is implied, with a touch of satire, in the author's explanation of the prevalence of impotence among well-to-do Scythians. The cause is the upper-class practice of horse-riding. If the disease came from the gods, as the Scythians suppose, it would attack all classes equally, or rather especially the poor, who cannot worship the gods as lavishly as the rich and also blame them for their poverty. In reality 'such a disease arises among the Scythians for the reason I have stated, and the rest of mankind is equally liable to it' (22).

The theory of *On Airs, Waters, Places*, together with the assumptions which it implies, is the culminating product at this time of that biological approach to humanity, that conception of mankind as a single species requiring rational study, which we have seen in Anaximander, Anaxagoras, Antiphon and Thucydides. It maintains man's unity, yet admits his diversity, and seeks a reasoned explanation for it in the place of tradition and prejudice.

CHAPTER III

SOCRATES AND THE FOURTH CENTURY

SOCRATES

THE ferment of ideas towards the close of the fifth century B.C. brought to the fore a number of conceptions relevant to our theme, which we shall find further developed and elaborated in later generations: the notion of a single universal and permanent 'human nature'; the belief that certain physical attributes are common to all men; the concept of a human unity made up of diverse elements; the rejection of traditional divisions between men as artificial and relative, not natural or absolute; the picture of 'civilised man' as the human norm. We have seen that among an intellectual minority some of these trends of thought led towards an egalitarian outlook far removed from the traditional Greek point of view. If the ideas voiced by Protagoras, Antiphon and the medical writers had persisted and spread, they would have gone far towards undermining the accepted discriminations and prejudices which shaped the prevailing contemporary picture of mankind. This, however, is not the main development that we find in thinkers after the fifth century B.C. The actual sequel, very different from egalitarianism, owed its derivation principally to another line of thought—the attitude chiefly represented by Socrates.

At first glance Socrates might be regarded as having nothing to say that concerns us here. He avoided wide horizons, and notoriously confined his movements and activities to his beloved Athens. He wrote nothing that has survived, and we know of no pronouncement of his about mankind as a whole; yet he had a profound influence on Greek ideas about the unity and the division of the human race. If we briefly review what appear to have been the essentials of his outlook, we shall not be surprised that his companions and admirers derived from him a common emphasis on a distinctive, though by no means new, line of differentiation between men—the reply of the fourth century to the budding egalitarianism of the close of the fifth.

One of the few certainties about the historical Socrates, a common factor in our conflicting evidence about him, which is confirmed by the outlook of his various followers, is that he upheld a different standard for man, a different conception of what is important in human life. For him it was not external goods—high birth or wealth, for example—that mattered. He himself was of humble birth, and Plato regularly represents him as having no money. Although he was no ascetic, his simple clothes and habits were a deliberate contrast to the fine clothing and fine ways of the rich aristocracy. Nor did he regard the body as the important part of man: in Plato's *Phaedo* (97b ff.) he tells how he rejected Anaxagoras' physical explanations of human movement; and although he constantly borrows analogies from the art of medicine, he had no sympathy with what I have called the 'biological approach' of the medical writers.

Socrates' whole life and thought centred round the belief that the *psychē*—'soul' is a translation with confusing overtones—is the vital part of us; and that the primary feature of the human *psychē* is its possession of *logos*, 'reason', closely connected with articulate speech. We have seen that this idea was far from new. It had its roots as far back as Homer's stock descriptions of men as creatures endowed with the gift of speech.

Socrates' development of this conception still maintained the link between speech and reasoning, so that he regarded thought as essentially a dialectic process involving discussion, and Plato, following in his footsteps, later described even individual thinking as a kind of dialogue within the *psychē*. What Socrates did was to make our possession of *logos* the key to the good life. Through the right use of *logos* we can attain wisdom, and through wisdom, happiness—*eudaimonia*, no longer contingent on the benevolence of a kindly *daimōn*, but the fruit of the wise man's own attitude of mind. Men need no longer depend on the whim of the gods to save them from the wretchedness which Homer saw as their common lot: in reason they possess the secret of happiness within themselves.

One aspect of Socrates' insistence on the right use of *logos* was his habit of seeking definitions. If he had applied this process to man, he might well have defined him as a reasoning animal, marked off from others by the common power of thought, in anticipation of Pascal: 'L'homme n'est qu'un roseau le plus faible de la nature; mais c'est un roseau pensant.' The idea had been implied long before in Heraclitus' doctrine that 'the *Logos* is common', and we have seen it emerging at a number of points in the fifth century B.C. With Socrates' new emphasis on *logos* as our most precious gift, we seem not far away from the conception of the common possession of reason as a bond between all human beings, overriding all divisions, whether between man and woman, or barbarian and Greek, or slave and free. But this was not a road that Greek thought easily followed. Rather than concentrate on the common link, as the medical writers did, most Greek thinkers still tended to think in terms of Odysseus and Thersites, high and low, worthy and worthless—and so, where *logos* was concerned, in terms of wise men and fools. The 'wise man', shrewd in counsel and provident as law-giver, was a regular ideal figure in the traditions of the Greek cities. Heraclitus, although he saw the *Logos* as common, proclaimed that most men are unaware of it. The Pythagoreans looked upon themselves as a small, select community of wisdom in a world of folly, and are said to have divided humanity into three types comparable with the three kinds of people who come to the Olympic Games: those who come to buy and sell, those who come to compete, and those—the best of all—who come to look on.

Socrates was no exception to this general Greek trend. He also did not concern himself with the implications of the idea that all men possess the power of reasoning, but with the need for making the *right* use of *logos* in order to achieve *true* wisdom. In Plato's *Apology* he tells how in his search at Athens for someone wiser than himself he rejected those traditionally regarded as the wise men of the community, the poets and politicians, and found that even the craftsmen's knowledge was limited to their own skill. Man's rise to civilisation through the arts, proclaimed by Aeschylus and Sophocles and Protagoras, had not brought him the wisdom Socrates was seeking. We have seen how in the *Phaedo* he denies wisdom to Anaxagoras and, by implication, to others with a materialist approach. In other Platonic dialogues his object is to expose the Sophists' pretended wisdom as a sham.

Amid all this Socrates makes no higher claim of wisdom for himself than that he, alone among men, is aware of his own ignorance. Nevertheless, the effect of his teaching and example was to strengthen still further the distinction between the wise man and the rest of foolish humanity, treating reason not as a common bond but as the basis of a barrier cutting across mankind. In spite of his modest pretensions, Socrates himself was naturally regarded as the typical 'wise man' by his contemporaries— idealised by his admirers, ridiculed by his critics and enemies. In the *Apology* he tells how the label *sophos*, the wise one, was attached to him by the Athenians (23 a, cf. 18 b); and Aristophanes was following popular opinion when he caricatured him in the *Clouds* as head of a 'thinking-shop of wise souls'.

This division of humanity into the wise and the unwise had a remarkable appeal to the Greek mind, and proved as long-lasting in its effects as the Homeric distinction between heroes and rabble. After Socrates, the question of the relation between the wise man and the rest became a crucial issue in discussions of the nature of human society and the unity of mankind. Where should the wise man stand—inside or outside society? How is the distinction between wise and foolish related to the accepted categories— male and female, free and slave, Greek and barbarian? Does it coincide with any of these, or transcend them all?

One possible line of thought was the creation of a new aristo-cracy of wisdom, a new *élite* to supersede the old, now largely discredited, aristocracy of birth. The wise man must not stand outside the community, but replace the hero and the noble at its head. The 'Old Oligarch' claimed that the upper class was the wisest: Socrates' followers could maintain that the wisest should be the upper class.

It may be that suspicion of such political ambitions was one of the causes of Socrates' indictment and condemnation. But the evidence rather suggests a popular conception of him as an eccentric standing aside, and drawing others aside, from normal society. This is the picture we find in Aristophanes' *Clouds* and in a passage of the *Frogs* (1482 ff.), and drawn again by Callicles in Plato's *Gorgias*:

Even though highly gifted by nature, such a person comes to be unmanly. He avoids the heart of the city and the market-place, where, as the poet says, men win true glory: instead he slinks away and spends the rest of his life whispering with three or four lads in a corner, and never makes any utterance that is worthy of a free man or important or effective.[1]

This conception of the seeker after wisdom, the philosopher, as outside the everyday life of the community, carried with it the idea that wisdom united its possessors everywhere, placing them above the ordinary divisions of mankind. 'The vertical classifica-tion of men into sages and fools', writes Ferguson, 'had as its necessary complement a horizontal grouping of them as kinsmen, it being a matter of no consequence in either case whether they were Greeks or Barbarians, rich or poor, free or slave.'[2] We have already seen this thought expressed by Euripides, and shall find it again in Socrates' contemporary, Democritus. The Pytha-goreans, we are told, based their behaviour to each other every-where on the belief that 'men of worth, even though they live far apart, are friends to each other before they meet or speak'.[3] For later generations, the idealised figure of Socrates was the embodiment of wisdom which lifts its possessors above the prejudices of the day, but also separates them by a great gulf from the unwise majority of mankind.

In comparison with this paramount distinction other divisions might fall away into insignificance—a line of thought which we shall find among the Cynics. But there was another possibility with a more ready appeal to minds so deeply imbued with the habit of discrimination as the Greeks: the idea that in the possession of *logos* or the lack of it a rational basis could be found for maintaining the old lines of difference, for taking what had hitherto been a matter of emotional prejudice and crystallising it into an intellectual pattern; and this, as we shall see, was the path followed by the outstanding thinkers of the fourth century B.C.

DEMOCRITUS

It would be surprising if the trends of thought about mankind which we have been tracing did not find some reflection in the writings of Democritus of Abdera (about 460–370 B.C.), which seem to have dealt with almost every field of human experience. Unfortunately the evidence on which an estimate of his views must be based all comes from two groups of 'fragments' rejected by some scholars as spurious.[4] What they contain suggests no view peculiar to Democritus, although there is nothing incredible in them as a picture of ideas on the subject of man at the end of the fifth and in the early decades of the fourth century B.C.

'Since we are human', says one 'maxim', 'we should sorrow over the misfortunes of human beings, not laugh at them' (107a). Another bases this need for sympathy with one's fellow-men on the subjection of all mankind to chance, the common source of both suffering and happiness: 'Those who find pleasure in their neighbours' misfortunes do not realise that the workings of chance are the common lot of all, nor do they understand the source of their own joy' (293). Fellow-feeling within a community can bring untold blessings: 'When the powerful have the heart to provide for those who have nothing, and to help them and fulfil their needs, here at last is pity, and an end to isolation, and comradeship, and mutual aid, and harmony of mind among the citizens, and other good things too numerous to tell' (255). The same spirit recurs in several other statements on the value of friendship.5 But it is noteworthy that this appeal for co-operation is made within the framework of the *polis*; and elsewhere such local *homonoia* is combined with acceptance of war against other states: 'From unity of mind (*homonoia*) come great achievements: only with this can cities crush their enemies' (250). Slavery is likewise accepted as a normal part of life: 'Use slaves like parts of the body, each for his own work' (270). The inferiority of women, too, is stated in several fragments without question.6 There is no indication that Democritus challenged, or even doubted, these basic divisions in Greek society.

Distinction between free men according to birth or wealth has no place in the picture presented by this evidence, and would indeed be inconsistent with some of the sentences quoted already. But the division between wise men and fools, good men and bad, is reiterated in many forms; and with it goes here also the further thought that friendship naturally arises between men of like mind. 'Unity of outlook creates friendship' (186). 'Not all kinsfolk are friends, but only those who agree about what is expedient' (107). These may seem mere truisms; but in combination with the idea of wisdom as the hall-mark of a separate section of mankind, extending beyond the city-state, the same line of thought leads to that notion of the world-unity of intellect which we have already found implied in the thought of Socrates and the Pythagoreans and expressed by Euripides. Here the same conception is put into words which show that Democritus also—if they are his—was capable of transcending the limits of the *polis* on this level: 'To a wise man every land is open; for the whole world is the native country of a good soul' (247). The genuineness of this fragment has been questioned, but its content, at any rate, is no ground for doubting its authenticity. If Democritus wrote these words, he was only expressing an outlook which others made familiar in the fourth century as they developed ideas already put forward in the fifth.

THE FOURTH CENTURY

For the period from the end of the fifth century B.C. to the death of Alexander the Great we have five major sources of information about the development of ideas relevant to our theme: the works of Xenophon, Isocrates, Plato, and Aristotle; and the evidence, such as it is, for the views of the early Cynics. Each of the five presents us with a distinctive attitude, although of course they have some features in common and some connections can be seen between them. In what ways any or all of them are typical of contemporary thought, is a difficult, if not impossible, question to decide; for apart from these five, indications of any realisation of human unity or rejection of divisions within mankind are limited to a few statements by intellectuals who are unlikely to be typical, and some themes and passages of comedy which are difficult to evaluate.

There is some evidence that the questioning of accepted prejudices continued. Comedy seems to show that discrimination against women was criticised in some quarters; at any rate, the idea of its reversal was well enough known to be a target for the comic poet. The presentation of Aristophanes' *Women in Parliament* some years before the earliest likely date for the appearance of Plato's *Republic* suggests that revolutionary ideas about the status and abilities of women may then have been common talk in intellectual circles at Athens, although Aristotle attributes such schemes only to Plato. Later, both Alexis and Amphis produced comedies called *Woman in Power*. Superiority of birth was flatly rejected by the Sophist Lycophron in words quoted by Aristotle: 'The splendour of high birth is imaginary, its majesty mere talk' (A 4). In a period when the gap between rich and poor was increasing, comedy gives us echoes of popular demand for a fairer distribution of goods—again Aristophanes' *Women in Parliament*, for example, with its burlesque of the welfare state, and his *Plutus*, in which the god of wealth regains his sight.

Slavery also had its critics. Both Plato and Aristotle, as we shall see, refer to contemporary controversy about the rights and wrongs of slavery and the proper treatment of slaves. In our extant evidence, however, only one lone voice is raised at this time in strong dissent from the general assumption that it is normal and right for some men to be slaves. This is a sentence from a speech by the Sophist Alcidamas, delivered after the Messenians in 369 B.C. had been freed from their subjection as helots to Sparta—an event which must have roused wide discussion, at any rate of the enslavement of Greeks by Greeks. Championing the liberation in opposition to Isocrates, Alcidamas made one of the most categorical statements against slavery in antiquity: 'God has left all men free; nature has made no man a slave.'7 Some lines preserved from a comedy by Anaxandrides, perhaps first performed in 352 B.C., express once more the thought that slavery is a matter of chance rather than nature; but it seems likely that the author's main point is to satirise the ease with which slaves can become citizens by admission to the Attic deme of Sunium:

> Slaves have no city anywhere, my friend.
> Chance gives men first this status, and then that.
> Many who have no liberty today
> Tomorrow become Sunians; the next,
> They're in the market-place. So Fortune shifts
> The helm for each.8

To complete the picture, mention must be made of one thinker who is represented as rejecting the *polis* itself—a line of thought which we shall find again in the Cynics, and later in the Epicureans. This is Aristippus of Cyrene, whom Xenophon portrays in conversation with Socrates. To Socrates' argument that those who seek another lot than rule or subjection are only crushed by the strong, Aristippus replies: 'Well, for my part, to avoid suffering this fate, I do not shut myself up within the confines of a state, but am a stranger everywhere' (*Mem.* II. I. 13). The words cannot be regarded as Aristippus' own, but are likely to be true to his outlook; and we can safely place him in the line of those who turned their backs on the *polis* and looked to a wider unity of the wise for their spiritual home.

As a contrast with these scraps of evidence for more radical views stand the varying degrees of conservatism which we find in Xenophon, Isocrates, Plato and Aristotle, all of whom, in different ways and with different reservations, tended to accept or excuse or even strengthen the framework of differentiation which we have seen reflected in most fifth-century literature. Which outlook was more typical of the majority of Greeks in the fourth century B.C.?

In comparison with the few passages so far mentioned there are many in the orators and elsewhere that repeat without question the accepted assumptions and prejudices, so that the balance in favour of orthodoxy seems greater in the fourth century B.C. than in the closing decades of the fifth. An impression gained from information so scanty and so limited may well be wrong. Most of it comes from Athens, and very different points of view may have prevailed elsewhere, especially (as we shall see to some extent in Xenophon) among those whose life brought them into association with 'barbarians'. Literary sources, it may be further argued, voice the mentality of the upper class, and quite other ideas may have existed among the less articulate majority—the scores of thousands of Greeks, for example, who went to serve as mercenaries in the armies of 'barbarian' rulers. Even among the rich, commercial interest was likely to foster an outlook that transcended the old limitations. Just before the beginning of the century the orator Lysias attacks the contemporary equivalent of the internationalism of high finance: those who, though born citizens, find their fatherland 'in any country in which they have business'— in short, 'not in their city but in their wealth'.9 Profit, as well as wisdom, could raise a man above the limits of the city-state.

The importance or extent of such trends cannot now be judged with any certainty. It may well be that the general attitude of most of the Athenians, at any rate, in this time of increasing contact with the non-Greek world, is fairly reflected in another fragment from the comic poet Anaxandrides, in which Demos—the People of Athens—addresses the Egyptians. He is familiar with their peculiar ways, but cannot see himself drawing into closer association with folk who turn all his customs upside-down:

> I couldn't well ally myself with you:
> Neither our customs nor our ways agree,
> But differ far. You fall before the ox
> In reverence: I slay him for the gods.
> You make the eel your greatest deity:
> With us he's best of all good things to eat.
> You don't eat pork, but I do, with a relish.
> You worship your dog: I give mine a beating
> If he steals meat. Our priests we keep intact:
> Yours you make eunuchs. If you see the cat
> Fall sick, you weep: I gladly kill and skin her.
> The mouse has power with you: to me she's nothing.[10]

Our information is clearly insufficient to provide an adequate picture of fourth-century public opinion on these matters at Athens or elsewhere. It can only be said that the documentary evidence gives us no ground for belief in any general growth of the idea of human unity or brotherhood in the decades between the Peloponnesian War and Alexander, or any widespread opposition to discriminations based on sex and class and race; no ground for supposing, as is sometimes done, that the majority had called in question or even cast aside the prejudices which Plato and Aristotle try to reassert. There is no basis for this view in the contemporary evidence, nor, as I shall hope to show, in the state of opinion in the Greek world after Alexander. The fourth-century philosophers are not to be seen as endeavouring to stem a tide of more enlightened opinion which, in spite of them, spread over Greece at the beginning of the Hellenistic age.

Although the five main sources to which we must now turn appear to the modern mind conservative or reactionary in comparison with earlier more radical ideas, the documentary evidence at any rate seems to suggest that in their different degrees and ways they gave intellectual crystallisation to the prevailing outlook of their day, rather than opposed it. Where they differed from it, they were often in advance of their times rather than behind them. Some of the lines of thought on which they travelled further than most of their contemporaries—Panhellenism, for example, and the contrast between wisdom and folly—led towards a limited unity rather than a universal kinship of mankind. But in so far as they saw the human race as a whole, however divided, they promoted the idea of its unity. For all the narrowness and inhumanity of some of their beliefs (a criticism which the whole of fourth-century Greece must share) all the writers now to be considered made some contribution towards the fuller conception of mankind that eventually emerged.

XENOPHON

Xenophon was the least intellectual of these fourth-century figures, the least likely to seek general principles underlying particular facts or to arrive at a synoptic view. His *Hellenica* narrates the history of his time from a Spartan standpoint and shows little realisation of Panhellenic trends[11]—a sorry contrast in intellectual quality with the work of Thucydides to which it forms a sequel. How inadequately he understands the significance of Socrates is shown by comparison with Plato. It is not surprising that we do not find in his writings any fundamental questioning on theoretical grounds, such as we have seen in the Sophists and shall see in Plato, of the accepted pattern of humanity. His book on household management, the *Oeconomicus*, takes the inferiority of women and the subjection of slaves for granted, although the position of both is regarded from the benevolent point of view of an enlightened country squire. The wife's place is the home, for God made her nature fit for tasks and cares within the house: her physique is not suited to life outside, which must be left to the men (7. 22-3). The position of the slave is justified by a simple application of the idea of *logos* as the ground of differentiation between high and low, ruler and ruled. The free man is assumed to have *logos*, the slave, like the beasts, to have none; and so he is seen—with no unkindly eye—almost as a species of domestic animal. After speaking of the training of ponies and puppies by rewards and punishments, the landowner Ischomachus goes on: 'One can make men (*anthrōpoi*) more obedient by showing them by *logos* ("word of mouth" or "reasoning"?) that obedience is for their good. But for slaves the training usually associated with animals is an effective way of teaching obedience; for you will get good results from them by giving their bellies what they desire' (13. 9). The implication that slaves, devoid of *logos* and scarcely *anthrōpoi* at all, have the mentality of animals reappears in the *Cyropaedia*, Xenophon's idealised biography of the sixth-century ruler of Persia. It was Cyrus' practice 'to serve all the servants' food from his own table, for he thought that this encouraged some measure of goodwill in them, as it does in dogs' (VIII. 2. 4). He always took care that slaves should not go without food or drink, as free men were sometimes required to do. When they acted as beaters in a hunt, he ordered food to be brought for them, but not for any of the free men; 'and when a ford was reached, he would lead them to the water like the baggage animals'. Hence the slaves, no less than the nobles, called him 'Father', because 'he took care of them so that they should always without question continue to be slaves'.[12]

All this is far away from Antiphon and Alcidamas. But if not outstanding in intellect, Xenophon was exceptional in experience. His association with Socrates, limited though it must have been, gave a philosophical turn to the idea of benevolent dictatorship, whether in the household or the state, which was his natural trend of thought: like Isocrates and Plato, he developed the notion of the wise ruler whose subjects are ruled for their own good, although his conception of him is far from the philosopher-king of the *Republic*. Secondly, the expedition to the East which he describes in the *Anabasis* brought him first-hand knowledge of non-Greek peoples and admiration for the traditions of the Persian aristocracy; above all, for the young Cyrus, in whose cause he had enlisted. 'I consider', he writes, 'that no one, either Greek or barbarian, has ever been more generally beloved' (I. 9. 28).

Approval of Cyrus was not accompanied by any respect for Persians in general, or doubt of their inferiority to the Greeks. Xenophon puts into Cyrus' own mouth a speech to the Greeks, when battle with the Great King's forces seems imminent, which rests on well-worn Greek assumptions and even applies the word *barbaroi* to his own people:

Men from Greece, it is not because of shortage of barbarians that I am leading you into battle at my side. I have obtained your help because I regard you as better and stronger than a host of barbarians. See then that you prove worthy of your freedom, which I think you happy to have: for be assured that I would rather have freedom than all my possessions, and many times more. To give you an idea of the sort of fighting you face, I will describe it for you from my own knowledge. Their numbers are great and they will advance with a deal of shouting; but if you stand up to this, I am ashamed at the thought of what sort of men, in every other way, you will find we have in this land (I. 7. 3–4).

One Greek is as good as many barbarians; Greeks are free, barbarians enslaved; barbarians make much noise but with little meaning. These are familiar themes. But to Cyrus, although he is Persian born and bred, they do not apply. 'Of all the Persians after Cyrus the Elder', writes Xenophon on his death, 'he was the most kingly and the most fitted to rule' (I. 9. 1). The same estimate is put into Socrates' mouth in the *Oeconomicus* (4. 18). When Xenophon wants to set forth his conception of the wise and beneficent ruler he exemplifies it not only in the Spartan Agesilaus, but still more in the description of the education and life of Cyrus the Elder which fills the eight books of the *Cyropaedia*; though the final chapter (if it is by Xenophon) takes care to counter the idealisation of sixth-century Persia by dwelling on the degeneration into which the mass of the Persians have now sunk.

Xenophon does not work out the theoretical significance of all this for the nature of humanity, any more than he is aware of the theoretical significance of a passage in the *Anabasis* which assumes gradations of barbarism, those barbarians being 'most barbarous' who are 'furthest removed from the customs of the Greeks' (v. 4. 34). But his outlook is of interest to us because there were implicit in it some of the main trends of thought about mankind which came to the fore in the fourth century and were brought into the open by others: that wisdom and merit transcended racial divisions, and therefore not race, but some other criterion, provided the important dividing line among men; that civilised standards were not confined to the Greeks, but other peoples had something to contribute to the concept of civilisation; or that if all civilisation was indeed Hellenic, then Hellenism was not a matter of blood.

ISOCRATES

Isocrates comes into our picture primarily as the untiring advocate of a Panhellenic crusade against the Persian 'barbarians'. 'Concord among Greeks and war against barbarians' is the stock theme of his political pamphlets; and although he tells us that this was a common topic of contemporary oratory,[13] we know of no speaker or writer who reiterated it so persistently as he. Whether under joint Athenian and Spartan leadership, as he proposed in the *Panegyricus* in 380 B.C., or with Philip of Macedon at their head, as he advocated thirty-four years later, the Greeks must unite in military action against their hereditary foes, their *natural* enemies. Homer owes much of his fame to his glorification of the men who fought against the barbarians—a striking distortion of Homer's real attitude to the Trojans. Through war against the foreign enemy lies the road to Greek peace and harmony.[14] Also, to Greek prosperity; for although Isocrates denies that the riches of the East are his main objective, the contrast between Greek poverty and supposed Persian plenty is clearly a strong material motive behind his eloquence.

If this were all, Isocrates could be regarded as one who attempted to strengthen Greek unity and anticipated future events, but had no conception of any unity or brotherhood of mankind. More closely scrutinised, however, his political works are found to contain much more than mere propaganda for a racial war. 'There is something of philosophy in the man's nature', says Socrates of him in Plato's *Phaedrus* (279 b); and although he was no abstract theorist or creator of a philosophical system, several passages show that his *Herrenvolk* doctrine was based on general principles which are very relevant to our theme.

How far he came under Socrates' influence in his early years, is doubtful; certainly in later life he tended to think in terms characteristic of the Socratic way of thought, such as 'reason', 'wisdom', and 'philosophy'. But in his mind these concepts took on a shape, perhaps inherited from the fifth-century Sophists, which fitted the outlook of the orator concerned with practical policies, so that for Isocrates *logos* meant the spoken word, eloquent and persuasive speech, quite as much as 'reason', and his *philosophia* centred on practical wisdom (*phronēsis*) rather than abstract speculation. These were the qualities which Isocrates looked for in the new intellectual *élite* which, as Jaeger says,[15] he sought to create in place of the old aristocracy of birth. Like Xenophon, he idealised the wise ruler; and in what might now be called an open letter to the young prince Nicocles of Cyprus he emphasises that the successful kings' first need is superiority in wisdom: they 'should see to it that they excel all others in wisdom. For experience has shown that the merits of their reign will depend on their preparation of their own minds for the task. Hence no athlete needs to train his body so thoroughly as a king should train his soul' (*To Nicocles*, 10–11). Or again: 'It is you who will give yourself the greatest encouragement, if you regard it as outrageous that the worse should rule the better and the less intelligent have command over the wise; for the more emphatically you disapprove of others' stupidity, the better will you train your own understanding' (14). In this and other passages Isocrates reaffirms the familiar distinction between the few wise and the many foolish. But his conception of the place of *logos* in the scheme of things is far wider than this, and provides the basis for the whole pattern of the animate world as he sees it. Although the idea of humanity as a whole is abstract and remote for him compared with the immediate issue of Greek against barbarian, he does regard all men as sharing the common gift of *logos*. It is this that raises them above animals, against whose savagery all mankind rightly wages a perpetual war (*Panath.* 163); and presumably it is this that brings about the common human respect for agreements to which Isocrates appeals, with some exaggeration, in an early lawcourt speech:

Their effect is so binding [he claims] that most things in the life of both Greeks and barbarians are controlled by agreements. We rely on them in making journeys to each other and supplying the goods which we both happen to require. It is with their help that we bring about contracts with each other and make an end of either personal feuds or general wars. This is the only common instrument of which all men continually make use. (*Ag. Callim.* 27–8)

In a passage of the *Nicocles*, which Isocrates thought important enough to be repeated later in the *Antidosis* (253–4), he describes all human civilisation as the product of speech (*logos*) and the wisdom that speech makes possible—'that power which of all the faculties inherent in man's nature is the most fruitful in blessings':

In the other characteristics that we possess we are not at all superior to other creatures: we are really inferior to many in speed and strength and other resources. But there is in us the ability to persuade each other and to explain to each other what we desire; and by this we not only escaped living like beasts, but came together and founded cities and established laws and invented arts. Practically everything we have devised has been brought into being with the help of speech. It is this that created laws distinguishing what is just or unjust, right or wrong— laws without which we could not live with one another. (5–7)

Thus all men have some share of *logos*. But Isocrates is of course far from thinking that all share in it equally, or are equally capable of the use of it. Like Plato and Aristotle, he sees mankind in a pattern graded according to possession or lack of *logos*, and it is their different degrees of participation in this gift that separate men into divisions with different levels of civilisation and culture. Hence the superiority of Greek over barbarian, and of the Athenians over all other Greeks. Isocrates tells the Athenians:

The reason why you excel and have the advantage over others is not the attention you pay to war, nor your admirable form of government and high regard for the laws which your ancestors handed down to you. It lies in those qualities which raise man above the other animals and the Hellenic race above the barbarians—in the fact that you have been educated better than all others in wisdom and in speech.

(*Antid.* 293–4)

Mankind is, in fact, a hierarchy. For Isocrates, however, the hierarchy is not rigidly fixed: there is room for advance from a lower level of *logos* to a higher. Seen in this light, the gulf which he proclaims between Greek and barbarian appears less insuperable than at first sight, and their 'natural' antagonism need no longer be an unchanging and permanent feature of human existence. The gap becomes one of degree, not of kind, related to the development of the intellect rather than to some peculiarity of physical make-up. 'The name "Hellenes"', he writes in the *Panegyricus*, 'now seems to belong not to a race but to a mental outlook, and is applied to those who share our culture rather than to men who share a common blood.'[16] The Persians, on the other hand, owe their servility, weakness and cowardice to their upbringing and their political institutions—a way of life which must corrupt the natures of men (*Paneg.* 150–1). But where human nature is deficient or corrupted, it can be improved. Isocrates justifies his own profession as a teacher of eloquence and general culture by insisting that the nature of man is responsive to *paideia*, education, and *epimeleia*, the attention which a guardian can bestow on those put in his care. If bodily weakness can be overcome by exercise and effort, surely the *psychē* can be made better through education and *epimeleia*; if lions can be tamed and bears given skill by training, still more can be achieved in changing the nature of human beings.[17] An example has already been provided by the good effects of the wise rule of Evagoras in Cyprus, which has made the fierce and hostile inhabitants friendly to the Greeks and eager to acquire Greek culture (*Evag.* 47–50). At the close of his appeal *To Philip*, which some translators have misinterpreted, Isocrates restates from this point of view the object of his anti-Persian campaign. Philip should have a three-fold purpose, corresponding to three levels of mankind:

> I suggest that your aim should be to work for the benefit of the Greeks, to be king over the Macedonians, and to bring as many barbarians as possible under your rule. If you follow this course, all will be grateful to you: the Greeks for the benefits they receive; the Macedonians because you reign over them not as a tyrant, but as a king; and the rest of the peoples, because through you they are set free from barbarian despotism and come under the guardianship (*epimeleia*) of Greece. (154)

Epimeleia here does not mean merely 'protection'; it implies— and the implication is, I think, more than a rhetorical flourish— that under Greek guardianship the barbarians can be raised above the slavish level at which despotism has kept them. As we have seen, Isocrates had various immediate motives for his advocacy of war against Persia, and these, no doubt, were his chief concern; but in so far as he saw it in this longer perspective, in its relation to the general principles on which he believed his teaching to be based, it contained an element which made it not a destructive crusade, but a civilising mission, intended to raise inferior peoples (as he regarded them) to the level of Greek civilisation. The principal effect of his campaign on the contemporary view of humanity must have been to strengthen the sense of division between the *Herrenvolk* and the rest. Even his underlying belief that all might one day rise to the Greek level involved the assumption that Greek culture, and Greek culture alone, was superior to all others. Nevertheless, this belief did constitute a certain advance in the direction of awareness of the unity of mankind.

As a result of the preservation of his works, Isocrates now stands out as an isolated individual; but in addition to being an orator and a pamphleteer he was also an educator, and his importance lies partly in his great influence on others. Before we leave him, one example of this influence must be mentioned: a speech in the *History* of Diodorus in which we may safely detect the hand of Isocrates' pupil Ephorus (about 405–330 B.C.), the chief source for this section of Diodorus' work.[18]

Diodorus' narrative has reached 413 B.C.: the Athenian invaders of Sicily have surrendered, and the Syracusans are debating their fate. A proposal has been put forward that their general should be put to death under torture, and the rest of the army thrown into the quarries; but an old man called Nicolaus, who has lost his two sons in the war, comes forward and appeals for a policy of mercy. His main emphasis falls on the fellow-feeling between Greeks, which the Syracusans must not violate. 'Among Greeks', he says, 'there should be enmity only till victory is won, punishment only till the enemy is beaten' (24. 3). In earlier days the Greeks set up victory trophies of wood, not of stone, so that when they disappeared hostility should be forgotten. The Athenians above all have in the past been the creators and champions of this civilised spirit—a eulogy of Athens which on this occasion cannot be historical.

All this is closely in line with Isocrates' Panhellenism and his praise of the Athenians as protagonists of the Hellenic tradition. But here, as in his works, Athenians and Greeks are seen only as the outstanding representatives of qualities which belong to all mankind. The Syracusans, says Nicolaus, must not expect that 'after murdering so many men in violation of the traditional customs of the Greeks, they can appeal in life's changes of fortune to the usages common to all humanity' (23. 4–5). The universal human qualities stressed in this speech are not *logos*, but those attitudes of sympathy (*philanthrōpia*) and compassion (*eleos*) which arise as an answer to our common helplessness in the face of our fate. 'The spirits of civilised men', Nicolaus declares, 'are

71

overcome above all by compassion, because of the fellow-feeling which nature has implanted in us' (24. 2). Or again:

What honour is there in killing a man who has fallen? What glory in inflicting vengeance on him? He who inflexibly maintains a callous attitude towards misfortune does not do justice to the common weakness of mankind. For no one is so wise as to be stronger than fortune, which delights in human sufferings and ends prosperity with sudden change. (21. 4-5)

Such sentiments, now put into fourth-century language, are of course as old as Homer, and recall the last book of the *Iliad*. But their expression here confirms the breadth of the outlook underlying the strongly Hellenic and Athenian attitude of Isocrates and his pupils. Nicolaus ends with a last appeal for the defeated Athenian, fortune's latest victim, which typically combines the thought of universal humanity with a final reference to Greek superiority over the barbarian:

With his hands bound behind his back, in a dirty tunic, he has experienced the pitiful fate of captivity, as if fortune wanted to use his life as a demonstration of her power. When fortune smiles, we should accept her kindness without forgetting that we are only men, and should not show barbarous callousness towards men of our own race.[19]

PLATO

Plato believed that the first need of human society, the essential remedy for its contemporary ills, was unity and concord; yet he was equally insistent on divisions that separate men. The combination may seem paradoxical, but it was no more than a variation on the traditional Greek outlook, which from Homer onwards had divided men into high and low, good and bad, worthy and worthless, and held that it is through the acceptance of such distinctions, the recognition that all men are *not* equal, that peace and harmony in the community are to be maintained. We have seen that in the fifth century B.C., and especially during its last decades, this tradition had become weaker and lost much of its hold on the Greek mind. Plato wanted to restore it.

To this extent his political thinking was traditional and can be called 'reactionary'. In another, and to his contemporaries probably more obvious way it was revolutionary, in that although of high birth and wealthy family himself, Plato rejected birth or property as the ground of discrimination, and followed Socrates in seeking a new basis in the inner character and mentality of men themselves. Socrates had held that true wisdom, the right use of reason, was the real hall-mark of quality among human beings—not possessions or noble blood or the pretended knowledge of those usually regarded as wise. Plato carried this view further by moulding it into a coherent picture of human society, based not on tradition or convention but on nature, and related to an interpretation of reality as a whole.

Several strands of thought were interwoven in the formation of the pattern of human society as Plato saw it. One was the idea of differences in natural aptitude, easily acceptable when many skills were traditionally handed down from father to son. We have seen how Protagoras uses this concept in the myth which Plato makes him tell, and Xenophon and Plato agree in attributing it also to Socrates. In Plato's works it becomes a commonplace, especially in the *Statesman*. In the *Republic* it is the foundation for the division of labour and the creation of a professional army from those naturally fitted for soldiering; and above all, the distinction between philosophers, men of true wisdom, and the rest of the community is justified by their natural aptitude for reasoned thought.

A second feature of Plato's approach to the subject is his view of individual psychology, which has been compared with the Pythagorean distinction between the three kinds of men at the games.[20] The *psychē*—according to the *Republic* version of the matter—is made up of three elements, appetitive, spirited, and reasoning; and men fall into natural divisions according to the predominance of one or other of these aspects of their make-up.

Most important of all is the relation which Plato sees between these human groupings and their metaphysical context, his ultimate analysis of all experience. Just as there is a great gulf between the Forms known to the mind and the appearances perceived by the senses, between the dark cave of illusion where we live and the bright realm of knowledge to which a few may escape, so there is a deep division between 'those who can apprehend the eternally immutable and those who lose their way amid multiplicity and change' (*Rep.* 484b). The gap between the wise and the foolish becomes as wide as that between two different worlds.

With an innate fitness for the task of *knowing*, guided by the reasoning element within him, lifted above ordinary humanity by the vision of the highest truth, Plato's wise man is thus *by nature* distinct from all others. His idealisation of him is expressed in many ways—he is gold, the others baser metal; he is akin to the divine, the others merely human—but most effectively of all, by the place given to Socrates in the dialogues.

Although Plato sees education as the most important thing in life for those who can profit by it, he has no belief, like Isocrates, that teaching can raise large numbers of men to higher levels of understanding. Those to whom nature has given the ability to become philosophers are very few, and this will always be so. What then is to be the relation between these few and the rest of society? For Plato, as the autobiographical passages of the *Seventh Letter* make clear, this was a crucial personal problem, demanding decision both in his youth and on occasions in his later years.

His conclusion was that while society is as it is, the philosopher's place is outside it. This is the attitude which he attributes to Socrates in the *Apology* and *Phaedo*, although he makes it clear in the *Crito* that the philosopher is not thereby exempt from obeying the law. In the *Republic* he draws a vivid picture of the wise man's plight amid the contemporary scene:

When those who belong to this small company have tasted the sweetness and happiness of their lot and have watched the folly of the multitude and realised that there is virtually no soundness in the conduct of public life, no ally at whose side one can win through in the fight for what is just; but that like a man fallen among wild beasts, unwilling to join in their villainy yet unable to hold out single-handed against the savagery of them all, the champion of justice must perish before helping his city or his friends, and so prove useless to himself or anyone else—he who has reasoned all this out keeps quiet and attends to his own affairs, like a man who stands apart by a wall to shelter from a driving storm of dust and hail. Seeing all other men filled with wrong-doing, he is satisfied if he can spend this life guiltless of wrong and wickedness, and take his leave of it with good hope in calm content-ment at the end.[21]

In the *Theaetetus* the philosopher is described as unaware of what goes on around him:

It is only his body that stays in the city and makes its home there. His mind, regarding all these things as trivial and worthless, scorns them and travels everywhere, as Pindar says, 'both beneath the earth', and measuring the surface of the earth, 'and beyond the sky', studying the stars, and exploring the entire nature of everything that is, each as a whole, never letting itself sink down to anything close at hand.

(173e-4a)

This was not far from the popular view, expressed by Aristo-phanes in the *Clouds* and Callicles in the *Gorgias*. But in his other proposition on the subject, reached perhaps partly by reflection on the way of life of Pythagorean communities, Plato was again revolutionary: in the ideal society, based on the natural divisions between men, the philosopher would be no outsider, but ruler with complete control. Plato's answer to the political problems resulting from the decline of the old aristocracy was a new aristo-cracy of real wisdom—not of 'wise statesmen' in the accepted sense, nor of men trained in the 'practical wisdom' of Isocrates, but of wisdom derived from knowledge of universal truth. Men like Socrates, whom the comic poets ridiculed and the Athenians executed, are the only possessors of the genuine art of statesman-ship, and must come back into the cave of ordinary life to bring good government to men.[22] Complete unity and partnership, involving the abolition of property and of family life, are only possible among the wise, but their rule would create concord between the different classes of the state, and so result in the greatest happiness a human community can attain. It is not surprising that when Socrates in the *Republic* first puts forward this view that philosophers must become kings or kings philosophers, he speaks of it as his most startling and paradoxical proposal, and Glaucon warns him to expect a storm of criticism.[23]

'Some men', in short, 'are fitted by nature for philosophy and leadership in the state, while the rest should follow their leadership and leave philosophy alone' (*Rep.* 474c). Plato's ideal *polis* is a community divided into classes according to natural aptitude for wisdom; and on acceptance of this principle of inequality the harmony and unity of the state depends. How far did he envisage the application of these ideas on a wider scale beyond the *polis*, or attempt to formulate a pattern of the human race as a whole? How far did his belief in the overriding importance of wisdom, and of natural differences of degree in the share of ability for wisdom, affect his attitude towards the existing divisions of mankind?

His awareness of humanity as a single entity is beyond question. Perhaps because many critics of Plato's political thought concentrate on the *Republic*, he is often accused of limiting his outlook to the city-state; but a wider reading of the dialogues, especially the works of his later years, shows that—as we would expect in such a synoptic thinker—he had the conception of mankind as a single species constantly in mind; probably more so, indeed, than any Greek writer before him. The Idea of man, like the other objects of knowledge, must necessarily be the philosopher's concern, and 'he persistently and diligently inquires', says Socrates in the *Theaetetus*, 'into the question, what man is, and what distinctive powers or properties such a being should possess' (174b). The only passage in the dialogues where man is defined is a half-playful exercise in the technique of definition by division:

men are living creatures which are tame, live on land, have no horns, do not interbreed with other creatures, walk on two legs, and are without feathers (*Statesman* 267a–c). But in the *Timaeus*, where human life is related to the cosmic order, the structure and functions of man's soul and body are described at length; and the third book of the *Laws* outlines the early stages of all human history.

In the *Gorgias* we are given a glimpse of all mankind, along with the rest of the ordered cosmos, held together by the same bonds which maintain the harmony of the ordered *polis* in the *Republic*— a thought which Plato acknowledges to be derived from 'wise men', probably the Pythagoreans. The man who merely follows his appetites, Socrates tells Callicles,

will be beloved neither by his fellow-men nor by God: he is incapable of joining in a community, and where there is no sense of community (*koinōnia*), there can be no love. According to the wise, Callicles, both heaven and earth and gods and men are held together by sense of community and love and orderliness and self-control and justice, and this is why they call this universe a cosmos, a world of order, and not a world of disorder or licence.[24]

The myth included in the *Statesman* presents an imaginary picture of the fulfilment of this ideal, in a distant golden age when God was the shepherd of mankind. The people of that era are referred to as a single 'human flock' (*agelē*, 274e), and they are not divided into states; there is no possession of wives and children among them, since all are born from the soil (272a).

These passages show that Plato did envisage the unity of man; but he has no thought of it as a possibility for the present age, his picture of which is sadly different. Today the prospect of concord is limited to the *polis*, and there is little enough hope of it there. The ideal state of the *Republic* must be prepared for war against its neighbours, and especially against the barbarians.[25] In the *Laws*, the Cretan spokesman maintains that the community must be organised on the assumption that there is a perpetual undeclared war between all states (626a). It is true that the Athenian, who doubtless represents Plato himself, criticises the Cretan and Spartan emphasis on warfare and military prowess, claiming that peace and friendship are the highest goods, war should be a means to peace and not peace a means to war, and bravery in the field is only fourth among the virtues. Nevertheless, Plato clearly has no thought that in the foreseeable future war or the antagonisms that lead to it can be brought to an end.

His view of the wider categories into which mankind was divided has to be gathered from a number of passages and incidental references in various dialogues. All-important as these aspects of Greek life appear to us, Plato is not primarily interested in them, and rarely devotes his attention to them as subjects of discussion for their own sake. For the same reason he is by no means clear or consistent in his attitudes towards them: in this sphere he does not fulfil his own often repeated requirement— to follow his thought through to the end. The direction in which his mind moved is evident enough. Exclusive emphasis on the antithesis between the small company of the wise and the folly of the multitude could lead, as we shall see in the case of the Cynics, to disregard of all other divisions of the human race, and there are places where Plato is not far from this attitude. But as might be expected from the hierarchical organisation of the *polis* in the *Republic*, he turned more readily towards an alternative conception of mankind which he never clearly formulates: a hierarchy graded according to natural potentiality for wisdom, with male Greeks on the highest level and women, barbarians, and slaves lower in the scale. The *Gorgias* passage already quoted[26] continues with a reference to the importance of *geometrical* equality in the cosmos—a principle which does not give the same status to all, but assigns to each his rightful place; and we shall see that Aristotle, following lines of thought not far removed from Plato's, did come to think in terms of a graded system which partly excused, partly revised the traditional distinctions of sex and class and race. What we find in Plato is evidence in plenty that implies such a trend of thought, but no clear or definite pattern; and in the lack of it he often—though not so often as is sometimes alleged—tends merely to reproduce the assumptions current in his time.

He is most radical and original in dealing with the distinction between male and female, which he cites in the *Statesman* as the obvious central division of the human species, comparable with the division of number into odd and even. His view of the relation between them was a startling change from the traditional Greek suppression of women, but also remote from the outlook of our own day. He was no 'feminist' in the modern sense. Aristophanes' brilliant Praxagora, laying down the law to her stupid husband Blepyrus, is not the Platonic picture of the balance between the sexes. Plato always regards women in general as by nature inferior to men; and the reason for this inferiority is clearly indicated when Socrates discusses the point with Glaucon in the *Republic*. Natural talent for something, he says, consists in the ability to learn easily and to make the body serve the mind; in other words (we may add) in possession of *logos* to a superior degree. It is after this explanation that Socrates goes on to ask (455c): 'Do you know of any human occupation at which the male sex is not superior in all these ways to the female?' The same view is maintained in the *Timaeus*: at the incarnation of souls in mortal bodies, 'human nature being twofold, the superior kind was that which thereafter was to be called "man"' (42a). In the subsequent transmigration of souls, those who fail in their life as men become women at their next birth (42b); and when Timaeus has completed his story up to the creation of man and turns to that of 'the other living creatures', it is woman that heads the list (90e). In the *Laws* the Athenian argues that public meals and other state institutions must be for women as well as men: otherwise 'the section of humanity which is generally more inclined by its weakness towards secrecy and cunning—the female sex—is left to its disorderly state through the lawgiver's mistaken concession'.[27] Such neglect of the control of women creates more than double the problem that arises from the men, 'in proportion as the female disposition is inferior in goodness to that of males'.

If women are inferior beings, why does Plato advocate their emancipation, and propose that they take their place beside men in all the occupations of the ideal state? His answer is that the sex distinction is a different kind of division from that grouping according to natural aptitudes on which the organisation of the *polis* is to be based. With the exception of their functions in the production of children, man as such and woman as such are not fitted for any particular pursuit. Women can and should undertake any role in the community, even those of soldier and ruler, although in each they will normally be less successful than men.[28]

Plato might have applied a similar argument to the division between Greek and barbarian, and claimed that since natural aptitude transcended this barrier also, there could be barbarian ideal wise men, barbarian philosopher-kings. He might well have gone further and contended, as Eratosthenes did later,[29] that in the last analysis the differentiation of barbarian from Greek is unimportant, for all that matters is the distinction between good men and bad. But except in one passage of the *Laws*, to which we shall return, he does not envisage this logical conclusion from his own principles. Nor, on the other hand, does he take the course of placing all non-Greeks on a lower level of ability for wisdom than Greeks. His attitude towards them is far from consistent, and his statements on the matter vary with the context in which they occur.

The passage which is usually cited for his view on this subject is in the fifth book of the *Republic*, where he discusses the usages of war (469b–71c). Fighting between Greeks is civil strife to be avoided: the term 'war' should be reserved for fighting against barbarians, who are the Greeks' natural enemies. This view, reminiscent of Isocrates, is echoed occasionally elsewhere in Plato's works, especially in the *Menexenus*: Greeks must fight against those of their own race only till victory, but against the

barbarians till their destruction; Athens is by nature barbarian-
hating, because the Athenians are pure Greeks and—unlike some
so-called Hellenes—have no admixture of barbarian blood (242 d,
245 c–d).

It is difficult to tell how far the *Menexenus* is satirical in its
purpose. Certainly passages and references elsewhere in the
dialogues follow lines of thought very different from its crude
hostility towards the foreigner, or from the 'natural enmity'
belief expressed in the *Republic*. It must not be forgotten that the
story of life after death which closes the *Republic* itself comes from
'a man of valour, Er the Armenian, a Pamphylian by race' (614 b);
and in the myth of punishment after death in the *Gorgias* all men,
stripped of their earthly trappings, seem to be judged alike,
whether they come from Asia to stand before Rhadamanthus or
from Europe to face Aeacus. In a number of places Plato adopts
a point of view which recalls Thucydides and the medical writers,
implying that the distinction between barbarian and Greek is not
absolute, but relative to time or place or political conditions. In
their attitude to nakedness, in their religious beliefs, even possibly
in their language, the early Greeks were like the present barbarians. Any man must have both Greeks and barbarians among
his ancestors—a statement directly contrary to the race purity
claimed for the Athenians in the *Menexenus*. Other passages
remind us of *Airs, Waters, Places*, attributing the character of
Greeks or other races to climate or natural surroundings; while
in the *Symposium* Pausanias declares that it is despotism that causes
the love of boys and philosophy and athletics to be frowned upon
among the barbarians, for—as an Athenian tyrant once learned
to his cost—the high thoughts and close companionships which
such practices engender are dangerous to autocratic rule.[30]

On the basic distinction between Hellene and 'barbarian'—
intelligible speech—Plato by no means follows the current view.
It has often been pointed out that he was no exception to the
general unilingualism of the Greeks—a limitation of great
importance in its effect on his philosophy. Yet the *Cratylus*, the

chief dialogue in which language is discussed, does not repeat the accepted contrast between Greek as the only reasonable form of speech and the unintelligible chatter of barbarian tongues. The conversation opens with a reference to the use of words among both Greeks and barbarians; and later, when Socrates advances the strange theory that each object has a 'natural' name, he does not merely mean its Greek name. The 'lawgiver' must know how to embody the 'natural' name in different sounds and syllables, just as smiths create the same type of tool in different pieces of material and good tools are produced 'whether it is done here or among the barbarians'. 'So you will judge', concludes Socrates, 'that the lawgiver also, whether the one here or the one among the barbarians, as long as he assigns to each object the appropriate form of the name, in whatever syllables, is no worse a lawgiver, whether here or anywhere else' (390 a). The passage gives Greek and non-Greek speech an equivalence of status rare in Greek literature.

It is especially in his later works that Plato seems to incline towards disregard, or occasionally even explicit rejection, of contemporary prejudice against the foreigner. In the *Statesman*, on the pretext of illustrating a mistake in the process of definition by division, he puts forward an outspoken criticism of the separation of mankind into Greeks and barbarians:

> *The Young Socrates:* What sort of mistake do you say we made just now in our division?
> *The Stranger:* The kind of mistake a man would make if he were trying to divide humanity into two, and adopted the popular division whereby most people in this part of the world treat the Greeks as a single class separate from all the rest. All other nations, although their number is unknown and they do not intermingle or share any common language, are called by the single term 'barbarian', and because of this one term it is supposed that they constitute one class.[31]

A comparable example, the Stranger goes on, would be to divide number into the number 10,000 and all others, whereas it is correct to split number into odd and even, or the human race (as we have seen) into male and female. Plato further satirises the accepted distinction by talking not of distinguishing Greeks from all the rest, but of an imaginary division setting the Lydians and Phrygians—the most despised of barbarians as the Greeks saw them—apart from all other peoples: the 'chosen nation versus foreigners' antithesis could be made from other points of view besides the Greek. Similarly cranes, he adds a little later, 'might give themselves airs and contrast cranes as a single species with all other living creatures, while they put all the rest, including men, together and called them by the single term "beasts"' (263 d).

There is more than methodology in this remarkable passage, which suggests an outlook very different from contemporary prejudice and from other writers of Plato's time, including Isocrates and Aristotle. Further signs of this wider perspective are to be found in the *Laws*. Apart from references to the Persian Wars, defeat in which would have led, it is said, to an unhappy intermixture of Greek and barbarian (693 a), there is little emphasis on the division between them in Plato's last and longest work. They are often put together as a means of describing all humanity. Patriarchal rule is said to be still common among Greeks and barbarians alike (680 b). Barbarian ways are not condemned wholesale, but some approved, others criticised. The condition of Persia in the days of Cyrus is idealised, as it was by Xenophon, and one of the causes of its excellence is said to be the opportunity given to the wise to contribute to the policies of the state: 'consequently at that time they enjoyed general progress, as a result of their freedom, amity, and joint participation in reasoned counsel' (694 b). Later Persian history is described as fluctuating according to the training and character of the Great King (694 c–7 d).

The cleavage which the Athenian Stranger in the *Laws* mainly stresses is not between Greek and non-Greek, but between the citizens of his imaginary state and *all* other men. Outside the city he describes lie many other cities and countries with their various laws and customs, and it is against all these, without distinction of race, that the city is perpetually at war.[32] A significant passage is the account in Book XII of the regulations for foreign travel (949e–52d), which contain some interesting parallels with the outlook of some modern nations. The new community's standing in the world, says the Athenian, requires that travel shall not be prohibited altogether, but it must be strictly limited and controlled, lest corrupting ideas be introduced from abroad. For our present purpose the important point is that apparently all other peoples, Greek and barbarian alike, lie beyond the iron curtain with which the city is to be surrounded: it is 'the institutions among other men' that the selected traveller must report on when he returns home; and the test of what is valuable and worth imitating in the outside world lies not in its racial origin, but in the wisdom of the men that produce it. There are always such men to be found, even in badly governed states, and they must be sought out wherever they may be:

Among the mass of men there are always some, though not many, who are of superhuman excellence. Association with such men, who spring up in badly governed communities as well as in those with good laws, is a privilege of the highest worth. It is always right that an inhabitant of a well-governed state, if he is himself proof against corruption, should go forth in search of these men over sea and land, with a view to confirming those practices of his own community which are good and correcting any that is defective.   (951b–c)

We are not far here from the view that the only distinction which matters is between wisdom and folly, whether among Greeks or those who speak another tongue.

Although he adopted a radically different view from his contemporaries on the position of women in society, and in some passages of the dialogues rises above prejudice against non-Greeks, no such major divergence from public opinion can be found in Plato's attitude towards slavery. In the *Laws* he himself refers to the extent of controversy on the subject in his day, and we have seen that one voice at any rate—that of Alcidamas—was raised against slavery as contrary to nature; but in the many references to it that occur here and there in the dialogues there is no suggestion that the institution is unnatural or wrong. His acceptance of it indicates, no doubt, how completely it was taken for granted by the vast majority of the Greeks. It is also evidence, however, of the fundamental inegalitarianism of Plato's own outlook; for where he does show some originality of attitude towards slaves, most of his proposals are less liberal, more calculated to emphasise the distinction between slave and free, than current practice at Athens.

The main principle underlying his attitude is that of differentiation according to natural fitness for wisdom. We have seen this in a simple form in Xenophon: slaves, like animals, are devoid of *logos*, and should be treated as such. In the *Statesman* (289 c) Plato describes the slave as a kind of domestic animal, but elsewhere his version of the matter is less simple than Xenophon's. Where the free man is capable of knowledge, reached by reason, the slave can attain only to opinion, gained by experience. The free doctor understands the science of medicine; the slave doctor can give no rational account of an illness, but treats it according to empirical belief (*Laws*, 720). The ideal ruler, we read in the *Statesman*, will reduce to the slave class 'those who wallow in ignorance and gross subservience' (309 a). Differentiation on such grounds, of course, really applies to all who are inferior in their possession of *logos*, and therefore fitted by nature to be subject to others; in some degree, it applies to all below the level of the philosopher-king. It is not surprising that Plato frequently applies the terminology of the master-slave relationship to the general theme of the distinction between ruler and ruled, high and low. In some passages it is difficult to know whether he is referring to slavery in the strict sense, or only to this wider meaning of the word.[33]

This approach follows logically from Plato's general pattern of thought—far more so than the variety of views which he puts forward on the division between Greek and barbarian. But the slave was not merely a subject, ruled by his master: he was a chattel, his owner's property. This aspect of his position is also completely accepted by Plato, but he does not state or even imply a reason for it. His attitude towards it emerges in most detail in the *Laws*, and especially in the sixth book (776c ff.), where slaves are discussed as a form of property that involves particular difficulties.

The discussion begins with an interesting glimpse of contemporary controversy. 'Probably the most debated problem in all Greece', says the Athenian Stranger, 'is that of the merits or demerits of the Spartan helot-system' (the cause of Alcidamas' protest); and he cites other instances of the enslavement of a whole people which rouse criticism. As for ordinary slaves, some base their attitude towards them on the view that in the past 'many have proved better in every way than brothers or sons, and have preserved their masters and their masters' property and families'; while others declare 'that there is no soundness in the heart of a slave, and no man of sense should ever trust the slave class', and consequently treat their slaves like wild beasts, and lash them till they are slaves at heart many times over.

None of the critics, one notices, is said to advocate the abolition of all slavery. The Athenian himself goes on to speak of the difficulties of dealing in practice with the 'necessary distinction' between free man and slave. His proposals for solution of the problem are two: to 'divide and rule' by having slaves of different races; and to treat them wisely. Outrage and wrongdoing against servants should be avoided even more carefully than in relations with one's equals; but on the other hand 'one must chastise slaves when they deserve it, and not encourage impudence by merely admonishing them as if they were free men. The normal form of address to a servant should be a simple command' (777e). There is of course one law for the slave and another for the free. The gap between them becomes particularly clear later in the dialogue (868a–c), when the penalties for murder are under discussion: if a slave in passion kills his master or another free man, the dead man's relatives must put him to death; but if a free man kills a slave, he is to pay the owner twice the damage; and if the slave is his own, he must purify himself. The killing of a slave, unlike that of an animal, at any rate involves pollution.

There is nothing here, or elsewhere in the dialogues, to justify the suggestion that Plato was really opposed to slavery, or even to the contemporary treatment of slaves at Athens. Some of his provisions—that children of mixed unions, for example, must be regarded as slaves, and that a freed slave can be enslaved afresh by his master34—are harsher than the Attic law of his day and tend to consolidate the 'necessary distinction'; and in the *Republic* the most extreme phase of democratic licence, a ready soil for despotism, is reached when 'the slaves of both sexes are not less free than those who bought them' (563 b). In such a community even the dogs and horses and donkeys walk the streets as though they were free men! Plato is not far here from the attitude of the 'Old Oligarch'.

Elsewhere in the *Republic*, in the discussion of war already mentioned in connection with the distinction between Greek and barbarian, Plato is at pains to condemn the enslavement of Greeks. 'Is it right', asks Socrates, 'that Greek cities should sell Greeks into slavery? Should they not refuse to allow this, as far as it can be prevented, and adopt in its place the custom of sparing the Greek race, for fear of being enslaved by the barbarians? . . . They must not own any Greek slave themselves, and they must advise other Greeks not to do so' (469 b–c). In its historical context this was a call for a more enlightened policy in advance of current practice, for Greeks were still commonly enslaved in the conflicts between Greek states: Philip of Macedon later reduced the entire populations of captured Greek cities to slavery. But Plato is of course only shifting the dividing line, not abolishing or weakening it: he implies that enslavement of barbarians is unobjectionable, in accordance with the prevailing popular equation of barbarian with slave. On slavery he has nothing to say that differs greatly from the more explicit treatment of the subject by Aristotle.

ARISTOTLE

Aristotle presents us with the same difficulty as Plato, in that although the exposition of his thought in the extant works is more systematic, they contain no one passage from which we can draw an account of his views on the unity or division of the human race. Information on the subject must be sought from treatises written at different times, and the collection which results contains inconsistencies probably due to the combination of different stages of his philosophical development. We have no means of deciding how far Aristotle himself ever consciously co-ordinated the several aspects of his thought on this issue into a single whole. But in spite of all the variations of emphasis and detail, if we draw together the threads to be found in his writings a pattern emerges which is far more coherent than we have seen in Plato; and we come nearer here than anywhere else in Greek literature to a synthesis of Greek thought on the nature of man.

On this topic, as on others, there are two lines of approach which Aristotle especially follows and brings together. On the one hand, he continues the scientific tradition, if it can be so called, with its emphasis on the unity of the human species. At the end of the fifth century, as we have seen from Antiphon and the medical writers, this way of thought led towards egalitarian conclusions and disregard of the accepted divisions of mankind; but Aristotle combines it—how systematically or completely, we cannot tell—with the idea of hierarchical gradation which we have seen in Isocrates and Plato, and which must have become familiar to him during his years in the Academy; so that in many passages he only seems to be reformulating more definitely doctrines already stated or implied in Plato's dialogues. At the same time he maintains, here as elsewhere, that attention must be paid to the general prevailing opinion on such matters; and if he seems much further away from modern ideas than the medical writers and more 'reactionary' in his conclusions than even Plato, the possibility must not be forgotten that he reflects more closely the common assumptions and prejudices of his time. His aim was to co-ordinate and clarify the issues raised by all contemporary thought on the subject, from the advanced speculations of intellectuals to the views of the man in the street. The result, as it emerges at various points in his works, is a remarkable example of the formulation of theory to fit the passing phenomena of what we now see to have been a transient phase of human history.

As a biologist surveying and classifying the world of living creatures, Aristotle sees mankind as a single fixed and unchanging species, 'simple and admitting of no differentiation' in the biological sense, standing by itself at the head of the *scala naturae*.[35] It is marked off from other species by a number of physical characteristics, which are mentioned incidentally here and there in various works. Thus man is the only animal that stands upright, looks straight in front of him, and sends his voice straight in front of him. He is the only creature that laughs, and therefore the only one susceptible to tickling. He alone in the animal world has eyelashes on both lids and hair that goes grey. He is unique in his ability to learn to make equal use of both hands, and his inability to move his ears.[36]

Aristotle's references to these and other observed physical peculiarities prove his awareness of the concept of man as a single physical type, distinct in many ways from all other species. He holds, however, that the chief distinguishing feature of the human species is a psychological one—Aristotle's version of the idea of man as a speaking and thinking animal, which we have seen to be an important aspect of Greek thought on the subject from Homer onwards. In his view man is the only creature that has the faculty of speech, and this has a material cause in the looseness, broadness, and softness of his tongue.[37] But this is only a physical accompaniment of a difference between man and all other living things in *psychē*, which is expounded in the treatise *On the Soul* and elsewhere. Whereas the *psychē* of plants is adapted to nutrition, and that of animals to both nutrition and sensation, man's alone has the additional gift of *logos*. This is the divine element in him, through which he is akin to God. It is this that makes the ability to acquire knowledge one of his permanent and necessary characteristics, and renders him alone capable of making value judgments, distinguishing between good and bad and right and wrong.[38] Because of his possession of *logos* man has a distinctive end or function, through fulfilment of which he alone of all creatures can attain to happiness, *eudaimonia*, in the full sense of the word.

In this way Aristotle gives more definite shape to the familiar conception of mankind as a single species distinguished from all others by certain physical features, and above all by the possession of reason. It is for man's benefit, he says, that all the other animals exist (*Pol.* 1256b17). In a striking passage of the *Nicomachean Ethics*, in language which suggests that the biological approach is not far from his mind, he states that there is a bond of affection between all members of the human race:

Affection of parent for offspring and offspring for parent seems to be implanted in them by nature, not only among men, but among birds and most animals. Affection also exists by nature between members of the same species, and especially among men; and for this reason we praise those who love their fellow men. Even on our travels we can see how near and dear every man is to every other.   (1155a16–22)

This is a more definite picture of mankind as a unity than any put forward in Greek literature before. Yet Aristotle also goes beyond any previous writer in his insistence on the heterogeneity of the human race, on the divisions that split it up into dissimilar sections. How is such unity made up of diversity, reminiscent of Heraclitus, to be explained?

On this point, again, no single passage will provide an answer. But by correlating statements in a number of places, and especially by comparing parts of the ethical and political works with theories put forward in the biological treatises, it is possible to infer a fairly coherent picture of what was in Aristotle's mind, although we cannot be certain that he ever envisaged it in precisely this form.

The key to the human pattern as he sees it is the teleological character of his thought. Every species has its own *telos* or end, which its individual members fulfil to the extent that the limitations of matter allow. Hence although the human species has a single end, actual men, because of the intractability of matter, fall short of it in different ways and different degrees. Their individual shortcomings are many and various, but there are also certain major divisions of mankind marked off by common deficiencies, so that humanity as a whole consists not only of more or less imperfect individuals, but also of sections which can be graded according to their approximation to perfection.

The highest place in the teleological scale is given to the wise man, the philosopher whose activity is contemplation. In the thought of Aristotle's earlier years, as the fragments of the *Protrepticus* show, this figure occupied a central position recalling his role in the *Republic*.39 In the *Nicomachean Ethics*, the last book of which is partly concerned with this subject (x. 7–8), the wise man's contemplation of truth is still the highest ideal, but there has been a shift of emphasis and interest whereby Aristotle has moved away from the Platonic view and developed his own answer to the familiar fourth-century question of the wise man's relation to the remainder of the community—an answer nearer to the general opinion that the philosopher stands outside the rest of society than to the belief that he should dominate the whole.

The wise man devotes himself to the contemplation of truth, the proper activity of intellect (*nous*); and because this is the highest element in us, our sovereign and better part and indeed our true self, it is the wise man who most completely fulfils man's end and has the highest happiness. Through his own perfection he is the least dependent on others, the most self-sufficient of all men. But because intellect is the divine element in us and self-sufficient contemplation, as we learn in the *Metaphysics*, is the activity of God, the wise man is also more than human, almost outside humanity. Aristotle may well have this superhuman wise man in mind when he writes in the *Politics* of the man by nature cityless who is 'either low in the scale of humanity or *above it*' (1253 a 4–5). Or again:

That the state exists by nature and is prior to the individual, is clear; for if the individual is not self-sufficient in isolation, he will be like a part in relation to the whole. But the man who is incapable of social relationships, or *has no need of them because he is sufficient for himself*, is no part of a state: he is either a beast *or a god*. (1253 a 25–9)

This account of the wise man might seem to separate him sharply from the rest of humanity, allowing him alone true good-ness and happiness and the full right to the status of man—a view not far removed from that of the Cynics. But Aristotle is much nearer to normal Greek sentiment than this extremism. Devoted though he is to intellectual contemplation, the philosopher must in fact 'live on the human level'[40]—must share to some extent the needs and the life of normal human beings, ordinary civilised free men. There is a good deal of inconsistency here in Aristotle's use of terms, if not in his thought, for in spite of his description of contemplation as the proper activity of man, it is these more ordinary beings living on a lower level that he usually regards as characteristically human and rightly designated by the name *anthrōpos*. They are not self-sufficient as individuals, but only become so through association with others, first in the household but above all in the *polis*, which Aristotle regards as the most perfect unit of human society. In this sense man is a 'political animal', a being made by nature for life with his fellows in the city-state. He possesses *logos* and exercises it, but through practical wisdom, *phronēsis*; and through the practical virtues, given a certain measure of the other good things in life as well as the internal goodness of the soul, he also can achieve *eudaimonia*: after all, happiness is not limited to the philosopher or entirely depen-dent on his theoretical wisdom.[41] Within the wide range of such normal humanity, of course, there is great variation between individuals, and only a minority come near the level of which this section of mankind is capable at its best. In spite of his atten-tion to public opinion, Aristotle agrees with most other Greek writers in his contempt for 'the many' and 'the base'. Concord, which should bind the city together, is a feeble growth among them, and talk of theory can do little to push them in the direction of lofty principles:

> It is their nature to obey not a sense of honour but only fear, to abstain from wrong not because of the disgrace but for fear of punishment. Living as feeling guides them, they run after the pleasures that suit their nature and the means to these pleasures, and avoid the corresponding pains; but of what is noble and truly pleasant they have no conception, as they have never tasted it.[42]

Although there is this wide variation in their capability for goodness, happiness is attainable in some degree by all members of this main section of the human race. Somewhat inconsistently with the denial that theory can influence the mass of men, Aristotle writes earlier in the *Ethics* that 'happiness can be regarded as widely spread, for through some process of learning and training it can be achieved by all who are not defective in their capacity for goodness' (1099b18–20). The statement is less sweeping, however, than it might seem to be. For in Aristotle's view several categories of mankind, constituting the numerical majority of the species, *are* 'defective', and by nature fall short of that level of humanity, that degree of fulfilment of the human *telos*, which can be reached by normal, undefective, man. This doctrine is Aristotle's way of finding a rational and coherent basis for the accepted Greek attitude towards women, and towards slaves and barbarians.

His view of the distinction between the sexes is a sharp contrast with Plato's novel doctrine on the subject, and a return to the orthodox Greek outlook: the mental and physical differences between men and women are such that women are not only inferior, but fitted for a different role in life. Because these differences are due—in Aristotelian language—not to form but to matter, they do not make woman a separate species, as Plato almost seems to suggest in the *Timaeus*.[43] But they set her in a category which has a distinct and subordinate place in the pattern of human society.

The idea that the female sex is by nature defective in comparison with the male is put forward in the treatise *On the Generation of Animals*. Discussing the resemblance of children to their parents, Aristotle says there are some who

> are not even like a human being in appearance, but have gone so far as to resemble a monstrosity. Indeed anyone unlike his parents is already in a sense a monstrosity, since in these instances nature has in a sense diverged from the generic type. The first beginning of such divergence is the production of a female instead of a male: but this is a natural necessity, as the species of creatures separated into female and male must be kept in being; and also the inability on occasions of the male to dominate, because of youth or age or some other such cause, makes the production of females inevitable among living creatures.
>
> (767b6-13)

A later passage emphasises that lack of heat is a fundamental distinction between woman and man, and adds: 'We must regard the female state as being a kind of deformity, but one in accordance with nature' (775a15-17).

Elsewhere in his biological works Aristotle describes the main points of contrast in physique between the two, differences in what would now be called primary and secondary sexual characteristics. But more important for his view as a whole are the psychological differences, to be seen in other animals but most clearly in mankind. The *Historia Animalium* describes them thus:

> The female is less spirited than the male in every species except the bear and the leopard, where the female is considered to be bolder. Among all other animals the females are softer, more mischievous, less simple, more impulsive, and more concerned with the nurture of the young; whereas the males are more spirited, fiercer, simpler, and less inclined to intrigue. Traces of these characteristics occur more or less in all species, but they are more obvious where character is more strongly marked and above all in man; for man's nature is the most completely developed, so that these qualities are more obvious in human beings. Hence woman is more given to compassion and tears

than man, more inclined towards jealousy and grumbling, more ready
to scold and slap. She becomes dispirited and despondent more easily
than the male. She is more shameless and more hypocritical, more
ready to cheat and more inclined to remember. She is more wakeful,
more timid, and in general more difficult to stir into action; and she
needs less food.   (608 a 31–b 15)

Above all, women differ from men in regard to reason, the distinctive feature of the human species. All sections of mankind
possess the various parts of the soul, we are told in the *Politics*
(1260 a 11–14), but they possess them in different ways; for the
slave (to whom we shall turn later) does not have the deliberative
part at all, and the female has it, but without authority, while the
child has it, but in an immature form.

The implications of this statement can be gathered from Aristotle's account of the rightful place of woman in the human
community. Unlike Plato and the Cynics, he believes that the
family, founded on a monogamous union, is an essential natural
feature of human life:

Man is a creature that lives not only in a community but also in a
household. Among human beings the coupling of the sexes is not a
matter of chance, as with other animals: man is a creature that associates
with those with whom he has a natural family relationship. Hence
there would be association and a measure of justice among human
beings, even if there were no community.[44]

Woman's partnership with man, necessary for the procreation of
children and the survival of the species, is the basis of the family
unit; but the wife must be the subordinate partner, the husband
lord and master. 'The male is by nature superior in relation to the
female, and the female inferior, the one rules and the other is
subject.' 'The male is by nature more fitted for command than
the female, except in some cases that are contrary to nature.' In
politics 'when one rules and the other is ruled, they try to make
a distinction by means of outward forms and titles and honours;
but the male has a permanent relationship of this kind towards
the female'. Such authority as the wife has within the household

is assigned to her by her husband, in those aspects of family life which it is fitting for her to control. The woman's virtues are those which suit her subordinate role: for a woman, silence is golden, but not for a man.45

Aristotle thus endorses and justifies the position of women in Greek life, and will have nothing to do with contemporary proposals for their emancipation. But he does not regard his programme for them as suppression; rather, as the treatment which will enable them to play their natural part. It is not inconsistent with the rest of his theory that in the *Nicomachean Ethics* he paints a picture, in his austere way, of co-operation and affection between husband and wife, bringing happiness to both:

Among other animals the association of the sexes aims only at the production of offspring, but human beings live together not only for this purpose but to provide what is required for a full life. The functions of the man and the woman are distinguished from the first, and by pooling their individual abilities they satisfy their joint needs. Hence it is generally thought that affection between husband and wife combines utility and pleasure. It may also be founded on moral worth, if the pair are of good character; for either sex has its own excellence, and this can be a source of joy to both of them.   (1162a 19–27)

If Aristotle's account of the difference between men and women is strange to the modern mind, much more so is his assertion that the master-slave relationship is equally natural, both being essential for the maintenance of the household, and unable to exist without each other. Rarely, it may be said, has a great thinker so sadly mistaken a transitory man-made institution for one of nature's laws. But although Aristotle may be criticised for not seeing further, he cannot fairly be accused of being more 'reactionary' on this issue than Plato, or even described with any certainty as lagging behind the general opinion of his day. On the question of slavery he is particularly concerned to study public opinion, and in the second chapter of the first book of the *Politics*, which he devotes to this subject, he begins by citing two views held at the time—the belief that being a master is a definite science,

identical with household management and the art of the statesman and the king; and the claim, particularly significant for our
purpose, that 'it is contrary to nature for one man to be master
of another, since only by convention is the one man a slave and
the other free, whereas by nature there is no difference between
them; so that the relationship is based not on justice, but on force'.
Aristotle's own aim is not to support either of these opinions or
reject it outright, but to arrive at a better account of the matter
which will clarify and reconcile these and other contemporary
ideas.

His first step is to seek a theoretical definition of the slave. The
manager of a household must own tools, lifeless or living. If the
lifeless tools were automatic, Aristotle says with a striking anticipation of the machine age—'if every tool on command or by
anticipation of what was required could perform its own task,
if shuttles could weave and quills could play harps by themselves,
master craftsmen would not need assistants, nor masters slaves".
But as it is the slave is a necessary human tool for action, the
property of another man although a man himself.

This is the theoretical status and function of the slave. Do
people exist intended by nature to play this part? Aristotle's
answer is that they do, for the principle that some beings should
rule and others be ruled is valid throughout nature, and accordingly there is a category of mankind naturally fitted for being
ruled. He nowhere describes these natural slaves as 'defective',
but it is clear that they are so in the sense in which the word was
used of women, since they fall even further short of the *telos* of
men. They are mainly equipped for physical labour—natural
hewers of wood and drawers of water, 'whose function is the use
of the body and from whom nothing better can be expected'.
Their bodies are adapted by nature for this purpose:

Nature's intention is to endow free men and slaves with different
physique: slaves' bodies she makes strong for the work they have to
do, but to free men she gives bodies that are erect and well-suited to the
life of a citizen, though unserviceable for the tasks of a slave.

We are reminded of the Homeric assumption that the lords and the commons differ in physique, and the misshapen figure of Thersites is not far away. 'But as a matter of fact', Aristotle admits, 'often just the opposite comes about.'

What is the natural slave's mental equipment? He has no faculty for deliberation or power to follow a course of his own choosing; yet he is a man, and therefore—as Plato had held, but not Xenophon—he must have some share of reason.[46] The solution is that he does not possess *logos*, as even women do, but can apprehend it; so that it is right to reason with a slave, and those people are wrong who deny him *logos* altogether and say he should only be given orders.[47] Such beings can feel bodily pleasure, but can have no experience of happiness, *eudaimonia*, in the proper sense of the word. Nevertheless, since slavery is their natural place in life, it benefits them as well as their masters.[48]

Where in the world around him does Aristotle find these 'slaves by nature'? They do not necessarily coincide with those who are now slaves in fact, some of whom owe their lot only to convention and force. In these cases the objectors to slavery mentioned earlier are justified, for 'it cannot be said that a man who does not deserve slavery is really a slave'. (Aristotle does not go so far, however, as to suggest that such unnatural slavery should be abolished.) We are not explicitly told who are those 'who do not deserve slavery', but it seems to be implied that they include men of noble birth, and all Greeks. Aristotle follows the view probably held by most Greeks since the fifth century, and maintained by Plato in the *Republic*, that it is the barbarians who are natural slaves. He quotes with approval the line put into Iphigenia's mouth by Euripides: 'It is right for Greeks to rule over barbarians.'[49] Those who say that barbarians are slaves are really following the principle of natural slavery. The barbarians endure despotic rule without complaint because they are more slavish in character than the Greeks, so that (a claim which recalls Isocrates) 'the Greek race could rule all mankind, if it attained political unity'.[50] War, though it may sometimes lead to wrongful enslavement of those who do not deserve it, is justified when it is waged 'against wild beasts or against men who are fitted by nature for subjection but do not accept it', in order to 'become masters over those who deserve to be slaves'.[51] It is not surprising that according to Plutarch Aristotle advised Alexander 'to behave as a leader towards Greeks, but as a master towards barbarians, and while caring for Greeks as friends and kinsmen, to have the same attitude to barbarians as to animals or plants'.[52]

This is a harsh doctrine. How is it to be reconciled with the belief that there is a bond of friendship between all members of the human species? Is there to be no fellow-feeling transcending the barrier between the slave and his owner, as there is affection between husband and wife? In one sentence of the *Politics* (1255b13-14) Aristotle allows that there is not only a certain community of interest, but also friendship, between master and servant, where both are suited by nature for their status. But in the course of the discussion of friendship in the *Nicomachean Ethics* he writes as though he realised that his theory leaves no room for affection towards slaves *as such:*

We cannot have friendship towards a horse or an ox, nor towards a slave as a slave. For there is nothing in common between master and slave, the slave being a living tool, just as a tool is a slave without life. So there is no possibility of friendship towards him as a slave, but there can be friendship in relation to him as a human being (*anthrōpos*). It is held that there is some room for justice between every human being and every other capable of participating in the rule of law or in a contract; and so there can be friendship with anyone, in so far as he is a human being. (1161b2-8)

This admission that the slave is from one aspect a slave, from another a man, shows the artificiality of Aristotle's attempt to schematise humanity, which here results in the division of the individual slave into two. It is significant that when he turns to closer consideration of foreign races he is not content with sweeping assertions of their slavish mentality, but in a manner reminiscent of the Hippocratic *Airs, Waters, Places* talks of differences in mental capacity and capability for freedom, dependent on differences in climate, between the various non-Greek peoples. Significant, too, is his admiration for the constitution of Carthage, and its inclusion in the collection of constitutions made at the Lyceum.53 Elsewhere he goes against his own theory in practical recommendations, arguing in favour of the eventual emancipation of slaves: 'It is better that all slaves should have liberty set before them as a reward' (*Pol.* 1330a33). If men are natural slaves, it cannot be right, or to their benefit or that of their masters, that they should be transferred to the category of free men, for which nature has not fitted them. We are told, however, that Aristotle carried out his own advice, and left instructions for the immediate freeing of some of his slaves, and the later emancipation of others, in his will.54

Slaves are the lowest major section in Aristotle's pattern of mankind. The contemplative philosopher at the top of the scale is near to God: the natural slave's tough, bent body and poor mental equipment place him close to the beasts, so that in the life of those well enough off to own a 'human tool' he replaces the poor man's ox (*Pol.* 1252b12–13). Yet he is above the lower animals, in that he shares in *logos* at any rate by his ability to apprehend it. On the fringe of humanity, however, it is possible to sink even below this level, to the 'man like a beast'. In the first book of the *Politics* we meet him as the man by nature outside society, the 'clanless, lawless, heartless' man denounced by Homer, who is a poor sort of creature—unless he is superhuman (1253a3–6); and again as the man who is no part of the *polis*, and must be a beast if he is not a god (*ibid.* 29). Elsewhere we read that the type is rare, and although some cases arise from natural deficiency or disease or habit inbred by ill-treatment, such beings are found chiefly among the barbarians. Thus those who are by nature incapable of reasoning and live by sensation alone are 'like certain remote barbarian tribes'.55 Aristotle could well have argued that these brutish creatures, like Homer's Cyclops, fall altogether outside the human species, for they fail entirely to fulfil the distinctive *telos* of man and are not a necessary complement, as women and slaves are, to the life of another section. But here again he accommodates abstract theory to accepted fact, and brings all who have the appearance of men within his picture of mankind. Aristotle's spectrum of humanity ranges all the way from the almost superhuman philosopher at the top to the subhuman creatures at the bottom, but these extremes as well as the intervening sections—ordinary free men, women, and slaves—all fall within the complex pattern that we can infer from his works. His analysis is the supreme Greek attempt to provide rational grounds and a single rational framework for the assumptions on which Greek society was based.

THE CYNICS

Like Plato and Aristotle, the Cynics also regarded themselves as followers in the path of Socrates, and with some justice: they carried to its logical extreme the Socratic practice of stripping away cant and pretence, and presented themselves to their startled contemporaries as examples of the Natural Man—creatures so naked and unashamed that the public called them not men, but dogs, dog-like (*kynikoi*). These outsiders of antiquity were familiar figures in Athens and elsewhere in the fourth and third centuries B.C., and later in many parts of the Roman Empire. They are of importance for our theme because they brought forward a new conception of human nature and human relationships, and because the conventions they claimed to transcend included most of those accepted barriers between human beings which, as we have seen, few had hitherto called in question. Our problem is to consider how far their Natural Man was also Universal Man, how far their disregard of divisions led them towards the concept of a united mankind. Are some modern writers, like Zeller, Kärst, and Wilcken, justified in ascribing to them the vision of 'all mankind living together like a flock', 'an all-embracing society of all men'?[56] Was there a single Cynic picture of humanity, and, if so, what was it like? This is a complex and difficult problem, to which various answers have been given.

The greatest difficulty lies in the character of our evidence. Once he has passed the writings of Plato and Aristotle, the student of Greek thought becomes inured to the task of extracting some semblance of truth from a mass of fragmentary and unreliable information, but nowhere is the confusion greater than here. There seems little prospect of deciding with certainty the list of thinkers who should be called Cynics, and still less of giving any precise account of their views.

Of their writings we have many alleged titles, but little else. Diogenes Laertius (VI. 15–18)* gives the names of works by Antisthenes which filled ten volumes; but his list is clearly unreliable, and the surviving 'fragments', including some of doubtful authenticity, fill no more than a few pages. To Diogenes some fourteen dialogues are attributed by Diogenes Laertius, including a *Politeia*, and seven 'tragedies'; but he adds that according to Sosicrates (perhaps second century B.C.) and Satyrus (third century B.C.) Diogenes left no writings; while Sotion (probably early second century B.C.) gave a different list containing a few of the same items, but no tragedies or *Politeia* (80). On the other hand, it is clear that a *Politeia* existed under the name of Diogenes in the third century B.C. and was regarded as authentic by the early Stoics Cleanthes and Chrysippus, and probably by Antipater, who died late in the second century B.C.57

The puzzle is of some consequence, since speculation about the contents of this alleged *Politeia* has played a considerable part in discussions of the problems of Cynic doctrine. A widely accepted solution is that of von Fritz,58 who supposed that the rejection of Diogenes' works, and of the *Politeia* in particular, was due to a Stoic desire to improve the reputation of a thinker who stood in the direct line of succession between Socrates and Zeno: Sotion went further, and produced a more respectable list largely of his

* Bracketed numbers in this section, unless otherwise explained, refer to paragraphs of Diogenes Laertius, VI (early third century A.D.).

own invention. As Tarn points out,[59] however, Stoic opinion in Satyrus' time was dominated by Chrysippus, who frequently referred to the *Politeia* as genuine; and Satyrus and Sotion, at any rate, were not Stoics, but Peripatetics. Tantalising though it may be to think that Diogenes wrote a *Politeia*, in which he must surely have given some account of the Cynic's attitude towards his fellow-men, the question of its authenticity must be left unsolved. Perhaps it is fortunate that there are few statements of his views for which the *Politeia* is definitely cited as source, and doubt about their authorship can make little difference to our general impression of Cynic thought. Far more valuable for our purpose is the small collection of fragments which we can allot with some certainty to Crates, each of which is worth pages of the gossip or prejudice of later 'authorities'.

For the most part, however, it is to such later writers that we have to turn. To some extent their evidence is doxographical, purporting to summarise Cynic views. Of this character is a section of Philodemus' work *On the Stoics* (cols. 8–10), which sets forth a number of Cynic precepts obviously selected to show their authors in a disreputable light. This has the advantage of a comparatively early date (first century B.C.), but gaps in the text make it difficult to decide how far the author continues with the Cynics and when he returns to his main purpose of castigating Zeno. There is also a short but valuable piece of doxography in the 'Life' of Diogenes which, along with brief biographies of other reputed Cynics, fills Book VI of Diogenes Laertius and constitutes our principal source of information; but most of the book, and especially the account of Diogenes, is a compilation of sayings and anecdotes which, says Dudley,[60] belong rather to an anthology of Greek humour than a discussion of philosophy. Probably still less reliable are the numerous works produced during the revival of Cynicism under the Roman Empire, in which Diogenes appears as a figure of literary fiction: the sermons of Dio Chrysostom, for example, in which he is idealised, or the satirical dialogues of Lucian.

With such 'evidence' it is naturally difficult even to decide who merits inclusion in the list of Cynics, and especially whether the first name should be Antisthenes (who may be as early as 455–360 B.C.) or Diogenes (about 400–325 B.C.). That the Cynic outlook was partly derived from Antisthenes can hardly be denied, and it would be wrong to leave him out; but although for our purpose he can be considered here along with Diogenes, the views attributed to them by no means wholly coincide, and it seems unlikely that there can have been any direct contact between the two. On the character and teaching of the Cynics there is still less certainty: modern accounts of them have varied all the way from serious analysis of their supposed doctrines to condemnation of them as worthless charlatans; and it may well be that this variation in modern views reflects to some extent an actual diversity of outlook and conduct among very different individuals to whom the name was given.

The task of extracting truth from such confusion may seem hopeless, and at best we may expect a large possibility of error, especially in attempting to distinguish Cynic political ideas from those of the Stoics. Yet after surveying all the available information one retains at any rate a strong impression that certain things stand out as distinctively Cynic: a point of view, although we cannot be sure of this or that detail of doctrine; a way of life, although we cannot prove one or other particular feature of it; a manner of expression, a mordant wit which seems especially characteristic of Diogenes, although we cannot guarantee a single one of his sayings as authentic.

Whatever else is doubtful, it is clear that an ideal figure stood at the centre of Cynic thought: the *sophos*, the man of wisdom, whom they, like Plato, identified with the true and natural man. The Cynic *sophos* was a man apart: they carried to the extreme that emphasis on the antithesis between the wise man and the rest of humanity which we have seen in many earlier thinkers, and especially in Socrates. Plato held that in contemporary society the philosopher must needs retire and 'shelter by the wall', but

in the ideal community he will play the central part. Aristotle
saw him as an almost superhuman being close to God, but maintained that he must to some extent 'live on the human level' and
mix with his fellow-men. The Cynics, on the contrary, regarded
the wise man's separateness from others as his essential characteristic and his crowning glory, and their interpretation of the words
'wise' and 'natural' threw him into sharp contrast with the rest
of mankind.

The Cynic version of 'wisdom' was far removed from the
qualities which had usually earned the name in the past, and
carried still further that denial of accepted forms of wisdom which
was a prominent feature of the thought of Heraclitus, and again
of Socrates. In Plato's *Apology* Socrates tells how he found no
true knowledge in either poets or politicians. The same view
reappears in more graphic form in the sayings attributed to
Diogenes. The plays in the theatre of Dionysus were for him
'great marvels—for fools', political leaders 'lackeys of the crowd'
(24). At a reading, when the blank end of the roll at last came in
view, 'Courage, men,' cried Diogenes, 'land is in sight' (38). Dio
Chrysostom makes him say Prometheus was rightly punished for
bringing civilisation to man: it has only made life a greater
burden (VI. 29). Contemporary 'philosophy' received no kinder
treatment from him than contemporary culture. The mathema-
ticians gazed at sun and moon, he said, but ignored what lay at
their feet (28, cf. 39). Plato's lectures were a waste of time, his
Ideas fantasy, his definition of man—'a featherless biped animal'—
equally applicable to a plucked fowl (24, 53, 40). The outlook of
these later stories is confirmed by Menander's description of
Diogenes' disciple Monimus, who 'called all suppositions nothing
but hot air' (83).

It is typical of the negative character of Cynicism that we can
say what claims to wisdom they rejected, but can give no positive
definition of the quality as they saw it. Diogenes again echoes
Socrates in allowing some real knowledge to practisers of the
arts (70, cf. 24), and we may infer that his wise man was one who

understood and practised the true art of living. But the evidence has nothing more precise than this to offer. All that is clear is that this Cynic norm, the natural man, was likely to be regarded as completely abnormal by his contemporaries; a being far removed from the common run of men and from their conception of 'wisdom' and how to attain it.

The question 'What is nature?' receives an equally negative answer. The wise man's following of nature appears to consist in the rejection of convention. We have seen the growing importance of the contrast between *physis* and *nomos* in the development of thought about man from the middle of the fifth century onwards. No group made the antithesis more absolute or proclaimed it more strongly than the Cynics. It is true that one passage of Diogenes Laertius[61] attributes to Diogenes the view that *nomos* is civilised and one cannot live in a city without it; but this is to talk in terms of what is expedient for the crowd, not what is 'according to nature' and right for the wise man. Elsewhere disregard for all law and convention is a recurring theme. As if in reply to the passage just mentioned, Antisthenes declares that the wise man will live in his city not by the established laws, but by the law of virtue (11). Diogenes said that he valued freedom (*eleutheria*) above all else (71); and by freedom he evidently meant liberty from *all* restraint: complete freedom of speech (*parrhēsia*), which he described as 'the finest thing men have' (69); equally complete freedom in act—not only rejection of the conventions of this or that particular city, but *anaideia*, shamelessness, overstepping that sense of rightness and decency (*aidōs*) which was supposed to be common to all Greeks.

To preach denial of convention and restraint was not unprecedented. What was much more remarkable was that, at any rate from Diogenes onwards, the Cynics *practised* what they preached. To us there seems to be a good deal of *parrhēsia* and even *anaideia* in ordinary Greek life; how far they were carried on occasion is shown by the plays of Aristophanes. The Cynics, if the account of Philodemus and the stories of Diogenes Laertius are to be

believed, brought the freedom and outspokenness and shamelessness of comedy into the streets of Athens. It was their public
habits, not merely their doctrines, that placed them beyond
the pale, outside normal human society, in the eyes of their
contemporaries, and earned them the name of 'dogs'. Plato
is said to have described Diogenes as 'a Socrates gone crazy' (54).
To many the Cynics must indeed have seemed to be the lunatic
fringe.

All this set the wise man apart from the rest of society and outside its normal ways of life and thought. The most significant
point for our purpose is that the Cynics emphasised the cleavage
between wisdom and folly to the exclusion of other divisions:
among the unnatural conventions to be ignored by the *sophos* were
those distinctions of sex, race and class which still retained so
strong a hold on the Greek mind, and which Aristotle was so
concerned to justify. Antisthenes declared that goodness was the
same for women as for men (12). Diogenes advocated sexual
promiscuity dependent on *mutual* consent (72). When Crates
formed a union with Hipparchia, we have the contemporary
evidence of Menander that they went about in public together
both wearing the rough Cynic cloak (93). Diogenes Laertius adds
that Hipparchia went to dinners with her husband, which no
respectable Athenian lady would do, and was proud to have spent
on 'education' the time she might have wasted at the loom (97–8).
The evidence for the Cynic attitude towards prejudice against
'barbarians' and slaves is less clear, but it is significant that
followers of Cynic 'wisdom' were drawn from both these
sources: Diogenes' pupil Monimus is said to have been a slave
(82); Menippus, in the third century, a slave of Phoenician descent
(99). The list of works attributed to Antisthenes includes one on
'Freedom and Slavery' (16); and Diogenes Laertius points out
that when he cited Heracles and Cyrus as models of endurance,
he drew the one from the Greeks, the other from the 'barbarians'
(2). The same authority twice tells the story of the sale of Diogenes,
which is to the point even though it may be a later fiction by

Menippus: captured by pirates, put up for sale as a slave, and asked what he could do, Diogenes replied, 'Rule men', and 'Sell me to this man here—he needs a master'.[62] The mischance of slavery cannot affect the true distinction between the worthy and the unworthy, the wise men and the fools.

The wise man's superiority to convention, his freedom and independence and separation from ordinary men, were summed up in the one term 'self-sufficiency' (*autarkeia*). Aristotle described the philosophic practiser of contemplation as 'the most self-sufficient of men'. The *autarkeia* of the Cynic sage is complete. He is primarily an isolated individual, the very opposite of the citizen of Plato's ideal state. Like the existentialist, he must stand alone.

This self-sufficiency, this ultra-individualism, is the main theme behind Cynic statements on human society. Cities and their laws may be right for the common herd whom the politicians serve, but the wise acknowledge no city or law known to ordinary men.[63] They want nothing of any man, and therefore have no need of the ordinary means of conflict or commerce; for them weapons are useless, and so is currency: knuckle-bones—dice—will do just as well.[64] Diogenes said that like a figure on the tragic stage he had 'no city, no home, no fatherland—a wanderer, begging his daily bread'.[65] The same thought was put in another form, itself typical of the hold of the *polis* concept on the Greek mind, when he described himself as *kosmopolitēs*, a 'citizen of the universe', in answer to the question where he came from (63), or —probably a variant of the same story—declared that 'the only true citizenship was that of the universe' (72). These phrases, which have sometimes figured so prominently in accounts of the development of the Greek conception of mankind, do not contain any idea of a world-state or of the brotherhood of all men. *Kosmos* means the universe, the whole of nature, not mankind, and *kosmopolitēs* is a long way from 'cosmopolitan': far from suggesting that the Cynic is at home in every city, it implies that he is indifferent to them all. Independent of all the local affiliations

of ordinary men, the wise man admits allegiance only to the
universe. He is a vagabond with no fixed abode, and Nature is
his only address.

We cannot be sure, of course, that these remarks were ever
made by Diogenes, although the ascription of such language to
him is more convincing than its attribution elsewhere to Socrates.[66]
But for Crates we have the same thought not only in late anecdotes, but in quotations from his writings; from one of his plays,
for example:

> No single native tower or roof for me:
> The citadel and house of the whole earth
> Stands ready for us as our dwelling-place.   (98)

His country, said Crates, was ill repute and poverty; and though
he came from Thebes and Diogenes from Sinope, they were
fellow-citizens (93). Most significant of all was his description
of the Cynic Utopia. Parodying Odysseus' account of Crete in
Homer (19. 172 ff.), Crates wrote:

> Mid wine-dark fog a city, Pera, lies,
> Fair, rich, yet squalid and possessed of naught.
> Thither no fool or parasite can sail,
> No lecher whose joy is a harlot's charms.
> Heartsease it bears, garlic and figs and bread,
> Things for which men make no wars on each other,
> Nor take up arms for cash or for renown.[67]

The Cynic's ideal, lying like an island of wisdom in the midst of
the fog of folly and conceit in which most men live, is no community at all, but Pera, the philosopher's own knapsack, symbol
of that self-sufficiency through which he is independent of all
communities. No fool or glutton or lecher can make his way into
this Utopia: in it the wise man finds all the joys of the Golden
Age—satisfaction of his humble needs, peace, freedom, and
contentment; in short, to quote another line of Crates:

> A quart of fodder and to be free from care.   (86)

In a sense, of course, the *sophos* has fellow-citizens—not the other inhabitants of the particular locality where he happens to have been born, but the other wise men, fellow-bearers of the knapsack, who share with him citizenship of Pera and of the cosmos. It was in this sense that Crates of Thebes could describe himself as a fellow-citizen of Diogenes of Sinope (93). There is friendship and kinship between the wise (12, 105), so that Plutarch rightly includes Diogenes along with Plato and Zeno as one whose political thought was guided by the principle of concord.[68] Scattered over the world though they may be, they form together a well-knit unity, for 'when brothers are of one mind, their life together is stronger than any wall' (6). But this united *politeia* of men of wisdom is nothing like an all-embracing society of all mankind. If it can be described as a state at all, it is a super-state, a state outside all states, the members of which are cut off from the mass of humanity. Although the Cynic wise man, far in advance of most fourth-century thought, ignores the traditional barriers that make female inferior to male, slave to master, foreigner to Greek, the Cynics themselves enlarged and strengthened the other barrier which loomed so large in contemporary thinking about mankind. The Cynic conception does not unite the human race, but draws a single great dividing line across it, separating the few wise men from the many fools, whom Diogenes described as 'one finger removed from lunacy'.[69] We may guess that if Diogenes did write a *Politeia*, its subject was life within this fellowship of the wise, not an ideal state in the ordinary sense.

What of the majority on the wrong side of the line of division? The doxographical reference to the value of law, which I have already mentioned, suggests that they should continue their ordinary city-state existence, guided by the traditions and conventions above which the wise man is able to rise. But whereas other thinkers, such as Protagoras and Aristotle, held that such civilised beings had a primary right to be called 'men', Diogenes declared that the non-wise are *not* men. Hence the story of his walking through the streets of Athens with a lantern in broad daylight, saying 'I am looking for a man' (41); or his description of the gathering assembled at Olympia: 'a great crowd, but few men' (60). Only the wise man is truly man, and truly possesses the nature of man. The unwise are sub-human, unhuman, not human at all. 'Reason—or the noose' was said to be one of Diogenes' favourite prescriptions: those who do not follow reason might as well be dead.

Nevertheless, the Cynics regarded themselves as benefactors, like Heracles, of the rest of humanity; and Crates especially seems to have achieved a reputation for *philanthrōpia*, benevolence towards his fellow-men, in spite of the general Cynic contempt for the mob.[70] When Cynicism was revived under the Roman Empire, this aspect came more strongly to the fore, bringing with it the picture of the ideal Cynic ruler.[71] Even the early Cynics certainly turned outward from themselves and practised *philanthrōpia* to the extent that they tried to recruit other individuals to their own ranks, and much of their unorthodox conduct and striking talk must have had a proselytising purpose. 'Other dogs bite their enemies, but I my friends, to save them', said Diogenes (Stob. *Ecl.* III. p. 462). Lucian makes him call himself 'a liberator of men and healer of their passions', and this theme of the healing of souls occurs several times in our stories of him and Antisthenes.[72]

There is inconsistency here between the Pera ideal and *philanthrōpia*, between emphasis on the gap between wise men and fools and these endeavours to bridge it. Once more we have an instance of the recurring conflict between the tendency to isolate the wise, rejecting the common run of men as worthless fools, and the thought that all human beings are akin in the possession of reason and the potentiality of becoming wise. In other minds the idea of a common humanity was eventually to win the day. But it must not be supposed that Cynic thought of the fourth and third centuries B.C. was dominated by such a conception, or that *philanthrōpia* was for them ever more than a minor theme. They were healers of the few *individual* souls which they regarded as curable, and had no thought of any programme for ridding the world of the plague of folly that afflicts the great majority of mankind. In our evidence for them there is no trace of any vision of a united humanity; and although as individuals they practised what they preached, there is no suggestion of casting down in practice the barriers between man and man. It was not social change that they proposed, but change of individual hearts, or rather of individual minds: slavery, for example, was not to be abolished, but to be disregarded.73 Their effect on the thought of antiquity was limited accordingly. They stand out as truly radical critics of the accepted pattern of society in sharp contrast with Aristotle and others who sought to justify it, and their precept and example must have done much to loosen the rigidity of accepted prejudices and prepare the way for wider views. They exercised great influence through the Stoics and other thinkers who incorporated some Cynic doctrines into their own in a modified form, and we shall often come upon them again in this indirect way in the further development of our theme. But the appeal of Cynicism itself was always to isolated individuals: through the fourth and third centuries B.C., and again under the Roman Empire, it produced some striking individual figures, powerful critics of society and its follies, but it never passed beyond its negative contempt for conventional barriers to become a major positive factor in the movement of ideas towards the concept of a united mankind.

CHAPTER IV

ALEXANDER AND HIS INFLUENCE

ALEXANDER THE GREAT

ALTHOUGH our theme is the history of an idea, it becomes necessary at this point to turn our attention to a figure who was primarily a man of action: Alexander the Great. Alexander's impact on the Greek conception of mankind has been variously assessed. Estimates of him have ranged from the soldier concerned with practical policies for particular ends, to the dreamer who envisaged a world of universal brotherhood, and so must be regarded as the creator and earliest champion of the idea of human unity. It will be best to consider first how far this latter verdict, which would make Alexander the turning point in our story, can be accepted as valid.

The view that Alexander was philosopher as well as man of action, and held a conscious and explicit belief in the unity of mankind, had its supporters in antiquity as well as in modern times. In our extant Greek literature the chief exposition of it is a short work, *De Alexandri Magni Fortuna aut Virtute*, attributed to Plutarch and probably an early product of his pen. The treatise is the first of two speeches composed in reply to the claim that Alexander's achievements were the result of fortune; on the contrary, declares Plutarch, his actions and policies sprang from the inspiration of philosophy; moreover, Alexander was no mere theoriser like other philosophers, but went beyond them all in that he put his ideas into practice. All this is set forth in what is essentially a rhetorical exercise, and the author states his case with all the flamboyant exaggeration and display of superficial learning which were characteristic of the *declamatio*. One brief quotation, even in translation, will be enough to illustrate his style:

Alexander did not overrun Asia like a brigand or with the intention of ravaging and plundering it like booty and spoils which unexpected luck had brought him, as Hannibal later came to Italy, and earlier the Trerians invaded Ionia and the Scythians Media. The reason for the form of dress which he adopted was his wish to make it plain that all earthly affairs are subject to one principle and one government, and that all men are one people. If the divinity that sent Alexander's spirit hither had not speedily recalled it, one law would hold sway over all men and they would have turned their faces to a single form of justice as if towards a common light. But as it is that part of the world which did not behold Alexander remained in darkness. (330c–e)

Obviously such stuff as this, written about four centuries after Alexander, is worthless as historical evidence unless it can be shown to embody material from much earlier sources. In 1885 Eduard Schwartz put forward the view that a considerable section of the essay came from the great geographer Eratosthenes, of whom I shall have more to say later; and if this were correct, the picture of Alexander the philosopher, champion of the unity of mankind, would go back at any rate to the third century B.C. With various reservations many recent writers on the subject have followed Schwartz, but others have rejected his claim; to me it seems based on slender arguments and out of accord with the general character of the document.[1] The treatise is a patchwork in which ideas and illustrations from various sources, including Eratosthenes, are woven together to form the highly rhetorical texture of the whole, and there is no good reason to suppose that its portrait of Alexander is either old or authentic.

Plutarch wrote at a time when world unity of a sort had been brought into being by Rome. In the present century, when there is again much talk of world brotherhood, a view of Alexander reminiscent of Plutarch's essay has been put forward and widely accepted. Its most vigorous advocate has been Sir William Tarn, who stated it briefly in his early books and his chapters in the

Cambridge Ancient History, and then argued his case more explicitly and at greater length in his Raleigh Lecture in 1933, *Alexander the Great and the Unity of Mankind*. Tarn's claim had a mixed reception: the majority of continental scholars, in particular, adopted a negative attitude varying from polite scepticism to scornful rejection. But Tarn repeated and elaborated it in an article published in 1939, and in his great work on Alexander in 1948 devoted a lengthy appendix to elaboration and emphatic reassertion of his view.[2]

In 1933 [he wrote] I referred everything about Alexander to a single idea; it can now be seen that what we possess relates, I will not say to three ideas, but to an idea which had three facets or aspects, and these must be distinguished, though they are closely interconnected. The first is that God is the common Father of mankind, which may be called the brotherhood of man. The second is Alexander's dream of the various races of mankind, so far as known to him, becoming of one mind together and living in unity and concord, which may be called the unity of mankind. And the third, also part of his dream, is that the various peoples of his Empire might be partners in the realm rather than subjects. (p. 400)

From the rest of the Appendix it is clear that in Tarn's view the most important of these three aspects was the second, which he also called 'the unity of peoples' (p. 435).

Since 1948 a number of scholars have criticised Tarn's claim, but many other writers on Alexander and on the history of ideas have accepted it or reproduced it in a slightly modified form. Such is Tarn's dominating influence in Alexander studies, at any rate in Britain and America, that Alexander the Idealist, the Dreamer, the first believer in the brotherhood of man, continues to haunt the pages of books on the ancient world. The arguments in favour of this portrayal of him clearly deserve careful consideration if we are tracing the development of the idea of the unity of mankind.

The direct evidence cited by Tarn and his supporters is slight. According to his list the relevant passages are a sentence in Plutarch's *Life of Alexander*; a paragraph of Strabo and two short sections of the *De Alexandri Magni Fortuna aut Virtute*, which Tarn, partly following Schwartz, derives from Eratosthenes; and closely linked with these, the sentences in which Arrian describes the banquet and prayer at Opis. To this collection may be added a few lines from the plans attributed to Alexander in Diodorus, which Tarn omits because he does not regard the plans as genuine. On each of these items something must be said.

The important sentence for our purpose in Plutarch's *Life* comes at the end of his description of Alexander's visit to the oracle of Ammon in the Egyptian desert (27. 6). The prophet, says Plutarch, gave him salutation from the god 'as from a father', and in answer to a question assured him—according to most writers on the incident—that he was to become lord of all mankind. The account concludes thus:

He is also said to have listened to the philosopher Psammon in Egypt, and to have agreed especially with his saying that all men are under the kingship of God, since the ruling and dominant element in each individual is divine. But still more philosophical was his own opinion and assertion on this matter, that God is indeed the common father of all men, but makes the best of them peculiarly His own.

Tarn asserts that in this alleged dictum of Alexander the first clause is the important one. It is no mere acceptance, as others have thought, of the familiar Homeric description of Zeus as 'father of gods and men'; on the contrary, by using the word 'father' Alexander is deliberately correcting a different interpretation of Homer's phrase, which we find in Aristotle (*Pol.* 1259 b 10 ff.) and which Plutarch puts into Psammon's mouth—the idea of Zeus as 'king' of all. 'What we have got, if I may use modern language without offence,' writes Tarn, 'is the whole difference between God the Ruler of the universe and God the Father.' 'This, on the face of it, is a plain statement that all men are brothers, and, if true, is the earliest known, at any rate in the western world.'

One may well doubt whether the Psammon anecdote is reliable history; but even if it is, and even if we accept for the moment the assumption that the fatherhood of God implies the brotherhood of man,3 the sentence does not really uphold Tarn's striking claim. The distinction between 'father' and 'king', however important in Christian thought, would have little significance for the Greeks; and in any case both Greek idiom and the context indicate that the first clause is *not* the important part of the sentence, but rather a reference to a familiar notion taken for granted: it is the second clause, with its emphasis on the inferiority of the rest of humanity to those outstanding individuals who are especially God's sons, that links up with the main point of the chapter—the oracle's greeting and response. That this distinction is foremost in Plutarch's mind is shown by the way he continues his narrative, stressing the difference in Alexander's behaviour towards 'barbarians' and towards Greeks.

The other passages mentioned by Tarn are all connected, in his view, with the feast at Opis in 324 B.C. On this our principal source of information is Arrian, who draws most of his account from Alexander's own close associate, Ptolemy.4 The banquet is the concluding incident in Arrian's narrative of a meeting among the Macedonian troops, whose loyalty was restored after Alexander had made a show of regarding Persians as his 'kinsmen' in their place. I will give Arrian's description of the sequel in the translation of Sir Ernest Barker, whose view of the passage is based on Tarn's interpretation of it:

Thereupon Alexander offered sacrifice to the gods to whom he was accustomed to sacrifice, and afterwards made a public feast, sitting himself in person at the table, with all the Macedonians seated round him and the Persians next to them, and after the Persians men of the other races who were pre-eminent in reputation or in any other respect. At this feast Alexander and his fellows dipped their cups in the same bowl of wine and made the same drink-offerings, with the seers of the Greeks and the Magi of Persia taking the lead. As they did so, Alexander prayed for blessings, and especially for the blessing of human concord and of fellowship in the realm between Macedonians and Persians. The story goes that those who partook of the feast amounted to nine thousand men, and that all of them made the same drink-offering and thereupon sang in triumph together.5

If this version is correct, the incident is clearly of great importance for our theme, and Barker is justified in describing it as 'an epoch in the relations of "Greeks and barbarians" and a landmark of progress in the movement of the age towards human equality and general fraternity'. In fact, however, both the general character and importance of the scene, and various particular aspects of it, have been the subject of dispute. There are two points of special interest for our purpose, on neither of which, if the Arrian passage is taken by itself, can Tarn's interpretation be upheld.

First, who were present at this ceremony? Was it really the international gathering, the feast of international reconciliation, which Tarn describes? Clearly the chief participants were Persians and Macedonians, representatives of the two peoples involved in the trouble which led up to the banquet; and this is confirmed by the joint inauguration of the ritual by Greek and Persian priests. What were the 'other races' which were also represented? Kolbe, who in 1935 went even beyond Tarn in his account of Alexander's internationalism, asserted that members of *all* the peoples of the known world were at the banquet, and commented: 'The idea of a universal world brotherhood came to birth.'[6] According to Tarn, the phrase refers to 'the most prominent men from every race in his Empire and from at least one people not in his Empire, Greeks'. But without confirmatory evidence it is difficult to believe that guests from so far afield could have been brought together for an occasion which seems to have been swiftly improvised to meet an unexpected crisis. It is easier to suppose, with Wüst, that 'other peoples' means 'the remaining, non-Persian, elements of the Iranian population', while Greeks were also there not as representatives of the Greek people, but among Alexander's officers;[7] and in any case it seems likely, as Wilcken suggested, that the 'other peoples' were present only as witnesses of the Persian-Macedonian conciliation.[8] The international banquet, unparalleled in world history, shrinks to an assembly more limited, more relevant to the needs of the occasion, and much more credible.

Secondly, there is the problem of Alexander's prayer, which is the central feature in Tarn's picture.⁹ He claims that two translations of Arrian's words at this point 'are grammatically possible, and both are equally true to the Greek'. One, the usual rendering, is that Alexander 'prayed for the other good things and for Homonoia between, and partnership in rule between, Macedonians and Persians'; the other, that he 'prayed for the other good things, and for Homonoia, and for partnership in the realm between Macedonians and Persians'. Perhaps it is true that both of these versions are grammatically possible; but there can be no doubt that the first, which brings in *homonoia* not as a separate concept of world concord, but as a relationship between two antagonised groups, is more probable both as an explanation of the Greek and as part of the whole scene which the passage puts before us. Only strong confirmation from other sources could justify acceptance of Tarn's version instead of the usual interpretation of the sentence.

Tarn seeks such confirmation in Strabo and Plutarch, from whom, he claims, we can extract a 'fragment' of Eratosthenes which must go back to an independent eyewitness of the Opis ceremony. The passage in Strabo's *Geography*, which we shall have to consider in more detail in a later chapter, mentions Eratosthenes as authority for the statement that someone advised Alexander 'to treat the Greeks as friends and the barbarians as enemies', and that Alexander, 'disregarding his advisers, welcomed and favoured all men he could of good repute'.¹⁰ In the *De Alexandri Magni Fortuna aut Virtute*, as we have seen,¹¹ Plutarch repeats the story, naming Aristotle as Alexander's counsellor and characteristically elaborating his advice; and it is reasonable to suppose that here Plutarch's information also comes, directly or indirectly, from Eratosthenes. Plutarch goes on:

Rather he believed that he had come from God to be the common harmoniser and reconciler of all men. Those whom he did not lead together by persuasion he compelled by force of arms and brought elements from every side into a unity, mingling like wine in a loving-cup their ways of life and their customs, their marriages and their social habits. He bade them all think of the inhabited world as their fatherland, the army as their citadel and their defence, the good as their kinsmen, and the bad as foreigners. (329c)

Tarn, partly agreeing with Schwartz, claims that down to the words 'social habits' all this must also go back to Eratosthenes; and by identifying the 'loving-cup' of Plutarch's simile with the bowl used at Opis, he links the whole Eratosthenes-Plutarch passage with the Opis ceremony. The ideal of universal brotherhood implicit in Plutarch's words must have characterised the scene at Opis, too; and when three pages later Plutarch describes Alexander as intending 'to gain for all men *homonoia*, and peace and partnership with one another' (330e), these words are a reference to the prayer at Opis, derived again from Eratosthenes and the nameless eyewitness behind him, and their tenor confirms Tarn's translation of the shorter account of the prayer given by Arrian.

If this were right, Alexander the champion of world brotherhood would be established as a historical reality. But the similarity between Strabo's story and Plutarch's reference to Aristotle cannot justify us in tracing all that Plutarch says here back to Eratosthenes —least of all, as Badian has shown, the last part of it, 'where the differences between Strabo's citation and Plutarch are manifold and striking'.[12] As far as we know, the loving-cup simile is the creation of Plutarch, not a borrowing from Eratosthenes or an imaginary eyewitness at Opis; and if it is linked in any way with a real vessel—possibly, as Tarn claims, the great bowl of Darius which Alexander captured at Susa—its use at the Susa marriage ceremony is more likely to be in Plutarch's mind than the Opis banquet. Arrian must stand alone as our only important authority for the Opis ceremony, and Tarn's improbable version of his account, lacking other confirmation, must be set aside. What we do gather from the incident is not a belief in world unity on Alexander's part, but a fact illustrated by other events in his career, and by no means irrelevant to our theme: his denial of the idea of a single *Herrenvolk* and his readiness to treat at any rate one 'barbarian' people on the same level with the Macedonians. His adoption of this un-Greek attitude towards racial divisions *is* confirmed by the Strabo-Plutarch-Eratosthenes story of his rejection of Aristotle's advice.[13] I shall return later to the importance of this conduct and attitude for the development of the idea of the unity of mankind.

So much for the direct evidence which Tarn puts forward in favour of his account of Alexander's ideal; it seems to me to fall far short of proving his claim. The passage in Diodorus, which he does not use, is one of the proposals said to have been found in Alexander's papers and abandoned after his death: 'to combine cities and transfer populations from Asia to Europe and in the opposite direction from Europe to Asia, using intermarriages and family ties as the means of bringing the greatest continents into common unity of outlook (*homonoia*) and the friendship that kinsmen share'. Tarn himself has demonstrated the improbability of this grandiose item, at any rate, in Alexander's alleged plans, and believers in its authenticity have been singularly unsuccessful in their efforts to find anything comparable in the actions attributed to Alexander himself. Certainly no conclusion about his view of mankind could be safely based on this slight and shaky piece of evidence alone.[14]

The argument to which Tarn devotes most space, however, is not a question of direct evidence, but an inference from a certain version of the history of Greek thought: the claim that at this point there occurred a change in the Greek conception of mankind which could only have been inspired by Alexander. To quote Tarn's own graphic words:

Somewhere between the middle of the fourth century B.C. and the early third century there took place a great revolution in Greek thought. For long, prior to that revolution, Greeks had divided the world they knew into Greeks and non-Greeks. . . . But in the third century we meet with a body of opinion which discarded this division; it held that all men were brothers and ought to live together in unity and concord.[15]

This 'tremendous revolution', he argues, must have been due not to Zeno, as some have supposed, but to Alexander; and all who accept his view have taken for granted some such picture of the development of ideas.

The thesis of this book has been that the notion of the unity of mankind was an attitude of mind which existed in some sense from Homer onwards, but was given varying shape and content by different writers as time went on. Tarn's belief, on the contrary, is that Alexander's genius produced something entirely new, which sprang full-grown from his mind like Athena from the head of Zeus; and similarly Kolbe emphasises Alexander's complete originality, which enabled him to break away from all previous Greek thought. To fit this point of view, any evidence for the existence of the idea before Alexander must be belittled or rejected. If earlier thinkers spoke at all of human unity or brotherhood, they meant not a conception to which Alexander gave richer or fuller significance, but something as different from what was in his mind as chalk from cheese. Tarn goes so far as to declare: 'There is no doubt that when a Greek before Alexander talked of "all men", or used some equivalent expression, what he meant was "all Greeks"'—an assertion which we have already seen to be far from correct.

With this approach, individual thinkers before Alexander are necessarily given short shrift. Antiphon is dismissed with the comment that his statement on the common attributes of 'all men' 'cannot refer to all mankind'. There is no consideration of where Protagoras or Thucydides stands in this matter, or of the evidence of the medical writers. In any case, Tarn goes on, anything of this sort in the fifth century or earlier 'had no importance for history, for in the fourth century the whole thing was swept aside by the dominant idealist philosophies' of Plato and Aristotle. Plato, on the evidence of the *Menexenus* and the fifth book of the *Republic*, is quickly convicted of the narrowest anti-barbarian prejudice; no mention is made of the *Statesman* and the *Laws*. Comment on Aristotle is limited to his description of barbarians as 'natural

slaves' in the first book of the *Politics*. There is no recognition
of the fact that he went far beyond all previous thinkers in his
realisation of the unity of mankind as a single species, within which
all the various types—admittedly, unequal types—must be seen
as parts of a single whole. As to the passage in the *Ethics* where
Aristotle speaks of a bond of affection between all members of the
human race,[16] Tarn deals with this by a misinterpretation: the
Greek must mean, he says, that 'as beasts of the same species are
friendly to one another, so are men of the same species (for
example, Greeks)'. He sees Aristotle here as following the same
line of thought as Isocrates—*homonoia* limited to the Greek race.
His account of Isocrates makes no reference to the *Panegyricus*
passage in which community of culture, not of race, is made the
justification for the name 'Hellene';[17] nor, again, to the picture
of humanity sharing the common gift of *logos* which forms the
wider context in which Isocrates' *Herrenvolk* doctrine must be seen.

Earlier chapters have, I hope, shown that this is not an adequate
account of Greek thought about mankind before Alexander's
time. Equally mistaken, it seems to me, is Tarn's treatment of the
theme *after* the 'revolution in ideas' which he is trying to prove.
Two of the main figures concerned—Theophrastus and Zeno—
will be considered in some detail later, and I shall try to show that
in neither case is there a sudden leap forward to a view of human
unity different in kind from earlier conceptions. Of the other
individuals and documents that he cites to illustrate this supposed
revolutionary change, something must be said here.

Some of the evidence which he discusses belongs to a much
later period, and is brought into the picture in order to follow
the link between kingship and *homonoia* down to Roman imperial
times. These items—the revolt of Aristonicus at Pergamum in
133 B.C., the prophecy about Cleopatra in the third book of the
Sibylline Oracles, Tiberius' temple to *Concordia Augusta*—are
presumably not intended to be relevant to the point at issue. But
there are others which must be set aside as equally irrelevant, on
the ground that Tarn's early dating of them is probably wrong.

Such are the strange fragments attributed to the allegedly Pythagorean Diotogenes and Ecphantus in Stobaeus, which Tarn, following the view argued by Professor Goodenough in 1928,[18] places in 'the early third century' and claims as a reflection of Alexander's views. The fullest study of these fragments, by Louis Delatte in 1942, puts them in the first century A.D., and Goodenough, reviewing Delatte's book in 1949, accepted this late date.[19] The question is difficult, but I doubt whether any scholar would now have enough confidence in the early dating to use this material as evidence for third-century thought. The same applies with at least equal strength to Iambulus, in whose strange Utopia Tarn finds, rather surprisingly, the connection of *homonoia* with kingship which he derives from Alexander. Iambulus, he says, must lie between about 290 and 133 B.C.; 'but he belongs to the constructive period and ought therefore to be third-century'. A stronger argument than this is needed if it is to be maintained that Iambulus lived within a hundred years of Alexander's death.

Certainly close to Alexander in time is another odd figure, of whom Tarn draws a persuasive but, I fear, fanciful picture: Alexarchus, brother of Cassander, who founded on Mount Athos a city called Ouranopolis.[20] Alexarchus, we are told, 'dressed himself up as the sun'; and extant coins of Ouranopolis show the sun, moon, and five stars on one side, and on the other bear the image of Aphrodite Ourania and refer to the citizens as 'Ouranidai'.[21] Apparently this eccentric liked to think of his *polis* as the 'city of heaven', its citizens as 'children of heaven', and himself as the Sun which dominates the heaven—notions which could come from the East or from study of Plato's *Republic*, but which do not prove, as Tarn suggests, that 'he had set up a little World-State in miniature'. A further whimsicality was his use of peculiar word-forms, apparently of his own invention, which he employed in an unintelligible letter to the magistrates of the neighbouring town of Cassandreia. Tarn calls this an 'international' or 'universal' language, devised to suit 'the World-State of his dream'; but in fact there is nothing international about such bits of this verbal jugglery as we can understand: they are as Greek as *Jabberwocky* is English, and there is no hint of crossing the line between Greek and any 'barbarian' tongue. The letter begins with a salutation which Tarn translates, 'To the chief men of the Brethren, all hail'— a further allusion to world brotherhood. 'The sense is certain', he writes; yet the obvious explanation of the Greek word involved is a reference to the fact that Cassandreia was founded by Alexarchus' brother, and Professor Gulick is probably right in translating 'to the Primipiles of Brother's Town'.[22] All in all, there is no good ground for the claim that there was any conception of world brotherhood in Alexarchus' strange mind.

With Alexarchus Tarn links Theophrastus, to whom I shall return later, and also Cassander's associate, Euhemerus: 'Behind all three', he says, 'stood *something*—the same something—which influenced them all and which was later than Aristotle; and it does not appear what else that could have been but Alexander.' Euhemerus' membership of this trio rests, it must be said, on extremely dubious foundations. We read in Lactantius that in his *Sacred History* Euhemerus maintained that not Saturn, but Uranus, was the first ruler on earth (fr. 12 Jacoby); and also that Jupiter, travelling over the world after gaining power, *reges principesve populorum hospitio sibi et amicitia copulabat*—'bound the kings and rulers of the peoples to himself by ties of hospitality and friendship' (fr. 23). And Diodorus, drawing from Euhemerus, states that according to one view held by 'men of ancient times', 'some of the gods are eternal and imperishable, such as the sun and moon and the other stars in the heavens' (fr. 2). Diodorus also reports how Euhemerus described a visit he had made to a Utopian island called Panchaea. Out of this evidence Tarn constructs the remarkable claim that 'Euhemerus made of Heaven the first ruler to unite the whole human race in a World-State', with Sun, Moon and Stars as its gods; and that according to Euhemerus 'Zeus, when he reunited men in a universal State, joined them together in *amicitia*'—not 'to himself', *sibi*, but 'together', which is surely an impossible translation of Lactantius'

Latin. Tarn's Euhemerus, like his Alexarchus, belongs to the realm of fantasy rather than fact. There may well have been some link between their views, as their common concern with Ouranos and the heavenly bodies suggests; but this is a far cry from the claim that they were believers in a 'World-State', or held a radically new conception of the unity of mankind.

I have argued that the picture of Alexander as the champion of human brotherhood and unity is not supported by direct evidence or by scrutiny of the development of these ideas in Greek thought. There remains one other source from which proof might be sought: it might be asserted that such a conviction of the unity of mankind is the only possible, or at least the most probable, explanation of some of Alexander's actions. Tarn made little use of this line of thought, but it is a constant theme in Plutarch's rhetorical essay, and some modern writers have made great play with the striking results of Alexander's fusion policy as alleged confirmation of his belief in the unity of all peoples: the inter-racial marriages, for example, culminating in the mass wedding at Susa, with Persian ritual, between Alexander and his Companions and daughters of the Persian and Median aristocracy; the combination of Persian with Macedonian dress which was adopted by Alexander and appears on his coins; the mingling of populations, mainly Greek and native, in the new cities which he founded; the reorganisation of the armed forces, whereby men of different races were brought together in each small military unit.

Clearly these and other events, though by no means 'international' in the fullest sense, involved a different attitude towards 'barbarians' from the point of view that had become usual among the Greeks; and if there were other good evidence for Alexander's belief in a doctrine of world brotherhood, they might perhaps be explained as deliberate moves in the direction of this ideal. As it is, however, one must turn to other, more probable, ways of explanation, both for the causes that might guide the young Alexander into such lines of conduct, and for his motives in acting thus.

One cause may be found in Alexander's own background—in his native Macedonian tradition and in the methods which his father had pursued before him. Racial exclusiveness was not part of the Macedonian outlook: absorption of other peoples had been a feature of Macedonian development, and fusion with a ruling class so similar as the Persian was to that of Macedon might seem reasonable to a Macedonian, though outrageous to a Greek. Polygamy was probably a traditional practice of the Macedonian royal house, and Philip had certainly used marriage with wives from other peoples as an instrument of political conciliation. The founding of cities—it may well be, with mixed populations—also goes back to Philip. Alexander seems to have learned more from his father than from any thoughts inspired by philosophy.

If, on the other hand, one is looking for motives for Alexander's extension of these lines of action on to the grand scale, there is no need to seek them in a consciously held intellectual theory. The scale is characteristic of Alexander. Sufficient motive can be found in his case, as in Philip's, in the political strategy required to cope with situations created by events; and in spite of the dimensions of his actions, they were at the same time limited in a way which points to practical purposes, rather than theoretical principles, as the reason behind them. As Hammond says, 'the equal association of Macedonians and Iranians in government, marriage, and warfare was designed for the purposes of administration and conquest and not for any philosophical or religious ends. In consequence it was attempted only at the higher social levels of the Indo-European peoples.'[23] At the least it must be said that such moves *can* be accounted for without reference to any conscious conviction of the unity of man; and where other evidence in support of Plutarch's Alexander Philosophus or Tarn's Alexander the Dreamer is lacking, it is safer to seek an explanation in practical policies which link up with his origins and early experience than to accept the new Alexander legend which Tarn and others have created.

AFTER ALEXANDER

If the argument of the preceding pages is correct, Alexander as the conscious champion of the unity and brotherhood of mankind has no place in our story. But this does not mean, of course, that the historical Alexander is irrelevant to our theme. Whatever the purpose and attitude of mind which inspired him, there can be no doubt that his novel policies (as they were to the Greeks) and his spectacular practical achievements did much to transform the world of his day, making a powerful impact on men's minds as well as changing the physical conditions under which they lived. Many historians have emphasised the difference between the outlook of the Hellenistic age, which followed his conquests, and the ideas of earlier years.

One great change was the widening of the world. The area of the earth's surface known to the Greeks had been suddenly enlarged by Alexander's expedition, together with the remarkable voyage of Pytheas in the west, and in a few years geographical knowledge had taken its biggest step forward since the change between Homer and Herodotus. But whereas writers of the fifth century B.C. soon passed beyond the limits of knowledge into regions of marvel and fantasy with only hearsay as their guide, military conquest and Greek settlement now brought vast areas within an inhabited world, an *oikoumenē*, known to many Greeks not only from second-hand information but from personal experience. Within this extended horizon travel and trade became far easier and developed on a far larger scale; local ties were bound to lose much of their strength, and the individual was likely to turn towards wider affiliations.

Secondly, there was a lesson to be learned, for those willing to learn it, in race relations. We have seen that the account of the banquet at Opis, the Eratosthenes story of the rejection of Aristotle's advice, and many of Alexander's acts involved a transcendence or neglect of racial distinctions which cut right across the prejudices that most Greeks had accepted for so long. Obviously there was food for deep thought for the Greek mind in the thoroughly un-Greek attitude of this Macedonian towards 'barbarians' who had other gods and spoke other tongues, treating at least one 'barbarian' nation as on an equal level with his own.

Taken together, the extension of the geographical horizon and the mixing of peoples should have been enough to inspire some radical new thinking about the nature of mankind. It is often said that now, as never before, the time was ripe for the spread of belief in the brotherhood and unity of mankind: even those who do not attribute these ideas to Alexander claim that they emerged in the decades after his death, and were part of the 'climate of thought' which his achievements created.

The claim contains some truth, but it has often been overstated. In reality the situation after Alexander was still far from completely favourable for acceptance of such concepts. Although the world familiar to the Greeks became much larger than before, its unity is easily exaggerated. If Alexander had lived longer, the result might have been different; but as it was, his empire and the fulfilment of his policies lasted for so short a span that it was over almost before the Greeks at home had time to absorb the news. The situation which followed, the situation which *did* last, was very far removed from unity: while we may see it as a single whole, its multiple divisions and conflicts, military and political, were probably the more obvious feature to the Greeks of the day.

One source of disunity was the continuation on a larger scale of the strife which had torn the Greek world apart in earlier centuries. The Hellenistic age was a time of ceaseless military and political struggles, whether the long Wars of the Successors which began two years after Alexander's death, the violent competition for supremacy during the unstable balance of power, or the repeated efforts of city-states to regain their independence. Only Roman intervention in the second century B.C. brought a period of peace.

Conflict of this type produced chaos and confusion instead of unity. But probably still more far-reaching in its effect on the life and thought of the time was the cleavage on which the unity of the *oikoumenē* depended—the division between Greek and native, which was to be found in every part of the world opened up by Alexander outside Greece. His fusion policy had broken down completely after his disappearance from the scene; and although it is difficult to estimate the amount of inter-racial mixing that developed in the new cities and elsewhere in Egypt and the East, and the extent of it varied greatly from one region to another, it is clearly true that the Hellenistic world was deeply divided by the antithesis between Hellenic and alien standards and culture. Such unity as it possessed was not due to its being a single whole made up of diverse parts, bringing into one all the various peoples described by Herodotus. Its different regions formed a unity only in so far as they had a common denominator—the homogeneous *Greek* civilisation which now permeated them all. In the *Iliad* and *Odyssey* poetic imagination had imposed a single pattern on the different peoples in Homer's story. Now the same thing occurred in fact: the effect of Alexander's conquests, as Isocrates had foreseen, was to release the floodgates of Greek emigration, so that Greek settlers, bringing with them Greek goods and Greek ways, spread to all parts of the vast area which he had overrun. In the decades that followed, the flow outwards from Greece continued. In spite of the struggle for power and the military conflicts between the Hellenistic kingdoms, the penetration of Greek culture produced unity, at a certain level, throughout. The *koinē*, the modified Attic Greek familiar as the language of the New Testament, was the common speech of this enlarged Greek world, the only tongue a man needed to travel from one end of the *oikoumenē* to the other: although settled abroad, the vast majority of the Greeks remained unilingual, and ignorance of other forms of speech still limited their conception of mankind. The writers of the period, says Rostovtzeff, all 'take one cardinal point for granted. The new world which they describe or mention was in their eyes an extension, a continuation of the Greek world. The new kings are Greek kings and pursue a

Greek policy; they rule over Greeks and are surrounded by Greeks.'24

This 'Hellenic' unity, it must be added, was not racial. If it had been confined to those of Greek racial descent, the status of the Macedonian rulers would have been doubtful; still more so, the position of the descendants of those numerous Greek emigrants who married 'native' wives. Isocrates' claim, that the name 'Hellene' belonged to those who shared a certain culture and mental outlook, was now fulfilled, and the unity I have described was one of language, education and mode of life, not of blood. The more prosperous and enterprising 'natives' were attracted by Greek culture and the status which possession of it ensured. Encouraged by the policy of the rulers, they were absorbed into the ranks of the 'Hellenes', and brought with them some of their own customs and ways of life, their ideas and their religious cults. But although this gave 'Hellenism' a wider meaning and some local variation of content, it remained true that the basic character of these islands of Greek culture in a foreign sea was determined by the hard core of Greek settlers, filled with the settler outlook, clinging as settlers will to their traditional ways; and the desire of the Hellenised 'natives' to be marked off from the rest assisted, rather than hindered, the retaining of the traditional Hellenic stamp.

The unity of the Hellenistic world, in consequence, was the unity of a culture little, if at all, less Greek than that of Greece itself—more homogeneous, indeed, than the civilisation of Greece in earlier centuries, just as the *koinē* was more homogeneous than the dialects it replaced. The life of the Hellenic or Hellenised minority everywhere was based on the *polis*, usually laid out on the same rectangular plan. The institutions of the *polis*—theatres, gymnasia, temples, festivals—shaped the citizens' pattern of living, and education, business, and family life went on in the new cities very much as in the old. Along with other features, the traditional divisions and relationships within society continued without fundamental change. It is true that some princesses among the

Macedonian rulers rose to remarkable heights of distinction and influence, and many individual Greek women gained education and intellectual emancipation; but these were exceptions to the continued general acceptance of the inferiority and suppression of women. Slaves—except in the mines—were more liberally treated and more often set free; but there was no radical alteration in their status or the conditions under which they lived.

Between this 'Hellenic' pattern of existence, now extended into Syria and Egypt and elsewhere, and the varied ways of life of the 'native' populations, lay a gap which was never bridged. The division, which the rulers encouraged, was not one of political status, but of culture and civilisation. To quote Rostovtzeff again:

The unity of the Hellenistic world . . . was a peculiar phenomenon, unique of its kind in the evolution of mankind. It was a unity which comprised the whole of the Greeks (including those of the mother country), but not the whole population of the Eastern monarchies, where it was restricted to its Greek superstructure. The natives, forming the vast majority of the population, were not (with few exceptions) absorbed into this unity. The native population remained as diversified in its national, social, religious, economic, and cultural life as it had previously been, and retained all the principal characteristics of this life until the end of the Hellenistic period.[25]

The scene which confronted Hellenistic man was not a united world in the full sense of the term, not a multi-racial unity. It was a world divided not only by rivalries and wars, military and political conflicts, but by a cleavage of culture and class running throughout. The contrast between the Greeks of the homeland and the surrounding 'barbarians' was now blurred;[26] but it was replaced by an antithesis between Hellenic and alien standards and ways. There was no precedent here for the idea of unity made up of diversity, or of equality in wisdom among all men, but rather for the attitude, not unknown in modern times, of those who think the whole world kin in so far as it adopts their set of values and their mode of life. Although the effect of this situation in literature and thought remains to be seen, it is not likely to have been such a ready breeding-ground for belief in the brotherhood of men as is sometimes supposed.

The brief survival of Alexander's empire and policies, and the conflicts and divisions characteristic of the period that followed, were one reason why the Greeks were slow to learn the lesson which his achievements might have taught them. Another is that they were unwilling pupils. They had regarded the hegemony of Philip as a foreign domination with the League of Corinth as its instrument, and maintained much the same attitude towards his son. While the Greeks with Alexander were outraged by measures like his demand for prostration before him, the vast majority of the Greeks at home turned their backs on him and his achievements; and Alexander in his last years treated them in turn as a subject people, rather than as the source of the culture in which he still found inspiration.

Of all who knew Alexander [writes Hammond] the Greeks of the mainland were least impressed by the spell of his personality. In their eyes he was the Macedonian, the sacker of Thebes, the king whose authority was wielded by the capable but ruthless hands of Antipater. They had not co-operated in Alexander's campaigns with any sincerity, and they did not think at all in terms of Graeco-Macedonian civilisation.[27]

That the same refusal to recognise his greatness or learn from his example persisted after his death is clear from the pattern of our sources of information about him, presenting us, once we have passed the work of his own associates, with a long period of hostility, and still more of neglect.

With this background it is a mistake to suppose that Alexander's career had an immediate overwhelming impact on the Greek mind, resulting in the sudden creation of a new outlook quite different from the mental atmosphere of earlier times. 'Man as a political animal,' wrote Tarn, 'a fraction of the *polis* or self-governing city-state, had ended with Aristotle; with Alexander begins man as an individual.'[28] The statement is striking, but hardly true to the facts. It is all too easy to dramatise the impact of so dramatic a figure, and to impose on the comparatively slow-moving world of antiquity the rapidity of change in outlook which modern means of news dissemination and propaganda have made possible today. Perhaps even the change of label, from the Hellenic to the Hellenistic period, tempts us to imagine a sudden shift in the climate of thought, just as we tend to think of a transformation of ideas at the end of the Victorian Age, or between the nineteenth century and the twentieth.

Whatever the cause, it is common among modern writers to suppose that the attitudes and emphases typical of later Hellenistic times were already present, and even fully developed, in the literature and thought of the first decades after Alexander; a mistake made all the easier because the same tendency exists in those later authors from whom most of our knowledge of the period is derived, influencing the selection and interpretation of their material. Festugière, for example, writes of 'une certaine unité entre tous les hommes en vertu d'une communauté de nature. Or ce concept, qui apparaît comme un dogme fixe chez Zénon, n'a pris naissance qu'à la fin du IVe siècle. Il est tout absent dans l'œuvre d'Aristote.'[29] But the complex processes of the history of thought cannot be thus simplified. The truth lies not in a sudden change to a 'Hellenistic' world, but in a complicated sequence of development whereby trends already at work, stimulated and given fresh scope by the achievements of Alexander, grew in strength and had a cumulative effect over the next century or more. The tendencies which we now see, looking back from two thousand years later, may have been implicit from the first, but they took many decades to emerge clearly and be fully realised.

MENANDER

What we know of the literature of the years after Alexander confirms this impression of a complex development rather than a sudden change, for it contains less evidence of a 'new spirit' than the idea of a sweeping transformation would lead us to expect.

It is true that there is an output of prose works on many subjects, matching the wider range of knowledge now available. But literature in the narrower sense draws surprisingly little inspiration from the new situation created by Alexander: its tendency is to turn back to the old Greece. The extreme case is the poetry of Alexandria, where the 'Museum' under the patronage of the Ptolemies provides a remarkable example of an island of Greek culture isolated from the native population. The archaising verse of the Alexandrian scholars and librarians seeks its models in Homer and the early poets, and rarely reflects the cosmopolitan character of the city in which it was composed.

The writer most often quoted to illustrate the new spirit is Menander, who produced plays at Athens for about thirty years after Alexander's death. Athenian comedy must have been closer to the general Greek outlook of the time than the products of the Alexandrian Museum; and although Menander probably mirrors the ideas of the more prosperous and better educated section of his audience, this only means that he represents those to whom the new circumstances offered the greatest opportunity, those most likely to be alive to the potentialities of the world around them.

The surviving remains of Menander's plays indicate both the extent and the limitations of the change in attitude towards human relationships. The need for goodwill among men (*eunoia*) seems to have been one of his favourite topics, well illustrated by the recently discovered *Dyskolos*. Cnemon, the disgruntled old man whose character gives the play its title, is 'a man that scarcely *is* a man'[30]—a striking addition to the list, headed by the Cyclops, of those figures in Greek literature who stand apart from civilised society and are regarded as hardly human at all. He detests women, hates crowds, and is determined not to be 'one of the mass'.[31] The main theme of the comedy is the ridicule and discomfiture of this anti-social curmudgeon, who is finally forced to join in the common celebrations that end the play, and in terms reminiscent of the Cynics describes how there would be no law-courts or prisons or war if everyone followed his example (743–5).

The relationship between the rich Sostratos and the humble Gorgias also ends in conciliation, pointing the moral that friendship is better than wealth which is here today and gone tomorrow.

All this is seen within the limited context set by the scene of the play. There is nothing in the *Dyskolos* that looks beyond Attica, or suggests the wider world of Alexander's conquests. How far do the other parts of plays and fragments which survive from Menander go in this direction?

The quoted fragments, selected mainly for their philosophic content and therefore hardly typical of the plays as a whole, contain a number of pronouncements on the unity of man, including some striking references to our common nature and common lot. One of the longest is a reminder to a young man that his ill fortune is only part of the ordinary troubles of humanity:

> Since you inhale this common air of heaven
> (To use a phrase that sounds like tragedy)
> Under the same rules as the rest of us,
> You needs must bear your lot, and use your reason.
> The point is, you're a man; and there's no creature
> That suffers speedier change—up to the heights
> And down again to lowest degradation. (Fr. 531. 6–12)*

This takes us back to both Homer and Antiphon, and the emphasis on reason as man's special asset is one we have found repeatedly in Greek thought. Another quotation neatly sums up the conclusion that all men are akin:

> For me no man who's good
> Is foreign. The same nature have we all,
> And it is character that makes men kin. (Fr. 602)

The same thought reappears in the well-known lines from Terence's *Heautontimorumenos*, drawn from Menander's play of the same name. When Menedemus criticises Chremes for interfering in other people's affairs, Chremes replies:

> Homo sum: humani nil a me alienum puto. (77)

* Fragments of Menander are numbered as in Kock, *Comicorum Atticorum Fragmenta*.

The distinction between 'alien' and 'kin', so prominent in earlier
Greek thinking, falls away: the true common denominator among
men is *tropos*, individual character. Character as the individual's
safeguard in a wide world is the theme of a passage in the *Arbitrants* (875–86):

Onesimus: I will explain. There are in all about
          A thousand cities; and in each one dwell
          Some thirty thousand people. Do the gods
          Trouble to crush or save each one of these?
Smicrines: What! That's a hard life that you're giving them!
Onesimus: 'Then have the gods no care for us?' you'll say.
          To each they send a captain of the watch—
          His character. He's always at our side
          To crush the man who seems to treat him ill,
          And save another. He's our deity,
          And he's the cause of how we fare in life,
          Success or failure.

These lines are certainly an advance on the limited outlook of
local city-state patriotism. They may seem to present a picture
of the whole Hellenistic world, at once cosmopolitan and individual, the other barriers that divide men forgotten. But it is
unlikely that Menander is making such a complete break from
earlier ideas as this. Aristophanes in the *Wasps* (707) had already
spoken of the thousand cities of the Athenian Empire, and Onesimus, too, probably has *Greek* cities in mind. Certainly for
Menander the characteristics which tend to make all men one
are not just features of the general human make-up, equally
shared by all: they are primarily Greek, and their spread is the
spread of the Greek spirit, not dependent on birth or race, but on
acceptance of the Greek outlook and Greek ideals. Several fragments repeat the belief that reasoning is the most important
human quality; but reason is the special possession of Greeks:

> Greeks are men, not creatures without sense,
> And all they do is done with reason's help.   (Fr. 617)

The spirit of conciliation, so strong in the *Dyskolos* and elsewhere, is a mark of the Greek character:

> I like such talk: 'I'll go halfway to meet him'.
> To accept amends when things go well with you
> Is proof of true Hellenic character.   (*Perikeir.* 887–9)

The same thought is probably present in the fragment which most strikingly transcends kinship ties and racial barriers, and points most clearly to merit, rather than blood, as the criterion by which men should be judged. A member of the younger generation is attacking the prejudices of the older:

> 'Good family' will kill me. Mother, please
> Don't bring the family into everything.
> If there are men who have no natural worth,
> They seek escape in this—in monuments
> And 'family', and rattle off their list
> Of grandpapas: they've nothing else to say.
> Yet without grandpapas there's no man born.
> But if through change of home or loss of kin
> Some cannot name them, are they of lower birth
> Than those that can? If nature's given a man
> Good character by birth, then he's well born,
> Even though he comes from Ethiopia.
> 'So and so's a Scythian?' Hell! From Scythia
> Came Anacharsis.   (Fr. 533)

The good, like the wise according to Diogenes, are on the same level whichever continent they come from. But it is significant that Anacharsis was a *Hellenised* Scythian sage. The young man is saying in effect: 'See how Greek these "barbarians" can be.' Conversely, a Greek can be 'barbarian' if he lapses from Greek standards. 'Barbarian, man without pity!' cries Charisius in the *Arbitrants* (683–4) as he reproaches himself for his ill-treatment of his wife.

If we look for evidence of an attitude towards the traditional sex and class divisions of society, we are confronted by the usual difficulty in drama, of deciding how far opinions expressed by particular characters can be taken as the author's own. For the most part the accepted social hierarchy seems to remain unchallenged, the old distinctions and prejudices are still taken for granted. The inferiority of women, for example:

> In talk the woman's is the second place,
> And in all things the man must take the lead.
> Disaster always comes upon a house
> Wherein a woman's first in everything. (Fr. 484)

Or again:

> Many wild beasts there are by land and sea;
> But woman is the worst wild beast of all. (Fr. 488)

Odd lines echo the usual attitude towards slaves:

> That slave I like not well who thinks more deep
> Than suits a servant. (Fr. 796)

And the equation of 'barbarian' and slave is once more implied:

> A. I want a drink. B. No. That barbarian girl
> Has cleared the table and taken the wine as well. (Fr. 451)

Yet another fragment effectively expresses an outlook often found in later Hellenistic and Roman times:

> Be free in spirit, though you are a slave:
> Then slave you'll be no longer. (Fr. 857)

And a quotation from Menander's contemporary, Philemon, flatly denies the idea of 'natural slavery':

> Even a slave is made of flesh and blood.
> No man was ever born a slave by nature:
> Slavery's of the body, and comes by chance.
>
> (Fr. 39 Meineke)

Such variety, reminiscent of Euripides, must be taken as a reflection of that wide range of views on slavery in fourth-century Greece which Aristotle mentions in the *Politics*. If there is one dominant idea about humanity that seems from our limited evidence to recur throughout Menander, it is the thought that character (*tropos*) matters above all else, and can transcend all the divisions of race and class. Where others—notably the Cynics—had talked of the universal worth of wisdom, Menander sets up merit as a universal standard: a Greek standard primarily, but one to which others, even Ethiopians or Scythians, may conform. The true division of the human race, it is implied, is between the good and the bad, not between riches and poverty or between Greek and foreign blood. Thus Menander may be seen as taking his place alongside Alexander in rejecting the Aristotelian point of view,[32] and in this sense, that there is one standard for all, he repeatedly emphasises the idea of the unity of mankind; but his conception of it seems to have arisen as a natural development out of earlier Greek thought rather than a result of sudden awareness of the wider horizons opened up by Alexander.

CHAPTER V

THE HELLENISTIC PHILOSOPHERS

THE PERIPATETICS

THE philosophers were no exception to the general picture of failure to grasp the importance of Alexander's achievements and to draw conclusions from his example. There was much that was new in the outlook and vision of those who taught at Athens round about the turn of the century, but their views of mankind were by no means such a clean break with the past as is sometimes claimed. The same lines of thought on the subject which we have found in the decades before Alexander were still followed after his death, and our few remains of philosophical writing for the period contain no evidence of a striking advance towards any radically new conception of humanity.

Awareness of the new world situation might especially have been expected in the Peripatetic school, which from Aristotle onwards paid so much attention to the collection and study of factual information, including geographical knowledge. In the course of time, as we shall see, the Lyceum's persistent concern with facts became a strong influence in the direction of a new grasp of the idea of mankind as a geographical aggregate; but neither Aristotle nor his immediate followers seem to have given Alexander or his policies or the results of his conquests the consideration they deserved. Ehrenberg has emphasised how little effect Alexander had on the political thinking of Aristotle, who after all had a special reason for interest in him: Alexander's empire, he points out, never penetrated into Aristotle's political ideas, 'neither as a vision of Greek unity in the future, nor as a powerful reality in the present. . . . His great collection of polities hardly contained any non-Greek states—with the exception, perhaps, of

Carthage.... Aristotle did not even visualize the empire; he merely visualized the king, the Greeks, and the barbarians, Greek *poleis* and barbaric *ethnē*; but not the empire as unit and entity.'¹ After Aristotle, the school became bitterly antagonistic towards Alexander because of the execution of Aristotle's nephew, Callisthenes; and Theophrastus' book *On Grief* began a long-lasting Peripatetic tradition belittling Alexander's achievements as mere fruits of fortune. This is the background that must be kept in mind in considering the views of mankind put forward by Aristotle's successors, to which we will now turn.

Embedded in Porphyry's *De Abstinentia* are extracts from Theophrastus, head of the Lyceum from 323 till 288 B.C. or later, which include two passages concerned with the unity of man. The first occurs in a section certainly taken from a book *On Piety*, in which Theophrastus evidently argued against the sacrifice of animals:

The following point must also be considered. In spite of the kinship that we have with human beings, we regard it as necessary to punish and put to death all wrongdoers whose individual criminal impulses drive them to harm those they encounter. Similarly among unreasoning creatures it is perhaps right to kill those that are naturally wild and destructive and impelled by nature to harm those who come near them. But if animals do no ill to their fellow-creatures and have no natural disposition to do harm, it is presumably no less wrong to slaughter them and put them out of the way, than to kill men of such harmless character. This seems to show that there is no general principle of justice governing the relations between men and the other living creatures, since among them, as among men, some are harmful and destructive by nature and others not. (II. 22)

The second passage probably, but less certainly, also comes from the work *On Piety*. It gives a striking account of the various degrees of kinship, spreading outwards as if in concentric circles from the family to the whole of mankind, and beyond that to the rest of the animal world:

Theophrastus also used this argument. We describe as naturally akin to each other those who are born of the same father and mother, and we further regard as kin those descended from the same ancestors, and moreover those who are fellow-citizens, because they are partners in a single country and society. This relationship that we find between citizens is not due to common ancestry, except in so far as some of their first forbears may have been the same, being the originators of their stock or descended from them. So in my opinion there are two grounds for saying that there is kinship or a common relationship between Greek and Greek, and barbarian and barbarian, and indeed between all men: either because they spring from the same ancestors, or because they share the same upbringing and ways and the same stock. Hence we regard all men as akin and related to each other; and indeed for all animals the beginnings from which their bodies have developed are the same. (III. 25)

The passage goes on to give grounds for the kinship of all living creatures, attributing to them not only the same physical constituents but also the same psychological faculties—desire and anger, sense-perception, and even reasoning (*logismoi*). It is doubtful how far actual quotation from Theophrastus continues here, but noteworthy that presently the same line of argument reappears as in the first passage, whether in Theophrastus' own words or paraphrased and adapted by Porphyry, and this time there is a definite reference to kinship (*oikeiotēs*) between man and beast.[2]

To these extracts must be added another sentence of Theophrastus quoted by Porphyry, describing the world as 'the common home of gods and men' (II. 162. 6). All this is of great interest for our purpose, and the second passage in particular is one of the most definite Greek statements of the unity of mankind. It is not surprising that much has been made of this as marking a new phase in the advance of ideas about human relationships. Tarn, for example, found in it 'a revolution in thought at once simple and far-reaching', unlikely to have been made by a fact-collector like Theophrastus but for the influence of Alexander.[3] Others have pointed to these passages as evidence of the contrast between the Hellenistic and the earlier point of view, claiming that here we already have the conception of human brotherhood which was common in later Hellenistic and Roman times.

Such judgments seem to me typical of the tendency to see dramatic and radical change where in fact there was only development of existing ideas. Theophrastus was indeed more of a scholar than an original thinker, and more likely to elaborate and apply Aristotle's doctrines than to initiate new fundamental theories of his own; and it is an example of this elaboration and development that we have here. We have seen that Aristotle, in spite of his emphasis on the divisions of mankind, could also look upon it as a unity:

Affection of parent for offspring and offspring for parent seems to be implanted in them by nature, not only among men, but among birds and most animals. Affection also exists by nature between members of the same species, and especially among men; and for this reason we praise those who love their fellow men. Even on our travels we can see how near and dear every man is to every other.[4]

It is the thought of these lines, doubtless familiar in the Peripatetic school, that is mentioned as an assumption in the first passage from Porphyry ('In spite of the kinship that we have with human beings . . .') and re-stated with more elaboration and emphasis in the second. There is no evidence to indicate that Theophrastus also did not combine such talk of human unity with belief in the inferiority of women, slaves and non-Greeks.

If there is any basic difference between Theophrastus' view on the matter and Aristotle's, consideration of the second passage in conjunction with the first suggests that it lies not in their treatment of mankind but in their attitude towards animals, the status of which is here Theophrastus'—as it is also Porphyry's—main concern. Of this, too, there are anticipations in Aristotle, which in turn go back through earlier thinkers, like Protagoras, all the way to Homer's Cyclops. His gradations of mankind reach from the philosopher right down to the bestial element, so that there is no gap between the lowest men and the highest brutes, and men who will not submit to rule are classed with wild beasts as proper objects of warfare; while among animals he also distinguishes different levels, and sometimes ascribes human characteristics, even 'practical wisdom' (*phronēsis*), to some of them.5 But Theo-phrastus, whose works significantly included one entitled *On the Intelligence and Character of Animals*, probably went beyond his master in claiming that animals are capable of *logismos*, or suggest-ing that they, like men, are to be divided into 'just' and 'unjust', and the 'civilisation test' which other Greeks had applied to humanity is also applicable to the animal world.6 All this would tend to blur the distinction between men and other creatures, rather than to clarify the concept of the unity of mankind.

If this view of these passages is right, they do not indicate any revolution in Greek thinking about humanity. Yet they are important, because they show more definitely than anything in Aristotle's own works the contribution which the Lyceum, in spite of its concern with the divisions of mankind, had to make towards the development of the idea of human unity. We have seen how the biological approach, which began as early as the sixth century B.C. and was developed by Antiphon and the medical writers, was carried further by Aristotle, who attached compara-tively little importance to the antithesis between the 'wise' and the 'unwise' so much stressed by Plato and the Cynics. Theo-phrastus, at a time when the new schools of philosophy at Athens were putting their main emphasis on the great gulf between wisdom and folly, kept alive and handed on the abstract idea of a single human species which makes *all* men kin; although he extended the marks of their kinship even beyond humanity into the animal world.

A similar approach to the subject of human relationships is implied in our fragments from Theophrastus' contemporary and fellow-Peripatetic, Dicaearchus, who seems to have carried still further the belief that practical sagacity (*phronēsis*), in which many can share, is more important than *sophia*, the theoretical wisdom of the few.7 This impression of his outlook is confirmed by his concern with the theme so often echoed in Menander: the value to men of good relations with each other, the need for conciliation and avoidance of strife. Cicero tells us that in a book with the interesting title *On the Destruction of Human Life* Dicaearchus listed the other causes of disaster to mankind—flood, pestilence, famine, the mass onslaught of wild beasts—and remarked how many more men have lost their lives through human action, in wars or revolutions, than through all other calamities.[8] From this he must have drawn the same conclusion as Cicero, that since human beings themselves are the main source of harm or benefit to their own kind, our moral endeavours should be particularly concerned with winning the hearts of men and gaining their co-operation.

We have no information to show how Dicaearchus further developed this line of thought, but it evidently involved the belief that a condition of peace and harmony is man's natural state; and we do know something of how he expressed this idea by projecting it back into the past. It is Porphyry again who preserves the account given in Dicaearchus' *Life of Hellas* of the first state of man—a rationalised version of the primeval Age of Kronos described by Hesiod, and later in Plato's *Statesman* and elsewhere. After expounding the other blessings of those early days, Porphyry's version goes on: 'They experienced no wars or conflicts with each other, for there lay before them no prize of sufficient value to become the cause of such violent strife. Consequently their life was characterised by leisure, easy fulfilment of their essential needs, good health, peace, and friendship.'[9] It was only when possessions worth fighting for emerged, that 'war came upon the scene as well'. The thought, of course, is not new; what is remarkable is the re-statement of it by a follower of Aristotle, underlining the Peripatetic belief in the natural kinship and affection between all members of the human race.

The book from which this extract is taken has been called the first universal history. Dicaearchus was certainly an author with a wide view: the topics on which he wrote included the geography of the known world, and this historical work evidently contained passages on the Chaldaeans and the Egyptians.[10] The title given to it—*Life of Hellas*—is all the more significant. The history of civilisation, it implies, is the history of *Greece*. In spite of the idea that all mankind are akin, Dicaearchus, like his contemporaries, looks on the world scene with the assumption that all that is valuable in human culture is essentially Greek.

THE EPICUREANS

At the opposite pole to Theophrastus' assertion of the natural kinship of the human race stands the doctrine of Epicurus and his followers, who show the growing strength of the idea of the unity of mankind by the vigour with which they reject it. The Epicurean theory is summed up in a few words by Lactantius: 'There is no such thing as human society; each individual looks out for himself; there is no-one who feels affection for another, except for his own benefit.'[11] A pirate or robber chief, comments Lactantius, would say the same! The Stoic Epictetus puts the same view into the mouth of Epicurus—whether quoting his own words or not, we cannot tell: 'Do not be deceived or misled, men, do not go astray. Believe me, rational beings have no natural partnership with each other. Those who say otherwise use false reasoning to deceive us' (II. 20. 6–8).

These, of course, are hostile sources. There is no such explicit and forthright denial of human kinship in the little we now possess from Epicurus' own vast output of written works. But the same thought is implied in his whole outlook on society, as it is in the pronouncement of his follower, Metrodorus: 'There is no point in saving the Greeks.'[12] Still less, it may be inferred, should the Epicurean be troubled about the fate of humanity as a whole. It is the individual's own pleasure that matters: mankind is to be seen as a conglomeration of individuals each concerned with his own good, just as the whole material universe is a collection of individual atoms.

This extreme individualism clearly involved the rejection of any concept of natural fellowship among all human beings. In Epicurus' own surviving writings, the specific conclusion drawn from it is that no human society is based on nature. Whereas Plato and Aristotle saw the city-state as a natural institution founded on natural justice, man being by nature a 'political' animal and living in society 'for the sake of the good life', Epicurus regarded the *polis* as an artificial arrangement originating in a 'social contract' for mutual protection. Some peoples lack the ability or the desire to form such contracts, and remain like animals, devoid of either justice or injustice. Where a community is created, it has only the negative value of security against harm: the wise man will use it as a means of gaining peace and quiet, but will take no positive part in its activities.[13] 'Live unobtrusively' is the motto which determines his attitude towards his fellow men.

In Lucretius' *De Rerum Natura* this view of human relationships is given expression in a chronological form, as part of the Epicurean picture of the rise of civilisation; and although we cannot be certain that Lucretius is following Epicurus himself here,[14] his account might well have been written as a counterblast to Dicaearchus and the Peripatetics. Where Dicaearchus found the proto-type of natural human unity in the primeval Golden Age, Lucretius imagines the first men as living in isolation like wild beasts, each absorbed in the struggle for his own survival: 'They could not look to the common good, nor knew they the use of customs or laws in their relations with each other. Each carried off the spoils chance put in his way, having learnt to live and put forth his strength for himself alone' (v. 958-61). Only after the beginning of family life were the first communities formed: 'Then also neighbours began to join together in friendship, wishing neither to inflict harm nor to suffer it; and they sought protection for their children and womenfolk, claiming with inarticulate cries and gestures that it was right for all to take pity on the weak. Not always could concord be achieved, but most of them kept their agreements honourably' (v. 1019-25). The same motive later induced mankind to accept the rule of law: 'The human race, weary of a life of violence, grew weak from its quarrels; and so more readily of its own accord it submitted to rules and strict laws' (v. 1145-7). A slightly different version of this artificial origin of society, in which it is the perils of strife against wild beasts that first drive primitive man to link up with his neighbours, appears in Diodorus: 'The first men, they say, led an unorganised life like beasts. They scattered in individual search for food, taking the tenderest plants and fruit which grew without cultivation on the trees. When attacked by wild animals they learned in self-interest to aid one another, and collecting together through fear gradually came to know each others' characteristics.'[15]

No Greek theory of man goes further than the Epicureans in denying the natural unity of the human race or the existence of any natural bond between its members. But it is one of the paradoxes of the Epicurean position that there was no group of people in antiquity among whom friendship was more generally cultivated or more highly valued. We have seen that Democritus, from whom Epicurus derived his physical system, laid great stress on friendship, 'not between all kinsfolk, but between those who agree about what is expedient'.[16] The Epicureans carried this concept into effect: while the Peripatetic school theorised about friendship, they warmly practised it within the limited circle of those who enjoyed Epicurean wisdom and accepted the Epicurean view of the good. The high place they gave to it is described by the Epicurean spokesman, Torquatus, in Cicero's dialogue *De Finibus:*

Epicurus says that of all the means to a happy life which wisdom provides, none is more important or more fruitful or more pleasant than friendship; but he put forward this belief not only in words, but much more strongly in his life and conduct. The mythical tales of the ancients show how great a thing friendship is: many and various as they are, reaching back to the furthest antiquity, scarcely three pairs of friends are to be found in them, beginning with Theseus and ending with Orestes. Yet what companies of friends Epicurus held together in one small house, and what affection and sympathy united them! And this still continues among the Epicureans. (I. 65)

Torquatus' account is confirmed by some of the sayings ascribed to Epicurus. One goes so far as to call friendship 'immortal', presumably because it makes human life comparable with the bliss of the gods: 'He who is noble makes wisdom and friendship his first concern; of these wisdom is a mortal good, but friendship immortal' (*Sent. Vat.* 78).

All this makes strange reading in comparison with the doctrine that the individual's own pleasure is his sole concern and fellowship between human beings has no natural basis. That the Epicureans were aware of the inconsistency is shown by Torquatus' next remarks. Three theories about friendship in relation to pleasure, he says, have been put forward in the Epicurean school. One is that friendship is the preserver and creator of pleasure. The second, that friendship first springs from one's desire for pleasure, but then 'blossoms into such affection that our friends are loved for their own sake'. The third, a remarkable extension of the 'social contract' idea, is that 'there is a sort of agreement among wise men to love their friends no less than themselves', as the best means to happiness. We cannot date these views, although support for the first can be found in Epicurus' own writings (Maxims 27, 40). What is certain is that within the Epicurean 'society of friends' the spirit of brotherhood was as genuinely felt and put into practice as anywhere at any time in antiquity. 'In a world where the frameworks of city and family were tending to disappear', writes Festugière, 'Epicurus had succeeded in founding a new family.'[17] Between these fellow-sharers in wisdom as Epicurus saw it, who sought to enjoy together 'the security that arises from a quiet life and withdrawal from the multitude' (Maxim 14), friendship created a bond which was more than a substitute for the *polis*; a bond all the closer because the group felt itself isolated from the rest of mankind. One of the most vivid sayings attributed to Epicurus represents friendship as a joyous figure passing from one group of Epicurean friends to another throughout the *oikoumenē*, rousing them all to realisation of their common happiness: 'Friendship dances across the world calling on us to awake and praise our happy life.'[18]

Plato, the Cynics and others had set the ideal wise man above the barriers that divide normal human beings. Similarly, within the circle of participants in Epicurean wisdom, but only there, these divisions were ignored and all could join in friendship. Women, including courtesans, were admitted, although they were excluded from Plato's Academy; and their high status is indicated by the fact that one of them became president. Slaves were members of the school, and one of them, named Mys (Mouse), is mentioned as particularly prominent. We are nearer here than in Aristotle to practical brotherhood among men, even though Peripatetic doctrine asserted the natural kinship of the human race and Epicurus denied it. In theory, the Epicureans were entirely opposed to the idea of the unity of mankind; but by their way of life they did much to promote it.

THE EARLY STOICS

Although in their very different ways both Peripatetics and Epicureans made a contribution towards strengthening the idea of human brotherhood, the Stoics are usually looked upon as the school chiefly responsible for its full emergence in Hellenistic and Roman times. The concept of the unity of mankind is regarded as a necessary part of the Stoic outlook as a whole—the doctrine that the entire cosmos is permeated and governed by a *Logos*, a divine principle of rationality, which is implanted in the form of reason in every human soul. In the earliest considerable Stoic document now extant, the *Hymn* of Zeno's successor, Cleanthes, the universality of the common *logos* is an aspect of the complete supremacy of Zeus. His thunderbolt is

> Vehicle of the universal Word, that flows
> Through all, and in the light celestial glows
> Of stars both great and small.[19]

Cleanthes came to Athens from Assus, in north-west Asia Minor; Chrysippus, the third head of the school, from Soli or Tarsus in Cilicia; while Zeno himself was a native of Citium, in Cyprus, and may have been of Phoenician or mixed descent. From these

Eastern associations the inference is often drawn that Stoicism, including the Stoic attitude towards human relationships, was an Oriental strain now introduced by these 'foreigners' and previously alien to the Greek mind. There may be some degree of truth in this supposition: certainly Zeno is likely to have been bilingual, and that in itself might have an enlarging effect on his thinking. But if he or other leading figures among the Stoics were non-Greeks, which is itself doubtful, they mainly illustrate the fact that the Hellenic tradition, as Isocrates had said, was now no longer a matter of blood and racial origin, but of education and culture. The Stoic philosophy and the Stoic view of man rested on basic ideas which had long been present in the main stream of Hellenic thought. The Stoics themselves rightly looked back to Heraclitus as one of the sources from which they drew: the essentials of the doctrine of an all-pervading *Logos* in which all men share were, as we have seen, the central feature of his outlook. But similar ideas, and in particular the belief that all men have *logos* in common, had made their appearance at many points in the earlier development that we have been tracing. Whatever blood ran in Zeno's veins, there was nothing un-Greek in his philosophy; and in considering the Stoic conception of humanity, we are still dealing with the continuous evolution of Greek thought.

I have already pointed out that latent and implicit in the notion of reason as a common human possession was the concept of the unity of all mankind. There can be no doubt that the same idea was at any rate implicit from the first in the teaching of the early Stoics. The problem that now confronts us is how far this implication was explicitly realised and stated, how far it was elaborated and what emphasis it received.

In Cicero, Seneca and other later writers the concept is explicit enough: the world is now in fact a single community, in which the common gift of reason makes all men kin. To quote one of Cicero's many statements of the idea: 'The world is as it were the common home of gods and men, or the city belonging to both; for they alone make use of reason and live according to right and law.'[20] Marcus Aurelius (IV. 4) puts the same thought in the form of a logical sequence:

If the power of thought is common to us all, common also is reason (*logos*), through which we are rational beings. If so, that reason is also common which tells us what to do and what not to do. If so, law also is common. If so, we are citizens. If so, we are fellow-members of a community. If so, the universe is as it were a city. For of what other community can the whole human race be said to be fellow-members?

Many modern writers have ascribed these ideas in their full and explicit form to Zeno, seeing the rejection of all barriers and championship of human brotherhood as the proclaimed doctrine of the Stoic school from its earliest days. J. B. Bury, for example, wrote in *The Hellenistic Age* (p. 26):

One of the things which Zeno's philosophy did was to overcome the distinction of Greek and barbarian. He introduced the idea of cosmopolitanism, transcending patriotism; of the whole world, the oecumene, as a man's true fatherland; of a community embracing all rational beings, without regard to the distinction of Greek and barbarian, or of freeman and slave. According to this doctrine the philosopher feels himself citizen of a state to which all mankind belongs, a state whose boundaries are measured by the sun. In the ideal state of Zeno all human beings were citizens.

This view of early Stoicism has been general in recent years, together with inferences from it such as Stoic condemnation of slavery. If it is correct, the decades after Alexander's death saw a radical change indeed in Greek thought about mankind—a change so decisive and dramatic that one might well call in Oriental influence, as well as Alexander's conquests, in order to explain it. But it seems to me highly questionable whether any such explicit doctrine of human unity was ever formulated by Zeno or his immediate followers.

The central problem here is the nature of that 'ideal state of Zeno' to which Bury refers. His ideal was set out in a work entitled, like Plato's *Republic*, *Politeia*, which was jokingly said by his critics to have been written 'on the dog's tail'.[21] Cynosura, Dog's Tail, was the name given to several Greek promontories, including one near Athens; but whether this is the allusion or not, the implication of the jest was of course that Zeno produced the book while still under the influence of the Cynics, to whom he attached himself soon after coming to Athens from Cyprus near the end of the fourth century B.C. That it belonged to his early, wild oat days is confirmed by the claim which Philodemus puts into the mouths of its defenders—that its faults are excusable because Zeno was then still young and headstrong.[22]

Unfortunately the probable content of the book is no easy matter to decide. Although there are more references in ancient writers to the *Politeia* than to any other of Zeno's works, our information about what it contained is so slight and so open to dispute that modern conclusions from it have varied all the way from a world-state embracing all humanity to a small community comparable with Sparta. My own reconstruction of it is based on those statements in which there is a specific allusion to the *Politeia* itself.

According to Plutarch's *Life of Lycurgus*, the central feature of Zeno's Utopia was unity. He adopted as his basic principle the belief, which he shared with Plato and other political writers, 'that for a whole state, as in individual life, happiness depended on goodness and internal concord (*homonoia*)'. It was in accordance with this principle that he made *Erōs*, Love, a god in his ideal society, for Love promotes friendship and freedom and concord (*homonoia* again), and therefore helps to maintain the stability of the community.[23]

That unity and concord among the members of the state was the first aim of Zeno's ideal is confirmed by what little we know of his more detailed proposals, which are clearly intended as means of eliminating disunity and strife. Most of them are not only close to the Cynic doctrine of the life according to nature, but also take us back to Plato, criticism of whom is often implied. Although Plato must have seemed revolutionary to his contemporaries, Zeno's radicalism is more thorough at every point; and it may well be this work that Plutarch had in mind when he said that Zeno 'wrote in reply to Plato's *Republic*' (*SVF*, I. 260)*.

Like both Plato and the Cynics, he saw one of the main sources of social conflict in the institution of the family, and put forward startling views on sex relations which have a prominent place in our evidence, presumably because hostile critics found here the most promising material for attack. His proposal is often called 'community of wives', but 'freedom of intercourse between the sexes' would be a better translation. It is not limited by plans for organised breeding, as in the *Republic*, but implies complete promiscuity; and the ground for this is no doubt correctly stated by a later author, though the words are not likely to be Zeno's own: 'We shall then have fatherly affection for all children alike, and there will be an end to jealousy arising from adultery' (Diog. L. VII. 131). For the same basic reason, Zeno gave a place to homosexual relationships in the ideal community: 'The wise man will love boys whose physical beauty shows the goodness innate in their character' (Diog.L. VII. 129). Here we are not far away from Plato's *Symposium*, and the *erōs* felt by the wise citizen is in accord with that worship of *Erōs* which is to help to preserve the state. The same thought clearly lies behind the proposition that all the citizens, both men and women, should wear the same clothing (Diog.L. VII. 33): unity is to be promoted by the simple device of putting both sexes into the same uniform. One is reminded of the Cynic Crates, Zeno's teacher, and his wife Hipparchia, who both wore the rough Cynic cloak in the streets of Athens.

No less revolutionary and shocking to the ancient Greek mind were Zeno's statements on public institutions, or rather the lack of them, in Utopia. He prohibited, we are told, 'the building of temples or law-courts or gymnasia in the cities' (*ibid.*). So much for the Parthenon! So much for the Athenians' favourite pastime

* Von Arnim's *Stoicorum Veterum Fragmenta*.

of litigation, no longer possible in a united society: as Aristotle had said, 'justice is not needed among friends' (*E.N.* 1155a26). So much for the cult of physical perfection, the practice of athletics, the great Games! Presumably the instruments of war were to disappear as well.[24] The detailed grounds for this sweeping rejection of the main features of Greek public life are uncertain, but obviously the general effect of thus stripping away the buildings and institutions which gave individuality and distinction to the city-states would be to produce a more homogeneous—one might think, a more monotonous—form of society. A further natural feature of such a Utopia was the absence of coinage, which 'need not be introduced', said Zeno, 'either for exchange or for travelling abroad' (Diog.L. VII. 33). Where all are honest and all are united by friendship, there is no need for buying and selling and therefore no need for money, that evil source of strife in existing society. Plato had banned money for his 'guardians'. Diogenes showed what he thought of it by recommending that the only currency should be knuckle-bones. Zeno decided to get rid of it altogether.

It is not stated in our evidence for the *Politeia* that goods, like wives, are common to all the citizens of Utopia, but this sentence excluding the use of money probably points to that conclusion, which seems likely on general grounds. The Stoics held that among true friends all things are common,[25] and it may well be that the members of the ideal state, bound in concord by friendship, were to practise throughout their society a communism as complete as that of Plato's 'guardian' class.

It is clear that Zeno carried the idea of a unified society to extraordinary lengths. But whom did he have in mind as its citizens? This is the vital question for our purpose, and it is one on which there has been much dispute. Controversy has been chiefly concerned with the problem of the relation of Zeno's concept to the division between the wise and the unwise. While some have followed Zeller in regarding Zeno's ideal as a 'polity of the wise', others claim that both wise and foolish were included, although only the wise may have been citizens in the fullest sense.

There can be no doubt that the early Stoics, like Heraclitus and Plato and the Cynics and unlike the Peripatetics, laid great stress on the cleavage between the few possessors of true wisdom and the folly of the mass of mankind. The distinction is one of the main themes of Cleanthes' *Hymn*, and is still more strongly stated in another fragment: 'Look not to what men think, if you would speedily be wise, and fear not the ill-judged, impudent talk of the mob. For the mass of men has no judgment based on understanding, none that is right or good: in few will you find it' (*SVF*, I. 559). It is true that even for the early Stoics the division was not absolute, the barrier not insuperable: just as the Cynics sought and welcomed individual conversion to their way of life, so the Stoics envisaged the possibility of making progress (*prokoptein*) from folly to wisdom; without it, there could have been little point in their teaching. But the weight of evidence suggests that for Zeno and his immediate followers (again, as for the Cynics) this acceptance of individual advance and entry into the company of the wise did little to blur the sharpness of the antithesis between wisdom and folly which stood out so strongly in their picture of human life. The division must certainly have played a major part in Zeno's thought; and we are told that in the *Politeia* itself he emphasised one particular aspect of it—that only the wise, who through their wisdom are the good, are capable of concord and unity: 'he calls all who are not good foemen and enemies and slaves and alien to each other, even parents and children and brothers and relations; while again in the *Politeia* he represents only the good as citizens and friends and kindred and free men' (Diog.L. VII. 32–3).

This seems to me decisive for our problem. On the one hand, the fundamental principle on which Zeno's community is based is unity, concord, freedom from internal strife. This is embodied in its organisation, consolidated by the worship of *Erōs*, and the main purpose of its various rules of life. Harmony and friendship is the first essential for its members. On the other hand, only the wise and good are capable of living in harmony: the unwise inevitably turn to conflict. The conclusion seems to be inescapable. Plato had included the 'craftsmen' in his Utopia as an inferior class, because he believed they would contentedly accept their part in the whole. Zeno rejected this belief that those whose souls are not governed by reason could be free from strife, and regarded inclusion of the unwise, even with inferior status, as impossible. His ideal was a one-class, or classless, society, attaining unity through uniformity. The common denominator of its citizens was not mere rationality, in which all human beings have some share, but the high ideal of wisdom. Like the Epicurean circle of friends, with which Zeno's Utopia had not a little in common, they might be drawn from any of the accepted divisions of the human race—men or women, Greeks or barbarians, free men or slaves;[26] but wisdom they must have.

This concentration on the wise and exclusion of folly recalls the Cynics, and confirms the tradition that the *Politeia* was written 'on the dog's tail'. Zeno's thought here was nearer to Diogenes and Crates than to Plato, but it did not wholly coincide with the Cynic point of view. We have seen how little certainty, or even plausible conjecture, there can be about Diogenes' political ideal; and where both items in a comparison are so doubtful, the comparison may seem hardly worth making. Nevertheless, it seems to me likely that Zeno differed from the Cynics in one important respect: if Diogenes thought of a society of the wise, it was only in terms of the fellowship of the few true philosophers scattered over the world; but Zeno had in mind a single community of wise men and women, and laid down in his *Politeia* the way in which they should live. His Utopia was a crystallisation in a single society of that ideal of unity based on wisdom, and confined to the possessors of wisdom, which had already been voiced so often in earlier Greek thought.

One passage concerned with the *Politeia* has not yet been mentioned, although it is the most frequently quoted account of

Zeno's ideal. It is drawn from Plutarch's rhetorical essay *De Alexandri Magni Fortuna aut Virtute*, which has already been considered in discussing Alexander:

Indeed the *Politeia* of Zeno, founder of the Stoic school, which is thought so remarkable, is directed to this one main point, that our life should not be based on cities or peoples each with its own view of right and wrong, but we should regard all men (*pantas anthrōpous*) as our fellow-countrymen and fellow-citizens, and that there should be one life and one order, like that of a single flock on a common pasture feeding together under a common law. Zeno wrote this, shaping as it were a dream or picture of a philosophic well-ordered society; but it was Alexander who gave the theory practical effect.[27]

This is not a 'fragment' of Zeno, although it is often called so: 'Zeno wrote this' does not mean that we have here his own words, though it presumably does imply that Plutarch is describing a written work. The passage is someone's summary of what he believed to be the main point of Zeno's book; but I have put forward the view that there is no good reason for the belief that this 'someone' was Eratosthenes, and who he was—whether Plutarch himself or someone closer to Zeno in time—we do not know.

How correct a summary is it, in view of the rest of our evidence? For the most part, it coincides well enough with the information we have already considered. Its general theme is an expression of that need for unity and concord which we have seen to be the main principle running through Zeno's work. The details of this unity—in particular, the statement that 'our life should not be based on cities or peoples'[28]—may seem inconsistent with the references to 'a city' or 'cities' elsewhere in the evidence,[29] but the discrepancy is more apparent than real. Plutarch surely does not mean that there are to be no places where people live together, but only that men's lives should not be based on individual city-states, each, as he says, with its own version of right and wrong; and on the other hand we have seen that Zeno's 'cities', stripped of the distinctive features of the city-state, could be no more than 'places where people live together', centres of population in a closely united whole. The picture of such a unified community as 'a single flock on a common pasture feeding together under a common law' is not inappropriate, although we cannot tell whether the comparison goes back to Zeno himself. There was precedent for it in Plato's description in the *Statesman* of the single 'human flock' of the Golden Age.[30]

The real difficulty in reconciling Plutarch's summary with our other information lies in the statement that 'we should regard *all men* as our fellow-countrymen and fellow-citizens', where Plutarch clearly has in mind a world-wide brotherhood of the entire human race, comparable with the vision of an all-embracing unity of peoples which he attributes to Alexander. How can this be consistent with Zeno's limitation of Utopia to the wise, and exclusion of the foolish? If my conclusions about the *Politeia* have been correct, he cannot have said that in the present state of the world 'all men', in the sense of 'all mankind', are to be regarded as fellow-citizens. There is only one way of avoiding this difficulty, and that is by supposing that Zeno was thinking of some remote future time when (it might be hoped) all human beings will have attained to wisdom and goodness. This is a very different idea from the later concept, reflected in Cicero and Seneca and elsewhere, of world brotherhood as a present fact. The later Stoic is not concerned with changing the institutions under which he happens to live. His approach to them is one of acceptance, of sublime indifference. His belief in a world-state has nothing to do with political programmes, even of the most Utopian sort: it is a matter of mental outlook, of his mental attitude towards himself and his fellow-men. Zeno, on the contrary—if he indeed set his Utopia in a distant future when all men are wise—visualised a reformed world, changed to suit the changed mentality of its inhabitants; a world in which all barriers would be set aside, and there would be no families, no sovereign states, no division into barbarian and Greek, slave and free; a realisation in the remote future of the Golden Age of concord and happiness which others had pictured in the remote past.[31]

If this was the theme of the *Politeia*, Zeno's was a bold and radical conception, one of the most daring flights of speculation in antiquity; and it was the first full Greek vision of the possibility of the unity of mankind. But it would be rash to accept such a remarkable conclusion on the evidence of a single short passage in a highly rhetorical treatise written some four centuries later, the whole trend of which was to read back later ideas into Alexander's time. The view of Zeno's Utopia as an ideal for the far future is not confirmed by our other information about the *Politeia*. It is actually in conflict with such inferences as we can draw about one important, though neglected, aspect of the book—the form in which its contents were set out.

A striking feature of the surviving evidence is that Zeno's proposals are usually put forward as statements about what ought to happen: we are told that 'he lays down' this or that proposition; 'he says we should not think coinage need be introduced'; 'he proposes that men and women should wear the same clothing'; 'he recommended such practices', and so on. In the two places where his own words seem to be quoted, we find this jussive form; and it appears again in the Plutarch passage we are now considering: 'our life should not be based', 'we should regard all men', 'there should be one life'. On the other hand, nothing in the evidence implies *description* of an ideal society as existing or imagined to exist. It is admittedly difficult to draw inferences about the form of an author's original statements from later summaries or allusions, but the evidence in this case seems overwhelmingly in favour of the conclusion that the *Politeia* did not, like many Utopian works, give a description of an ideal community in narrative form, but rather set out Zeno's alternative to the present state of affairs in some such form as 'this is how things ought to be', or 'this is how things would be if people were wise'. Zeno's approach was thus more or less of the same type as that used by Plato in the *Republic*; and it is interesting to find that Aristotle summarises Plato's views in phraseology closely resembling that of the extant references to the *Politeia*.[32]

This interpretation of Zeno's point of view is in harmony with the statement by his Epicurean critic, Philodemus, that 'at the beginning of the book he declares that its proposals are relevant to his own place and times'.33 It does not leave room for a descriptive account of the remote future; and the future tenses here and there in the evidence, which in a descriptive narrative would be a clear indication of the timing of the ideal state, are probably no more than an alternative way of stating what is desirable or right: 'the truly wise man will act thus and thus'; 'if men are wise, there will be no need to build temples'. Desirable action not performed now is in a sense always an ideal for the future, but this is not the same as the deliberate relegation of Utopia to some future date. Zeno's proposals, like Plato's, are likely to have had no definite timing, rather than to contemplate an imaginary distant age when all men may have reached wisdom.

A similar indefiniteness is all we find when we try to investigate the other aspect of Zeno's ideal which is important for us here—its geographical extent. If his Utopia embraced all mankind, its area must have included the entire inhabited world. The rest of the evidence, however, contains no sign of this, but refers indifferently to a single 'city' or to 'cities', in a way which suggests a state of no particular size. The explanation again lies, I think, in the jussive manner of Zeno's approach. He was not *describing* a community of any definite extent, but stating how life should be lived in a city—or in cities in general. He clearly did not limit his vision to a single *polis*, like Plato; but he was not thinking of a definite number of cities either, still less of a Utopia covering the whole world known to man.

Plutarch's account, then, is not likely to be a correct summary of Zeno's theme. He or his source has given a twist to Zeno's ideas and attributed to the founder of the Stoic school the 'world-state' conception which was its normal doctrine in his time—a distortion which would hardly be surprising even apart from the general rhetorical character of his essay. If Zeno used the words 'all men' or their equivalent, he probably did so in a way more in keeping with the line of thought and form of expression which we have found in the rest of the evidence for the *Politeia*: that is, in the simple sense of 'everybody', 'all people'—'this is what everyone ought to do'—which is very different from talk of 'all mankind'. Although the thought of human unity was implicit in the rationality of all men, in which he believed, and although he was greatly concerned with the question of unity within society, his outlook was dominated by the contrast between the ideal of wisdom and the prevailing folly, and it was a community of wise and good men and women that he envisaged, not a world-state embracing the entire human race.

The *Politeia*, as we have seen, is likely to have been an early work. In the later, more respectable days of Stoicism, some leaders of the school tried to suppress parts of the book or even disclaimed it altogether (Diog.L. VII. 34); and similarly some modern writers on the Stoics have supposed that it did not represent Zeno's mature outlook. But in the rest of our evidence for his political ideas there is nothing that conflicts, except on points of detail, with our information about the *Politeia*, or suggests that in his later years its author saw humanity in a different light. Nor does it appear that any of his successors in the third century B.C. diverged very far in essentials from the same line of thought.

The attribution of a 'world-state' concept to Zeno, usually based on the Plutarch passage which I have already discussed, is not supported by any of the other surviving fragments. As Diogenes the Cynic is said to have talked of 'citizenship of the universe', it would not be surprising if the early Stoics also had described the cosmos as a *polis*, with at any rate the wise, along with the gods, as its citizens; and Zeno's pupil Ariston of Chios, who rejected some aspects of his master's teaching in favour of an outlook very close to the Cynics, comes near to their negative 'cosmopolitanism' in his statement that 'we have no fatherland by nature' (*SVF*, I. 371): patriotic feeling for a particular country has no natural foundation. But in the two passages which may

11-2

refer to Stoics of this period as comparing the universe with a state, they are thinking, as Anaximander did three centuries earlier (fr. 1), in terms of a cosmic society made up of the phenomena of nature or the heavenly bodies, not human members. 'All things in the universe are managed well, as in a well-ordered community', says an account which may reflect the views of Zeno (*SVF*, I. 98). The other relevant passage is in Plutarch, who in the course of criticism probably directed against Chrysippus ridicules the proposition that 'the cosmos is a *polis* and the stars its citizens' (*SVF*, II. 645).

It is to Chrysippus that we might well look for further development of the idea of the unity of mankind. It was he who elaborated Stoic theory in the course of answering the attacks of the Sceptics, and worked out in sometimes wearisome detail implications which had been latent in the thought of Zeno or Cleanthes. He might be expected to realise more fully and bring into the open the concept of human unity implied in the doctrine of the universal *Logos*. How far do our scanty remains of his works confirm the expectation?

It is clear that he spoke of man as 'the rational animal', marked off by his possession of *logos* from the other animal species, which exist for the benefit of man.[34] This is in line with Aristotle, and indeed with the general trend of Greek thought. Other fragments bring us nearer to the idea of a single human society through emphasis on the universality of law. Although the laws of particular communities differ—and Chrysippus seems to have shown typical perseverance in collecting examples of their inconsistency—his book *On Law* began with the proposition that 'law is lord of all things, divine and human' (*SVF*, III. 314); and Cicero preserves in Latin dress an important statement which relates this universal reign of law to the notion of a natural compact by which all men are bound:

It was well stated by Chrysippus that whereas all other things came into being for the benefit of men and gods, these exist for the sake of their own common welfare and fellowship, so that men are justified in using beasts for their own advantage; and since the nature of man is such that a kind of social code exists between the individual and the rest of the human race, he who maintains this code is just, he who departs from it, unjust. (*De Fin.* III. 67)

The little information we possess on Chrysippus' attitude towards traditional barriers and prejudices confirms the impression that he at any rate went beyond most of his contemporaries in seeking an overall unity more important than the usually accepted divisions among men. He scornfully rejects noble birth as a criterion of merit (*SVF*, III. 350). He defines the slave as 'a permanent hireling' (*ibid.* 351), distinguishable from the free labourer not by nature, but only by length of service—no condemnation of slavery, but at least a rejection of the 'natural slave' of Aristotle.

It is difficult to judge how far all this carries us. Belief in the universality of natural law, it may be said, had been stated long ago by Heraclitus and dramatised by Sophocles in the *Antigone*. Many others had criticised prejudice against the humbly born and the slave. How far Chrysippus gave these ideas new emphasis within the Stoic context, we cannot tell. It seems likely, however, that for him, as for Zeno, there was one division of mankind which played a more dominating part in his thought than any consideration of human unity: no Greek thinker laid greater stress than Chrysippus on the gulf separating the wise from the unwise. Between the wise there is the closest of bonds, so that any move they make from a good motive profits them all, even if they do not live together or know each other: 'If a single wise man anywhere but raise his finger with wisdom, all wise men throughout the world are benefited.'35 Between the unwise, it is implied, there can be only discord and strife. It is not surprising that our few scraps of information about Chrysippus' book *On Politeia* suggest that it followed the same lines as Zeno's work—a Utopian account of how a community of the wise should live, emphasising the ideal concord of the few philosophers, not that brotherhood of all which later Stoics saw as a present fact. In spite of the possibility of individual advance towards wisdom, the mass of humanity in its present condition, although possessed of reason, is still rejected and scorned and set apart for its failure to make good use of the divine gift. Bréhier seems justified in his estimate of Chrysippus' attitude:

Ces idées amènent naturellement, semble-t-il, à celle d'une humanité universelle. . . . Pourtant ne concluons pas trop vite; ce seront là les fruits qui mûriront à l'époque romaine, dans le moyen stoïcisme, où l'idée de l'humanité universelle est assez bien symbolisée par l'amitié de Panétius et de Scipion. Chrysippe n'est pas encore arrivé à cette largeur de vues; et nous allons voir, chez lui, la cité divine devenir le privilège de quelques sages.[36]

CHAPTER VI

THE IMPACT OF ROME

ERATOSTHENES

THE last few sections have attempted to show that in spite of changing ideas of human relationships after Alexander, and in spite of the implications of Stoic theory in particular, there was a wide gap between any conception of mankind in the third century B.C. and the view, primarily Stoic, which was widespread in the first. This later belief that not only the wise but all men, or at any rate all civilised men, are already fellow-citizens of the world city, is very different from anything that we find in Theophrastus, Epicurus, Zeno or even Chrysippus. When did this further development take place towards a wider, though also shallower, vision of humanity? And what were its causes?

It is an oversimplification to suppose that such a shift of thought can be given a date, and the reasons for it were, no doubt, many and various. But if one principal factor is to be singled out, it must be the impact of Rome, beginning in the third century and becoming the dominating feature of the situation in the second, and bringing to the Greeks a broader and more complex picture of the human race. In short, the idea of the unity of mankind in this broader sense was not Greek, but Graeco-Roman. It came into being not through the concept of cosmic unity, nor through further consideration of man as a species, but rather by the development of a line of thought which did not easily arise in the Greek environment and had comparatively little part in earlier Greek thinking about the human situation: the notion of mankind as an aggregate, the sum-total of individual human beings spread over all the various countries of the inhabited world—mankind, in fact, viewed *geographically*, as we find it easy to see it today.

It was characteristic of the early Stoics and the Epicureans that they took little interest in geography. Alexander's conquests, as we have seen, had sharply accelerated the expansion of the known world, and the decades that followed witnessed the increasingly clear emergence of the *oikoumenē*, the habitat of the human race as it was known to the Greeks. But there is no sign that this enlargement of geographical knowledge had much significance for Epicurus or Zeno or Chrysippus. Like many Greek thinkers before them, they were concerned with man rather than mankind, with people but not with the many peoples or the complex variety of the world in which they lived. The Epicureans rejected the conception of a spherical earth, and regarded it as a flat disc: the details of human distribution over its surface could have no importance for their limited society of friends. The Stoics, taking their cosmology from Aristotle, did see the earth as a globe with Antipodes, but what mattered to them was man's place in the order of the cosmos, not his physical grouping and environment. Zeno's Utopia, we noted, seems to have had no definite extent; and among the many titles of the works of Chrysippus none is geographical.

The attitude of the Peripatetics was very different. A glimpse of their interest is given by Theophrastus' will, which contained a clause providing for the safe keeping of the maps in the school. The geographical work of Dicaearchus has already been mentioned. But the full extent of the new geographical knowledge, and the importance of its effect on Greek thought about mankind, first become apparent when we turn to the greatest geographer of antiquity, Eratosthenes, who was approximately contemporary with Chrysippus. While Chrysippus elaborated the Stoic doctrine of man in the universe, Eratosthenes was mapping and measuring the earth. There may have been some truth in the nickname *bēta*, 'second-class', which his contemporaries are said to have given him, but he was one of the most remarkable men of the Hellenistic Age. He was head of the Alexandrian library, and a man of learning in so many fields that he was also called *pentathlos*, 'all-rounder'. The breadth of his outlook was shown in his attitude to geography, for he was no mere collector of facts. His approach was mathematical and scientific, and what we are told of his *Geographica* shows that he saw the study of the world and its peoples as a single whole. He estimated the circumference of the globe with remarkable accuracy; and what is more significant for our purpose, he measured and mapped the *oikoumenē* from Thule in the north to Somaliland and Ceylon in the south, from the Pillars of Heracles in the west to furthest India in the east—the great oblong island, entirely surrounded by ocean, which for him was the whole of the domicile of mankind. His work, now known to us chiefly through Strabo, must have presented a picture of variety within unity, and the third book included a survey of the products of this complex world and the races inhabiting it.

It is not surprising that Eratosthenes included philosophy in his wide range of interests and wrote various philosophical works. He cannot be assigned to any particular school of thought, but it may be significant for our purpose that one of the teachers at Athens who chiefly influenced him was Ariston, the Stoic who came near to Cynic 'cosmopolitanism'. The combination of geographer and philosopher is clear in the passage from Strabo which is our main evidence for his general view of mankind:

Towards the end of his treatise he declares that praise should not be given to those who divide the total number of mankind into two sections, Greeks and barbarians, or to those who advised Alexander to treat the Greeks as friends and the barbarians as enemies; the division should rather be made, he says, according to good qualities and bad. For many of the Greeks are bad, and many of the barbarians civilised—Indians and Arians, for example, and also Romans and Carthaginians, who conduct their political affairs so admirably. It was for this reason, he continues, that Alexander ignored his advisers, and welcomed and favoured all men he could of good repute. (I. 4. 9)

We have seen that this attitude was by no means new. Criticism of the antithesis between Greek and barbarian, together with the claim that the true division lay between good and bad, went back to various earlier thinkers—Plato and the Cynics, for example; in this case, perhaps especially to Ariston. But Eratosthenes' version of the matter was evidently different from the contrast, so much stressed by contemporary philosophy, between the few wise men and the misguided many. As might be expected in a writer with wide knowledge and less lofty philosophical ideals, Eratosthenes took a broader view: the distinction he put forward in place of Greek and barbarian was something like 'civilised' and 'uncivilised', with good government, practised in many parts of the world, as the criterion of merit.

Strabo goes on:

As if those who made such a distinction, allotting blame to one category and praise to the other, had any other reason in mind than that in some people the dominant tendency is acceptance of law and society and an attitude based on education and rational speech, whereas in others it is the opposite of these. So Alexander did not ignore his advisers, but accepted their view, and acted in accordance with their advice, not against it: he took as his aim the real meaning of those who gave him counsel.

Some commentators have supposed that here, too, Strabo is following Eratosthenes, who would thus fall into line with Isocrates and the general Hellenistic belief that civilisation was identical with Hellenism, and talk of civilised and uncivilised was only the old antithesis in new terms. But to attribute this further comment to Eratosthenes is to blur the main point that distinguishes his attitude—a point which is in fact a direct rejection of current opinion. Looking at the world of his day with the geographer's eye, he argues that there are other civilised peoples besides those who can be labelled Greek. His examples fit the contemporary scene—not the time of Alexander nor that of Strabo, but the middle or late third century B.C. India and Ariana, east and west of the Indus, are two of the main sections of the Orient as Eratosthenes saw it; both were opened up to the Greeks by Alexander, and later cut off once more from the west by the power of Parthia. In the west Rome and Carthage are balanced against each other, as they were in the time of the Punic Wars. These countries are cited not as regions to which Hellenic culture had spread, but as areas with an independent civilisation and language of their own. Here for the first time, or at any rate more clearly than ever before, we have the concept of a multi-racial and multi-lingual civilised humanity, put forward by a Greek whose picture of mankind included non-Greek centres of civilisation comparable with his own, to all of which the same standard must apply.

How far Eratosthenes worked out this view in detail, we cannot tell. But his interest in Rome is confirmed by a reference to Romulus, and a brief quotation from one of his philosophical works seems to be concerned with the point that the power to endure pain is not confined to one people.[1] It seems likely that the idea of multi-racial civilisation was for him no passing or isolated thought. One is tempted to see in him a Greek who lived before his time. With his wide view of mankind and his 'philosophical' outlook not tied to any particular school, he stands nearer to Cicero than to Isocrates, and his doctrine is not championship of Hellenic culture, but an anticipation of *humanitas*.

POLYBIUS

In the second century B.C. the shift of forces in the Mediterranean area produced a situation which must have impressed upon all thinking men the point of view already taken by Eratosthenes. Carthage disappeared as a great power, but Rome was transformed from a newcomer on the western horizons into the master of the Mediterranean world, bringing a temporary period of peace after the long succession of wars. The Hellenistic Age was over, and a new Graeco-Roman period had begun.

Much as many Greeks might resent the conquest and despise their conquerors, the more discerning among them could see that in the new situation there was no longer room for belief in a Greek *Herrenvolk*, or for the idea that Greek culture was the only civilisation or the Greek language the only speech of civilised man. Although the Latin comic poets jokingly referred to the Romans as *barbari*, the antithesis between Greek and barbarian was now manifestly out of date. The way lay open to a wider view of civilisation in which both Greek and Roman had their place; and men's minds turned, as Eratosthenes' had already done, to a picture which included not these two only, but also—thanks partly to Roman freedom from racial prejudice—all peoples worthy of the name of 'man'. A conversation which Cicero puts into the mouths of Scipio Africanus the Younger and Laelius in 129 B.C. well illustrates the new outlook. Scipio is arguing in favour of monarchy, and after offering to produce in its favour 'witnesses who are not very ancient and by no means barbarians', he cites Romulus. The following dialogue ensues:

Scipio: Tell me, was Romulus a king of barbarians?
Laelius: If we accept the Greeks' view that all men are either Greeks or barbarians, I am afraid he must have been. But if that description should be applied according to men's ways rather than their speech, I don't regard the Greeks as less barbarous than the Romans.
Scipio: Well, for our present purpose it is character that concerns us, not race. If the desire to have kings existed among men of good sense not so very long ago, then I am citing witnesses who are neither very ancient nor uncivilised savages. (*De Rep.* I. 58)

It is notable that in the last sentence the words *inhumanis ac feris* are used instead of *barbaris*: it is now not the non-Greek, but the brutish creature outside all human civilisation, who is beyond the pale.

The outlook here attributed to two Romans must have become widespread in the middle of the second century B.C., but it flourished most strongly where educated Greeks and Romans came together as they did in the so-called 'Scipionic Circle' at Rome. While Roman reactions to Greek culture varied all the way from the hostility of the conservative Cato to the enthusiasm of young men who earned the label *Graeculi*, the group of which Scipio and Laelius were the centre brought some of the best intellects of both Greece and Rome into contact and through their interaction reached a point of view which was neither Greek nor Roman, but combined and transcended them both. Although Terence's 'humani nil a me alienum puto' comes from a Greek original, the line had a fuller meaning for his patrons than for Menander's audience a century and a half earlier.

This background is the source of the earliest document which clearly presents the unity of mankind as a Graeco-Roman concept —the *Universal History* of Polybius, covering the years 220 to 144 B.C. Of the original forty books the first five are fully preserved, the rest in part. The circumstances of Polybius' life made him peculiarly fitted to adopt a Graeco-Roman point of view and to realise the unity of human affairs. Born at Megalopolis in the Peloponnese about the end of the third century B.C., he entered politics early and became a prominent figure in the Achaean League. After the battle of Pydna in 168 he was brought as a hostage to Rome, and soon gained a position under the patronage of the younger Scipio which gave him an exceptional opportunity to understand Roman ways of thought and the sources of Roman strength. When the Achaean internees were released in 150 B.C., he returned to Greece, but thereafter spent some further time in the company of Scipio and visited Rome at least once more. In addition to all this experience of Greece and Rome he travelled in many parts of the world: he was with Scipio at the fall of Carthage, and refers himself to journeys 'through Africa, Spain, and Gaul, and on the ocean that lies beyond' (III. 59). A man with such experience of the relations between states and such first-hand acquaintance with non-Greek peoples was not only likely to give due prominence to Rome and Carthage, hitherto neglected, as he complains, by other historians (v. 33), but also to go beyond his contemporaries in seeing the world of his day as a whole.

The geographical unity of the *oikoumenē* is a basic concept for Polybius, as for Eratosthenes. Like earlier Greek historians, he shows his interest in geography throughout his work, and Book XXXIV, now represented only by fragments, appears to have been entirely geographical. His insistence on a synoptic view is shown when he ridicules the absurdity of a man's imagining he 'has come to know the shape of the whole world, its entire disposition and arrangement, by visiting the most famous cities one by one, or even by looking at separate pictures of them' (I. 4). In describing Hannibal's march to Italy he rejects the mention of particular places as inadequate, and digresses into an account of world geography (III. 36). Past ignorance of the outlying areas, he says, was excusable, but now Asia has been opened up by Alexander, and the west by Rome (III. 59). Only the extreme north and south remain unknown, and they await future exploration (III. 38). Wrong as he was, within the limits of ancient knowledge he took a comprehensive view, transcending frontiers and racial distinctions. It is not surprising that he makes frequent mention of international law, or that he follows the author of *Airs, Waters, Places* in seeing climatic influences as the sole cause of national differences in character and physique (IV. 21).

Here there was nothing new, although such ideas were still far from general. Where Polybius did break new ground, and contribute a fresh element in the development of our theme, was in his insistence on the unity of human history, in the sense that happenings of the same period throughout the inhabited world must be seen as a single interconnected whole. That such a view was a natural product of the times is clear from his own account of the matter. He regards himself as a factual historian, a realist; and his belief in the unity of history, he claims, is drawn from the compulsion of events. Although his praise of Ephorus as the only previous 'universal' historian[2] implies that history *could* always be regarded in this light, he points to the Second Punic War as the time when its unity became definite and clear, so that from then on the story of the eastern Mediterranean and of Rome and Carthage *must* be seen as one.

This theme, so closely allied to the concept of the unity of mankind, is the burden of his introductory chapters. Whereas earlier builders of empire, including even the Macedonians, held only part of the *oikoumenē*, the Romans, he points out, had mastered nearly the whole of it in fifty-three years. Up to the 140th Olympiad (220 to 217 B.C.) 'world events had been scattered, as it were, undertaken and completed independently of each other, just as they were separate in locality. But from this date onwards history becomes an organic whole: events in Italy and Libya are interwoven with those in Asia and Greece, and all lead towards a single end' (I. 3).

The next chapter, attributing the convergence of human affairs at this time to Fortune, must be quoted at length:

There is a connection between the special intention of my work and the outstanding feature of current history: just as Fortune has guided nearly all the world's affairs in one direction and made them all incline towards one and the same end, so the historian must give his readers a single comprehensive view of the process whereby she has brought the entire series of events to pass. This was the point that chiefly invited and encouraged me to attempt this work, along with the fact that no contemporary writer has undertaken a general historical survey; otherwise I should have been far less eager for such an enterprise. But as it is I observe that whereas a number of historians concern themselves with particular wars and some of the incidents associated with them, no one, as far as I know, has even attempted to study the general overall scheme of events—the time and place of its origin or the way in which it reached fulfilment.

Polybius goes on to ridicule the belief that a comprehensive view of history can be gained from writers of mere episodes, comparing it with the absurdity of the idea, already mentioned, that one can learn the shape of the whole world from visiting particular places, or the notion that to see a number of scattered limbs is 'as good as being an eyewitness of the movement and beauty of the living creature itself'. The human race, in other words, forms a single unity analogous to the unity of its geographical environment, or to that of an individual body. 'Hence we must conclude', Polybius adds, 'that history limited to a partial view makes very little contribution towards any well-founded understanding of the general trend. Only by combination and comparison of all interrelated events, observing the resemblance and the difference between them, can one reach one's goal and survey the whole scene, and so gain both the profit and the pleasure that history has to give.'

The same line of thought is expressed at a number of later points; and as Polybius indicates in the chapter just quoted, the conception of the convergence of history into a unity in the 140th Olympiad determines the whole plan of his book. Down to this time he gives the history of each state in a continuous account; but after the battle of Cannae in 216 B.C. he follows an annalistic scheme which brings together events in different parts of the world under the same year, applying to all humanity the same kind of method which Thucydides had used for Greece in the Peloponnesian War. The main part of Polybius' work is indeed an embodiment of the idea of the unity of human affairs, springing directly from the rise of Roman power to balance the intellectual leadership of Greece.

Polybius' belief in the unity of history was not accompanied by any egalitarianism, any talk of need for change in the structure of human society. His vision transcended the frontiers, but left the traditional divisions of class and status undisturbed. He accepts slavery without question. Cattle and slaves, he says, are 'the first necessities of life' (IV. 38). Slavery is the normal fate of the defeated according to 'the laws of warfare', an inadequate punishment for the treachery of the Mantineans in 227 B.C., which 'violated the common code of mankind' (II. 58). He is no lover of the common man. Towards the masses his attitude is one of contempt: they must be restrained, as the Romans well understand, by religion. 'Since every populace is unstable, full of lawless desires, irrational anger, and violent emotion, the only possibility is to keep the masses in check by unseen terrors and theatrical effects of that kind.'[3]

THE MIDDLE STOA

In spite of the breadth of outlook which gave him a synoptic view, Polybius was essentially a historian, not a philosopher. His acquaintance with earlier thought seems to have been limited in both extent and depth; and although he must have learnt much from the Peripatetics and signs of Stoic influence have been found in his work, he is evidently right in claiming that it was the compulsion of facts, not philosophical theory, that led to his view of history as a unified process. He voices the scepticism of the practical man towards philosophy in his satirical remark, perhaps directed especially against Zeno or Chrysippus, that 'if it were possible to form a community of wise men', it would not be necessary to encourage fear of the gods.4

If we now turn from the historian to those who can be called philosophers, and ask what they had to say of mankind in this period of the rise of Rome to supremacy and the growth of Graeco-Roman civilisation, the answer is that their thought on the subject contained little or nothing that was completely new. They drew no fresh conceptions from Italy. Their fund of problems and ideas, and the general framework within which they reasoned, were taken over from their Greek predecessors. Yet their view of human society is marked by great differences of tone and attitude, even from the thinkers of a century before.

Two differences are particularly relevant to our theme. One of them recalls Polybius' attitude—a movement, even among the philosophers themselves, away from high philosophical speculation in the direction of more practical realism, linked with factual knowledge. We have seen this tendency at work among the Peripatetics, especially in Dicaearchus. How it would be increased by contact with Rome is indicated by Jaeger's comment on its suitability to the Roman point of view:

It is worth noticing that the Romans, when they incorporated Greek philosophy into their culture, left the ideal of the philosophic life behind. . . . When Cicero in his books *On the State* undertook to give

Greek philosophy a fixed place in the whole of Roman culture, he could combine the political spirit of his people with Greek science only by disregarding his deep reverence for Plato and Aristotle and adopting Dicaearchus' ideal of the political life.[5]

If this attitude was natural to the Romans, it may be regarded as a likely trend for the Greeks also amid the 'failure of nerve' that came upon a defeated people. However that may be, it became characteristic of Graeco-Roman thought long before Cicero. It involved decline from the ideal to the actual, acceptance of what is in place of insistence on what ought to be. But while the new outlook lacked height, it gained in breadth: it was not high enough to reach after ideal wisdom, but wide enough to embrace mankind.

The second change of attitude which concerns us is the movement towards synthesis; with the exception of the Epicureans and Sceptics, the various schools tended to come together. For our purpose, a particularly important development in this direction is one aspect of the fusion of Stoic and Peripatetic thought.

We have seen how a doctrine of kinship (*oikeiotēs*), varying in strength according to the different grades of relationship but extending in some degree to all mankind, was stated by Aristotle and developed by Theophrastus.[6] Among the early Stoics a theory arose with a similar name, but originating in a different approach. The Greek term here was *oikeiōsis*, defined by Plutarch as 'the perception and apprehension of what is akin to oneself' (*SVF*, II. 724)—the impulse which makes all living creatures seek in the first place self-preservation. The idea of this as the basic impulse of human life is a self-centred conception, one in which we might think there was no room for love of one's neighbour or human fellowship; yet by regarding relations with others as parts or extensions of oneself, it was possible to reconcile the two. Chrysippus, the earliest thinker to whom the concept is clearly attributed, extends it to our offspring as the next stage after the parts of our own bodies (*SVF*, III. 178–9). By further extension

outwards the doctrine could be seen as coinciding with the Peripatetic theory of *oikeiotēs*; and so the notion of human unity,
implicit in early Stoicism, could be made explicit and given
definite form by a pattern of kinship extending from self-love
to a bond connecting the entire human race. I shall take the view
that this fusion with Peripatetic ideas, without Theophrastus'
further extension of kinship to animals, came about during the
'Middle' period of Stoicism, in the second and first centuries B.C.,
but we cannot be sure of placing it more precisely than that. We
shall see that whoever was responsible for the synthesis, it was at
least partly realised in the thought of Panaetius, and is to be found
complete in Antiochus. One source may put even earlier a
simplified form of the doctrine, in which we pass straight from
affection for children to the fellowship of mankind. In the third
book of Cicero's *De Finibus* (62–3), which some regard as derived
from Chrysippus' pupil, Diogenes of Babylon, or from a Stoic
handbook of the time of his successor, Antipater, Cicero makes
the Stoic Cato stress the importance of understanding 'that nature
implants in parents love for their children, and this is the beginning
from which we eventually reach the common fellowship of
mankind. . . . Our love for our young is the starting-point of the
universal natural affection felt by human beings for each other,
which makes one man seem akin to another simply because he is
human.'

Panaetius, the first notable figure among the philosophers of this
period, was a thinker of great importance for the development of
the concept of the unity of mankind. In him also Hellenic and
Roman influences came together to produce a fresh attitude
towards the old problems and ideas. He was born on the island
of Rhodes early in the second century B.C., gained a thorough
knowledge of Greek, and especially Stoic, thought by studies at
Pergamum and Athens, and was head of the Stoic school for
twenty years before his death in 109 B.C. But the most remarkable
aspect of his life was his association with the leading intellects of

Rome, as a result of which a number of them are described as his 'disciples'. Several references mention him along with Polybius as one of the company gathered around Scipio Aemilianus, including a remark which Cicero makes Laelius address to Scipio himself in their discussion on the state: 'I remembered that you often used to talk with Panaetius in the company of Polybius, two Greeks perhaps superior to all others in their knowledge of political matters; and that you marshalled many arguments to show the supreme excellence of the form of government bequeathed to us by our ancestors' (*De Rep.* I. 21). The allusion to Panaetius' experience of political affairs and the comparison with Polybius indicate that Panaetius, too, greatly concerned himself with the facts, as he saw them, of human life and human history. The possibility that he wrote geographical works fits the same picture, and so also does our information that in philosophy, although himself a Stoic, he paid much attention to the writings of Plato and Aristotle and other thinkers of the Academy and Lyceum. He had a range of interests and knowledge which clearly justified the epithet *eruditissimus* applied to him elsewhere by Cicero, although in earlier times the adjective had suited the Peripatetics rather than the leaders of the Stoa.7

The writings of Panaetius are lost, and our knowledge of them is so slight that it is disputable whether they were many or few. Fortunately, however, an account of his ethical views has been preserved in the works of Cicero. In some passages of Cicero where Panaetius has been suggested as a source, the ascription is doubtful; but in the first two books of the *De Officiis* Cicero himself states that he is following him, although his version is not merely a translation and he makes additions, mainly illustrative, of his own. The work he is using is one *On Duties*, for which *De Officiis* is Cicero's Latin equivalent.

The doctrine expounded in these books of the *De Officiis* is of course Stoic, but it is Stoicism with a difference when compared with the outlook of Zeno. The keynote is an attitude which may be labelled realism, whereby the mind is concentrated not on a remote ideal related to the cosmic *Logos*, but on the world as it is and the duties of the ordinary man in that world. Consonant with this shift of emphasis is Panaetius' insistence that the philosopher's attention must be given not only to man as an abstract type, but also to the characters of individuals.[8]

Typical of this realism, and of great significance for our theme, is Panaetius' attitude towards that antithesis between wisdom and folly, the ideal wise man and the waywardness of the multitude, which, as we have seen, had already had a long history in Greek thought, extending from Heraclitus and other Pre-Socratics through Socrates and Plato down to the Cynics and early Stoics. For many thinkers, including Zeno and Cleanthes and Chrysippus, it had been the principal division of mankind, a deep cleavage which seems to have mattered more than the unity given by the common possession of reason. Scipio and his associates, we may suspect, took a very different view, echoed in Polybius' satirical reference to the 'community of the wise' as if it were an impracticable dream. Panaetius, whether because he came to share this outlook under their influence, or because of his wide knowledge of human affairs, or because his own temperament turned him towards acceptance of the actual rather than striving after the ideal, gave the concept of the perfect wise man little more than nominal assent. He brought to the fore that belief in the universal possession of reason by *all* men which had been a commonplace of Greek thought, including that of the early Stoics, but had sometimes been pushed into the background by the call for wisdom, the perfection of reason, and the contrast with the worthlessness of reason when misused. He virtually ignored the view so emphatically stated by Zeno and Chrysippus, that without wisdom men are incapable of any degree of virtue or co-operation, and concentrated his attention on principles of conduct for the ordinary man; or rather, in writing on 'duties', he produced a moral code for the sage and the ordinary man alike.

Consideration must be given not only to the wise, but to every man who shows any sign of merit: 'Since our life is spent not with men who are perfect and completely wise, but with those who do well if they have in them some semblance of goodness, I think we must conclude that no one should be entirely neglected in whom some trace of goodness is to be found' (I. 46). Panaetius wrote at length, says Cicero, on the theme of the contribution of lesser men to the achievements of the great. History is not only the story of great men; the common man also plays his part (II. 16): 'Who does not find self-evident the point which Panaetius illustrates at length—that no one, whether war leader or statesman, could have achieved great things for the welfare of the state without the enthusiastic support of other men?' An anecdote told by Seneca fits the same picture:

I find very neat the reply that Panaetius gave to a young man's question whether a wise man would become a lover. 'With regard to the wise man,' he said, 'we shall see later. But you and I, who are as yet far away from wisdom, must not make the mistake of falling into a condition that is unbalanced and beyond control, involving enslavement to another and worthless even in its own eyes.'

(*Epist. Mor.* 116. 5)

The question of the wise man's conduct can be postponed. It is 'you and I' who are our immediate concern.

All this opens up the way for an ethic directed *mihi et tibi*, framed not merely for the wise man, but for the whole of mankind; a code that will democratise, or perhaps water down, the early Stoic ideal, but will also broaden it out. Such a code will involve respect not only for the highest, but for all men: 'In our relations with our fellow men we should show what may almost be called reverence, not only for the best but for the others as well' (I. 99). Panaetius seems to have found the basis for this ethic in that combination of the Peripatetic doctrine of *oikeiotēs* and the Stoic theory of *oikeiōsis* which I have already described, and which may, as we have seen, have been put forward in at least a simple form by one of his predecessors in the Stoic school. Cicero is presumably drawing on Panaetius when in the first book of the *De Officiis* he expounds a view which brings the two doctrines together, although without the particular grades of relationship which we find in Theophrastus. The basic impulse of *oikeiōsis*, resulting in desire for self-preservation and reproduction and care for offspring, is extended through the power of reason in man to affection for others and readiness to associate with his fellow men:

To every species of living creature nature has given an instinct for preserving its own life and body, avoiding things that seem likely to harm it, and seeking and providing all the necessities of life—food, shelter, and other essentials. Another attribute common to all creatures is sexual desire with the production of young as its object, and some degree of concern for the young. . . . Nature also by the power of reason brings man into association with man both in speech and in life; she endows him above all with a special love for his children, and she impels him to want to create and attend gatherings and assemblies; and in consequence she makes him eager to provide the needs and conveniences of life not only for himself, but for his wife and children and all others who are dear to him and require his protection. (I. 11–12)

The importance of the idea of human fellowship for Panaetius' ethical doctrine becomes evident in the discussion of justice later in *De Officiis*, I. We have seen that Chrysippus spoke of the universality of justice and of one code of law for all men, although he counterbalanced this by emphasis on the cleavage between wisdom and folly. In Cicero's version of Panaetius' book the subject plays a large part. After little more than a page devoted to the virtue of wisdom, nearly twenty are concerned with justice and other social virtues which are subsidiary to it, before Cicero passes on to fortitude and temperance. The discussion begins (I. 20):

Of the three sources of duty that remain the widest in application is that principle, whereby the association of human beings with each other and their participation in a common life are maintained. Of this there are two parts: justice, the crowning glory among the virtues and the ground on which men are described as 'good'; and akin to justice, charity, which may also be called kindliness or generosity.

The most striking characteristic of Panaetius' thought on the subject is made clear in this first paragraph. Justice not only is a negative protection against harm, but also has a positive function, the promotion of communal life. Only Plato's *Republic* need be mentioned to remind us that this conception of justice was far from new, but here it receives fresh emphasis and is extended to human society as a whole. It is in accordance with the same line of thought that *beneficentia* is said to be closely linked with *iustitia*.

The positive aspect is brought into prominence again two paragraphs later, though the references to Plato and the Stoics here may be additions by Cicero:

As Plato has finely said, we are not born for ourselves alone, but our country and our friends each claim a share in our making. And as the Stoics believe, while all that is created on the earth is made for the use of man, men were brought into being for the sake of men, so that they could be of value to each other. In this, therefore, we should follow nature's lead and contribute to the common welfare by an exchange of services, by giving and receiving; and we should use our skills, our hard work and our talents to strengthen the bonds of fellowship between men.

If men are born to help other men and promote the common good, peace must be superior to war; and when armed conflict does occur, brutality must be avoided:

There are two ways of deciding a conflict—by discussion, which is characteristic of man, and by violence, the way of beasts; and we should resort to violence only if discussion is impossible. Therefore the only reason for going to war is to ensure that we can live in peace unharmed; and after victory those who have not been brutal or bloodthirsty in warfare should be spared.[9]

The universality of justice is stressed by mention of the need to exercise it even towards slaves, who should be treated in accordance with Chrysippus' definition of slavery:

Let us remember that we must adhere to justice even in our relations with the most humble of men. The most humble lot and position is that of slaves, and we are well advised by those who tell us to treat

slaves like hired workers: labour must be required from them, but they
must be given their dues.   (I. 41)

Cicero now turns to a lengthy discussion of kindness and
generosity; and presently the statement that human fellowship
will be best maintained if kindness is shown 'to each according
to the closeness of his relationship' leads to a general account of
human society and its foundations (I. 50–1):

We must go more deeply into the basic principles of fellowship and
association set up by nature among men. The first is to be found in the
association that links together the entire human race, and the bond that
creates this is reason and speech, which by teaching and learning, by
communication, discussion and decision brings men into agreement
with each other and joins them in a kind of natural fellowship. There
is nothing in which we are further removed from the nature of beasts:
we often say they have courage—horses or lions, for example—but we
do not allow them justice or equity or goodness, because they have no
share in reason or speech.

This is the most comprehensive association that links men with each
other and joins all to all. Within it we must maintain the common right
to all things produced by nature for men's common use. Things to
which some special statute or civil law applies must be owned as the
laws prescribe; but everything else must be treated in accordance with
the Greek saying, 'among friends all things in common'.

We go on from this universal bond to an account of other
degrees of relationship within the unity of mankind as a whole,
recalling to some extent the pattern put forward by Theophrastus,
although the order of the items is not his and kinship with animals
is excluded. Closer than the link of our common humanity is
the connection between those belonging to the same people, tribe,
and tongue; closer still, the relation between citizens of the same
city-state; still more intimate, the union between kindred. Friendship is considered next, as a bond of fellowship than which none
is finer or more powerful. Finally—and here Cicero, writing in
44 B.C., has his own Roman reasons for emphasis—'of all bonds
of association none is more serious, none more precious than that
which links each one of us with our own country' (I. 57). So all

of us, according to Panaetius, are involved in a multiple scheme of relationships inside the larger unity of the entire human race.

In the intellectual circle associated with Scipio Aemilianus Polybius and Panaetius represented two different approaches to the understanding of human affairs. Polybius, the student of facts and events, concerned himself with history and geography, not with philosophical theory. Panaetius, though far from blind to the world around him, seems to have been primarily a philosopher.

In Posidonius, who listened to the teaching of Panaetius at Athens towards the end of the second century B.C., both points of view came together in a single remarkable mind. Few figures of antiquity have roused more dispute, but there can be no doubt that he was the outstanding intellect of his day and the foremost representative of the Graeco-Roman point of view, who in the great body of his writings, as Bevan put it, 'expressed with unique completeness the general mind of the Greek world at the Christian era'.[10] Posidonius does not rank as one of the great original thinkers of ancient times. On the subject of mankind he probably said nothing new that was of primary importance, but we shall see that he appears to have broadened and enriched the concept of humanity as a unity within the wider unity of the cosmos.

One side of Posidonius puts him near to Polybius and Eratosthenes, and far away from the attitude of Zeno and the early Stoics: he was an indefatigable inquirer into the facts of the universe around him, who seems to have combined the curiosity of Herodotus with the systematic approach and encyclopaedic range of Aristotle. His personal experience of the world and its inhabitants was wide. He was born in Syria, studied at Athens, and became a citizen of Rhodes, but travel also took him to North Africa and to many parts of the West, including Italy, Gaul and Spain. As Bevan wrote, drawing on the evidence of Strabo, 'he saw with his own eyes the sun set in the Atlantic beyond the verge of the known world, and the African coast over against Spain, where the trees were full of apes, and the villages of bar-

barous peoples inland from Marseilles, where human heads
hanging at the house-doors for trophies were an everyday sight'.[11]
He had the opportunity to study man and his ways both at the
periphery of the *oikoumenē* and at its centre, for although he never
taught in Rome, he went there more than once and had a number
of eminent Romans, including Cicero and Pompey, among his
pupils or admirers. The effect of Roman imperialism on the contemporary world must have had a great influence on his outlook,
as on that of Panaetius.

What we know of his voluminous works confirms the picture
of a tireless seeker after factual knowledge, whose store of information reappears in the writings of lesser men who lacked his
synoptic powers. The only specifically geographical book of
which we are aware is one on *The Ocean*, in which, in consequence
of thirty days of observation of the sea at Gades, he made a notable
advance in the explanation of the tides. But we know that he also
calculated the circumference of the globe, though less accurately
than Eratosthenes; and Strabo and others draw repeatedly on him
for accounts of countries and their peoples, especially in the
remoter areas of the *oikoumenē*. Like Eratosthenes and others
before him, he looked to differences of climate as a factor deter-
mining physique and moral character. Much of his writing on
places and their inhabitants must have formed part of the fifty-two
books of his *Histories*, which were a continuation of the work of
Polybius down to 88 B.C. Like Polybius, he took the view that
history must be universal, but for him the concept had a wider
meaning. It is commonly supposed that Posidonius was the source
for the description of the universality of history at the beginning
of the *Library of History* compiled by Diodorus in the middle of
the first century B.C.—a disjointed miscellany which is very far
from maintaining the ideal of unity set forth in the opening
chapters. It has been the ambition of authors of universal history,
says Diodorus,

to bring all men within one and the same pattern, participants as they
are in kinship with each other although separate in space and time. In

this historians have acted like servants of divine Providence. For Providence, having brought the arrangement of the visible stars and the natures of men into conjunction, guides them round on their courses continually through all time, dispensing to each what falls by fate to its lot; and likewise these writers, describing the joint activities of the inhabited world like the affairs of a single city, have made their histories a single record and common archive of the past.[12]

Posidonius the scientist, geographer and historian is a definite figure, although our information about him is limited. Posidonius the philosopher is much more obscure. The day of bold assertion about him is over, when extensive sections of the works of later writers were traced back to him as their source, and after a period of extreme scepticism when almost any statement about him was called in question, there is general agreement that many aspects of our picture of him must remain conjectural. There is much uncertainty about his doctrine of the nature of man. One thing that seems clear, however, is the point suggested by the passage just quoted from Diodorus: the two aspects of his outlook were not separate, but closely linked. Unlike Polybius, he looked upon the study of human affairs as only part of the understanding of the wider and truly universal processes of the cosmos. He followed Panaetius in regarding mankind as a single whole without emphasis on the division between the wise and the foolish: his version of the Golden Age, the period when government was conducted by philosopher statesmen for the benefit of all, makes an interesting comparison with Zeno's exclusive Utopia of the wise.[13] But Posidonius probably went beyond Panaetius in placing human unity in perspective within the organic unity of the world, intermediate between the animal and the divine. He saw mankind both as a whole made up of the many diverse parts which he knew and described in his writings, and also as itself a part of the complex unity of the universe.

Among the many passages of Cicero about mankind which have been thought to come from Posidonius none is more generally agreed, or seems more probable, than the last few pages of the second book of the *De Natura Deorum*, in which Balbus expounds Stoic theology. In the rest of the book there has been much dispute as to what source or sources Cicero is following; but the final paragraphs at any rate have a strong Posidonian stamp, and a mention of Rhodes alongside Rome and Athens and Sparta points to the same conclusion. Even if the passage is not derived from Posidonius, it remains significant for the outlook of his time.

The topic to which Balbus here turns is the care of the gods for mankind, and his first remarks contain a sentence summarising the idea of the universe as the common home of gods and men: 'The world is as it were the common home of gods and men, or the city belonging to both; for they alone make use of reason and live according to right and law' (154). Later, after a detailed account of how plants and animals exist for the sake of man, there follows a passage which illustrates well the way in which interest in geography and history enriched the philosophic concept of mankind, so that the abstract notion took on more definite shape and content through the thought of the variety and complexity of the human race. Posidonius supposes that mankind is spread over a number of areas of the earth's surface, and he turns from the human race as a whole to the more remote areas before concentrating on the 'world' as the Greeks and Romans saw it—the 'island' formed by the continuous land area of Europe, Asia and Africa:

Not only mankind as a whole but even individuals enjoy the care and providence of the immortal gods; for we can take what is true of the entire human race and apply it on a more limited scale, narrowing it down step by step to smaller and smaller groups, and finally to individuals. If we believe that the gods care for all men everywhere in every coast and region of the lands far from this continuous land area which we inhabit, then they also care for those who with us dwell in these lands between the rising and the setting sun. And if they care for the inhabitants of this great island which we call the world, they care also for those who dwell in the divisions of that island—Europe, Asia and Africa. Consequently they also feel concern for the divisions

of these divisions, such as Rome, Athens, Sparta and Rhodes, and for
the individual citizens of these cities as well as for the population as a
whole. (164–5)

The gods' providential care for human beings had been a
frequent topic in earlier philosophical literature, notably in the
tenth book of Plato's *Laws* (899 d ff.), where arguments are put
forward to prove that if the gods care for what is great, they must
also feel concern for the small. The contrast between Plato's
abstract discussion and Posidonius' geographical analysis is a
measure of the development and shift of emphasis in the conception of mankind.

A thinker far inferior to Posidonius in intellectual calibre, but of
considerable importance for our purpose, is Antiochus of Ascalon,
who seems to have carried furthest that synthesis of earlier ideas
which now became the prevailing view of the nature of man. A
younger contemporary of Posidonius, he too had much contact
with the Romans, for after visiting Rome in 88 B.C. he found a
patron in Lucullus, and when he was head of the Academy at
Athens many distinguished visitors from the West attended his
lectures, including Cicero and Varro, the two outstanding Roman
intellects of the day.

The philosophical position which Antiochus maintained was
that there was no essential difference between the doctrines of
Plato and Aristotle, the Academy and the Lyceum; while Stoicism
also was in fundamental agreement with these schools, and no
more than a corrected version of their theories. His view of
mankind was one aspect of this synthesis: the same fusion of
Peripatetic *oikeiotēs* and Stoic *oikeiōsis* of which we have found
some evidence in the thought of Panaetius and perhaps even
earlier, but now—as far as we can judge from our uncertain
information—more fully worked out than before.

One follower of Antiochus was Cicero's older contemporary
Varro, the most notable of all Roman scholars; and in St Augustine's summary of his beliefs in the *City of God* we have a brief

glimpse of this side of Antiochus' teaching, reminiscent of passages already cited from Aristotle and Theophrastus. 'Friendship' is seen extending outwards from the family until it includes even the gods:

They say that this happy life also involves one's fellow-beings. It loves the good of friends for its own sake, regarding it as its own good, and desires for them for their own sakes what it desires for itself; whether by 'friends' we mean those in a man's home—his wife and children and the rest of his household; or those in the locality where his home is, such as the citizens of his city; or those throughout the world, the peoples linked with him by the fellowship of mankind; or beings even of the universe, which is called heaven and earth—such as they say are gods and regard as friends of the wise man, while we, who have better knowledge of them, call them angels. (XIX. 3)

For a fuller account of Antiochus' view we must turn to the fifth book of Cicero's *De Finibus*, where Piso is made to expound his doctrines.[14] Following a line of thought which recalls part of Aristotle's discussion of friendship in the *Ethics*, Piso endeavours to reconcile love of self with affection for others, and to produce a moral code centred on self yet including not merely a negative 'social contract' with other men, but a positive doctrine of universal human fellowship. All living creatures love themselves, he argues, and therefore desire self-preservation and self-development. Man's self-love makes him want the perfection of every aspect of his nature, physical and mental, humble and high. This perfection is the good for man, desirable as an end in itself.

After a lengthy account of man's concern with himself and his own development, Piso turns to his relations with others:

In the whole realm of moral excellence there is nothing finer, nothing with wider implications, than the interrelationship of men with each other—the fellowship, as it were, that exists between them, their exchange of services, and indeed the affection which unites mankind. This affection comes into being right from our birth, in that children are loved by their parents and the whole family is held together by the bonds of marriage and parenthood. From there it gradually spreads beyond the home, first through ties of blood, then through marital

relationships, then through friendships, later by association with neighbours, afterwards to fellow-citizens and to partners and friends in
public life, and finally by embracing the entire human race.[15]

After this Theophrastean description of the different degrees of
human fellowship, it is identified with *iustitia*, to which Piso here,
like Cicero's version of Panaetius in the *De Officiis*, gives a
positive function; but every kind of moral activity, he adds, has
its outgoing aspect, linking us with our fellow men:

This attitude of mind, which gives each man his own due yet generously
and fairly maintains this human fellowship and unity of which I speak,
is called justice; and linked with it are sense of duty, kindliness, liber-
ality, benevolence, friendliness, and the other qualities of the same
sort which are particularly related to justice, although the remaining
virtues also share in them. For because there is innate in human nature
an element of civic and national feeling (which the Greeks call *politikon*),
every action of every virtue will be in keeping with the common
interest and with that affection and fellowship of mankind which I
have described; and justice in its turn, which in action must spread
into the spheres of the other virtues, will seek after them.

What follows makes clear the dilemma in Antiochus' thought
about mankind, one form of a problem involved in all Greek
thinking about the nature of man. Our fellow men are to be
sought after for their own sakes; yet they are not part of the Good,
the perfection of the individual self, but only 'external goods':

Since, therefore, every virtue involves a concern which looks outwards,
as it were, and seeks and embraces other men, the result is that friends,
brothers, kinsmen, relations by marriage, fellow-citizens and indeed all
human beings (since we hold that there is one fellowship of all men)
are goods to be desired for their own sake. Yet none of these is of such
a kind as to be part of the final and ultimate good. It follows that
there are found to be two classes of things desirable for their own sakes:
to one belong those goods of mind or body which constitute the
ultimate good; but these goods which are external, belonging to neither
mind nor body—for example, friends, parents, children, relatives, even
one's native land—these are precious on their own account, yet do not
belong to the same class as the first.

Piso's answer to the difficulty is the solution already implied, if not explicitly stated, by Aristotle—that action related to these 'external goods', our fellow men, is right action and benefits the doer, and therefore is a means to the good end of his self-development. In this way the movement of affection outwards from the self, reaching ultimately the whole human race, is reconciled with the centripetal tendency towards concentration on the individual ego. The good Samaritan's action was in his own self-interest, and so is the altruism of the champion of world peace. Egoism and 'love thy neighbour' coincide.

Probably also from Antiochus, although perhaps indirectly, comes the thought of some pages in the anthology of excerpts compiled by Stobaeus round about the fifth century A.D. The passage occurs in a summary of the ethical teaching of 'Aristotle and the other Peripatetics' by Arius Didymus of Alexandria, who became the philosophical teacher of Augustus.[16] It is clear from the summary as a whole that Arius' version of Peripatetic doctrine does not come from Aristotle or Theophrastus but coincides with the synthesis of Antiochus, though it may have come to Arius through the medium of a younger Peripatetic under Antiochus' influence.

In a context which contains numerous marks of Stoic thought,[17] we meet once again the Theophrastean conception of degrees of relationship extending outwards from love of children to the entire human race, but not beyond man to the animals. After insisting that parents love children for their own sakes, not merely for the services they can give, Stobaeus continues:

Children being thus loved like something desirable in itself, it goes without saying that parents, brothers and sisters, husbands and wives, blood-relations and other relatives and fellow-citizens all receive affection on their own account. For with them also we have certain natural ties of kinship, since man is a creature that loves his fellows and takes part in a common life. That among these bonds of affection some are more remote and others close to us, is beside the point; for every one of them is desirable on its own account, not only for the services it can provide. Now if affection for our fellow-citizens is desirable on its own account, so also is affection for men of the same race and the same stock, and consequently affection for all mankind.

The passage goes on to give illustrations of our duty towards our fellow men. In Euripides' *Helen* (501–2) Menelaus says no man will be so 'barbarous' as to refuse him food—once he has heard his name. Here such conduct towards *any* stranger is regarded as *inhuman*:

Who that saw a man overpowered by a wild beast would not rescue him, if he could? Who would not show a lost traveller the way? Who would not help a man perishing from want? Who that came upon a spring in a waterless desert would not leave marks to indicate it to those following the same route? Who does not take great care to avoid speech of ill omen for posterity? Who does not abominate, as contrary to human nature, such utterances as these?:

'When I am dead let fire consume the world',

or

'I do not care, for all goes well with *me*.'

It is evident, then, that by nature we feel goodwill and affection towards all men, which proves that this bond is desirable in itself and that the poet's words are right:

'One is the race of men, one the race of gods; from one mother we both draw our being.'[18]

That mother is Nature.

CICERO

It will be evident from the preceding pages that in their views on human society and the unity of mankind Panaetius, Posidonius and Antiochus had much in common. To their contemporaries they must have been very different figures, each with his own distinctive approach and his own ideas, but the uncertainty of our knowledge of them as individuals makes us tend to see their doctrines now as three of the main sources, not always clearly distinguishable, from which was built up a general 'philosophic' conception of man and his place in the world, held by most educated people. This common outlook was not attached in the minds of most men to any individual thinker. It was known to the reading public not so much from the writings of a single great philosopher, but rather through the easier medium of summarising handbooks or volumes of selections; and it was regarded as part of a general philosophical currency which cultured men, except the Epicureans and Sceptics, would accept.

This is the attitude that we find in Cicero, who despite his outstanding brilliance was in a sense typical of the educated and thinking men of his time. His writings present an invaluable picture of the prevailing attitude in such circles towards the ideas which we have been tracing, in all its breadth and with all its limitations, during the culminating phase of the development of our theme before it becomes complicated by the intrusion of conceptions from Hebraic or Christian thought or elsewhere. Although the passages from Cicero which I have used so far are traced with strong probability to particular sources, on this as on other topics his general aim in his philosophical works is not to reproduce the ideas of individual thinkers; rather he tries to draw from their writings, and from the current handbooks and anthologies, an account of the widely accepted 'philosophical' view which he is himself helping to create. There are many passages in him where the source cannot be decided with certainty; often we cannot assume that he is using any one authority, but must be content to say that he is putting forward, and to some extent himself developing, the conception of human society which Greek thought reached in this period of contact with and domination by Rome. In this conception the idea of unity and fellowship among all men was evidently a commonplace, although Cicero admits that it was a particularly favourite theme with him.[19]

I will cite one such passage, from the first book of the *De Legibus* (22–39), for which some find an origin in Panaetius, others in Antiochus, while others again deny that it can be attributed to any particular source—a passage in which various lines of thought that we have found in earlier writers reappear as elements in

Cicero's point of view. Here he does not treat human fellowship as an emotional bond derived from our natural affection for others, but in a way which suits the topic under discussion—as the result of subjection to a common law based on the common possession of reason. This is near to Chrysippus, and it has been suggested that Cicero is drawing on him; but whereas Chrysippus' attitude was complicated, and probably dominated, by the antithesis between wisdom and folly, so that the many who fail to use reason are far removed from the wise man and divided against each other, this passage insists that *all* men are alike in sharing reason (*ratio*) and the potentiality for wisdom (*sapientia*).

Cicero, who is himself the speaker, begins with a striking statement of the belief which had persisted throughout Greek thought on the subject—that reason is the common distinctive feature of men and gods:

This creature which we call man, endowed with foresight and sagacity, complex, intelligent, equipped with memory, full of reason and understanding, has been created by the supreme deity with a certain distinctive status: out of all the species and varieties of living creatures he alone has a share in reason and thought, which is lacking in all the rest. And what is more godlike, not only in man, but in all heaven and earth, than reason, which, once it is full grown and brought to perfection, is rightly called wisdom? Since therefore nothing is better than reason and reason exists in both man and god, reason is the first bond of unity between them. But those who have reason in common also have right reason in common; and since right reason is law, this also must be seen as a common tie linking men with the gods. Now those who have the same law must also have the same justice; and those who share law and justice must be regarded as members of the same community—much more so, if they obey the same authorities and powers; and they do obey the order of the heavens, the divine mind, and the god of supreme power. Therefore the whole universe must be seen as a single joint community of gods and men.

The growing and perfecting of reason into wisdom is nature's work on the gift of God; that is, the natural development of our natural endowment:

While God created and equipped man, giving him the first place above all other things, it must be clear without discussing every detail that nature of her own accord goes further: setting out without a guide from those things, the character of which she has learnt from the first rudiments of intelligence, she strengthens and perfects by her own efforts the faculty of reason.

As with the early Stoics, men's vices and mistakes are seen as keeping them unlike and apart; but Cicero's main emphasis falls on their likeness, which he here describes in exaggerated terms:

That justice is based upon nature will be evident, if you fully realise man's fellowship and unity with his fellow men. No two things are so closely and exactly alike as all of us are to each other. If degeneration of habits and false opinions did not pervert the weakness of our minds and turn it aside in whatever direction it begins to stray, no one would be so like himself as all would be like all. Hence, however man is to be defined, one definition is true of all men—proof enough that there is no difference within the species, for if there were, a single definition would not cover all its members. And indeed reason, our sole ground of superiority to the beasts, whereby we are able to form opinions, to prove or disprove, to discuss a point and settle it and draw conclusions —reason is certainly common to all men, variable in what it learns but equal for all in its power to learn. For the same objects are perceived by all men's senses, and the things that affect our senses do so in the same way in every man; the beginnings of understanding are imprinted on all minds alike, and speech, the interpreter of the mind, expresses the same thoughts though the words may differ. There is indeed no one of any race who, given a guide, cannot make his way to virtue.

Although our follies divide us, yet even our vices, as well as our virtues, make the whole world kin. Differences of religious belief do not prevent human unity:

The likeness that pervades the human race is evident in its bad qualities as well as in the good. . . . Troubles, joys, desires and fears haunt all men's minds alike; people differ in beliefs, but those who worship the dog and the cat as gods are afflicted with the same superstition as other races. But what tribe does not value friendliness, generosity, and a heart that gratefully remembers a kindness? What tribe does not reject and hate the proud, the vicious, the cruel, the ungrateful?

Justice is common to all men, and would be equally valued by all if they followed nature:

If in agreement with nature men considered 'nothing alien to them that concerns humanity', as the poet says, justice would be equally revered by all. For those to whom nature has given reason have also received the gift of right reason, and so the gift of law, which is right reason in the sphere of command and prohibition; and if law, then justice also. Now all men have the gift of reason; therefore justice has been given to all.

Atticus, summing up, brings in the natural affection between men as well as the link of law, and so states in brief the whole Ciceronian position. It has been proved, he says, 'first, that we have been equipped and endowed with what may be called gifts of the gods; second, that there is one rational principle by which we can live together, the same for all and common to all; finally, that all men are bound together by a sort of natural kindliness and goodwill, and further by their joint participation in justice'.

Cicero adds a statement which makes it clear that he claims to be speaking here for the majority of the thinking men of his time. These first principles that he has laid down, he says, have the approval of all the right-minded schools of philosophy—not the Epicureans or the Sceptics of the New Academy, but the Old Academy, the Peripatetics, and the Stoics alike.

It remains for us to ask what real influence this widespread belief in human unity exercised on men's minds and lives. We have seen that the concept of the brotherhood of mankind developed in Greek thought against a background of long-standing distinctions and barriers, between slave and free, between the sexes, between cities and between peoples, between rich and poor or high and low. How did the growth and increasing acceptance of this concept affect men's attitude to these divisions? How real, even for

Cicero and his contemporaries, was their sense of fellowship with *all* men?

According to one passage in the third book of the *De Officiis* (28), the same warmth of relationship extends throughout human society. Ignoring the Theophrastean idea of different grades of kinship, Cicero argues that we should make the interest of the individual and the interest of all men identical, for otherwise all human fellowship will be destroyed. We should show the same consideration towards fellow-citizens as towards our own family, and towards foreigners as towards fellow-citizens:

An absurd attitude is adopted by those who say that they will take nothing from a parent or brother for their own gain, but a different rule applies to the rest of their fellow-citizens. Their position is that no tie of obligation, no association for the sake of the common interest binds them to their fellow-citizens—a view which tears asunder the whole unity of society. Those again who say that regard should be had for fellow-citizens, but not for foreigners, rend apart the fellowship that unites mankind.

This is a lofty ideal; but Cicero's own real opinion and the general outlook of the time are probably better represented in other places where the kinship between all men seems to be something far more tenuous. We have seen that in the first book of the *De Officiis*, for example, where Cicero is following Panaetius, he says that kindness should be shown 'to each according to the closeness of his relationship';[20] and the extent to which Ciceronian charity begins at home is indicated in the examples that follow, which significantly restrict generosity to one's fellow men to cases where there is no cost to oneself:

Those things are thought to be common to all men which are of the type of which Ennius has given one instance, though it could be extended to many others:

> Who kindly shows a wanderer the way
> Does just as if from his own lamp he lit
> A lantern for the other; no less bright
> Shines his, when he has given the other light.

By this one example Ennius shows that even a stranger should be given anything that can be bestowed on him without loss to ourselves. On this principle we have the following instances of things in common: 'Deny no one running water'; 'Let anyone who will have fire from your fire'; 'Give true advice to him who seeks it.' All these gifts are of value to the receiver and cost the giver nothing. Therefore we should follow these examples and always be making some contribution to the common welfare. But since the resources of individuals are small and the number of those in need is infinite, the desire for generosity towards all must be kept within Ennius' limit—'No less bright shines his'—so that we may have the power to be generous to our own friends.

(51-2)

The examples given by Arius Didymus in the passage I have already quoted from Stobaeus are also minimal, and scarcely carry us beyond helping our fellow man in emergencies—again, at little or no cost to ourselves. Cicero seems to be expressing the normal attitude of his day, and his own real thought, when he makes Laelius in the *De Amicitia* (19-20) differentiate strongly between the weakness of our feeling towards mankind in general and the warmth of the affection between a few close friends:

This fact seems to me to be clear, that we come into the world under this condition, that there is to be a certain bond of fellowship among all, but increasing in strength according to the closeness of the connection. Hence fellow-citizens have more claim on us than foreigners, and relations than strangers; for friendship with the latter is the creation of nature herself, but there is not enough certainty that it will last. The point in which friendship is superior to relationship is that goodwill can be removed from relationship, but not from friendship; for where there is no longer goodwill the word 'friendship' cannot be used, but 'relationship' can. How great the force of friendship is can best be seen from this, that starting from the unlimited association of all mankind, which nature herself has knit together, this feeling is so concentrated and is brought within such narrow limits that the whole range of affection becomes a bond by which two individuals or a small group are united.

That the idea of human unity had no fundamental effect on Cicero's thinking is confirmed by his attitude towards the tradi-

tional divisions of ancient society. His outlook is one of acceptance, not of protest or call for change. His doctrine of universal
fellowship is evidently intended as a description of what is, not,
like the ideals of Plato and Zeno, a programme of what ought to be.
In his writings as a whole he normally assumes without question
such basic distinctions and prejudices as the inferiority of women
or the existence of slavery as a natural institution. Nor does he
or any of his contemporaries think of the concept of a universal
human community as pointing to any organisational results. The
societas humana already exists, and does not have to be created.
Nevertheless, the idea of the unity of mankind did carry with it
ethical implications, apparent in Cicero, which had no small
impact on history. To discuss the *ius gentium* and the *pax Romana*,
two aspects of Roman civilisation which embodied the conception
of human fellowship, would carry us beyond the limits of this
book. But to complete our sketch of the views of Cicero and his
contemporaries, and the point of development which the idea of
human unity reached in their time, something must be said of
one line of thought connected with this idea which, short-lived
though it proved to be, had a considerable practical effect on
the life of the day. This is the doctrine, if it can be so called,
of *humanitas*.

By *humanitas* Cicero does not normally mean 'humanity' in the
sense of 'mankind'. His Latin for the human race is *genus humanum*,
and its unity is *communitas* or *societas generis humani*. *Humanitas* is
the attribute of one who is *humanus*, and is equivalent to 'humanity' only in this qualitative sense. It might be argued, of course,
that every member of the zoological *genus humanum* is *humanus*,
and therefore *humanitas* should be the common quality which
makes us all men. But that this is not the usual meaning of the
word is shown by the numerous passages which imply that
members of the human species are not necessarily *humani* or
possessed of *humanitas*, but can become so if 'their minds are
turned towards *humanitas*', or the like. Cicero's use of the word
is derived from another line of thought, which we have found

among the Greeks from Homer onwards: the idea that only those who conform to certain standards are really men in the full sense, and fully merit the adjective 'human' or the attribute 'humanity'. The wise man, says Scipio in the *De Republica*, 'believes that while others may be called men, only those really *are* men who are accomplished in the arts characteristic of *humanitas*' (I. 28).

The standard set by the Greeks for the true man varied to some extent according to the point of view of the thinker, but always, with one notable exception, it involved the idea that a man really worthy of the name is one fitted to be a member of human society and play his part in the life of the community. Homer's Cyclops, Protagoras' 'misanthrope', and Aristotle's 'cityless' man all stand outside the true human pattern because they are incapable of social and political association with normal men. The exception which proves the rule is the paradoxical view of the Cynics, who regarded the mass of 'civilised' mankind as sub-human and claimed true humanity for those whom others nicknamed 'dogs'.

Cicero's standard of *humanitas*, it has been said, was that of the Roman 'gentleman'; and it was indeed partly shaped by the traditions and prejudices of the Roman aristocracy. But Cicero himself writes of the Greeks as the source from which his ideal has spread to others,[21] and it is clear that his conception continued the same line of thought which we have seen among the Greeks, although, significantly enough, there was no single Greek word for it—the idea of a common civilisation, now no longer equated with the outlook of the *polis* or with Hellenic culture, although it owed much to both, but enlarged to cover a far wider picture of civilised man. An essential attribute of the member of civilised society, an essential aspect of *humanitas*, was awareness of kinship with the rest of mankind. To quote the *De Republica* again (II. 48), the tyrant, 'although he has a human form, yet outstrips the most monstrous beasts in the brutality of his ways. How can we rightly describe as a human being a creature who will have no tie of justice, no partnership in human civilisation with his fellow-citizens or indeed with any part of the human race?'

The development and spread of the concept of human unity which we have traced from Homer to Cicero ends with the traditional divisions and prejudices still unbroken. It has roused no call for revolutionary change in the structure of society, and has had no more than a reforming effect on human relations. But at any rate a stage has been reached at which acceptance of the idea of human brotherhood is regarded as an essential characteristic of every human being worthy of the name.

NOTES AND REFERENCES

CHAPTER II

1 On the likelihood of ethnic relationship between Achaeans and Trojans, see G. S. Kirk, *The Songs of Homer* (Cambridge, 1962), pp. 17–19.

2 *Il.* II. 867 ff. Cf. Strabo, XIV. 2. 28. The inconsistency, which Strabo discusses, with Thucydides' statement οὐ μὴν οὐδὲ βαρβάρους εἴρηκε (I. 3) suggests that Thucydides rejected or did not know the lines, and the scholiast comments τὸ γὰρ βαρβαροφώνων Καρῶν νενόθευται (cf. Gomme *ad loc.*). *Il.* II. 867–75 seem to imply a special antipathy to the Carians, οἱ Μίλητον ἔχον, and Strabo says that according to Apollodorus the term βάρβαρος was particularly applied to them (cf. the later contempt for them as mercenaries or slaves: ἐν τῷ Καρὶ κινδυνεύειν, etc.). If this attitude goes back as far as Homer, it may be argued that βαρβαρόφωνος, unlike ἀλλόθροος, has an implication of hostility, and that βάρβαρος implied antagonism from the first, being used originally in particular cases and later extended to non-Greeks in general.

3 Phoenicians: 14. 287 ff.; 15. 415 ff.; 13. 271 ff.

4 Abii: XIII. 6. Ethiopians: I. 423–5; XXIII. 205–7; I. 22–6, etc.

5 Cyclops: 9. 124, 119, 190–1. Hesiod, *Theog.* 142 ff. includes the Cyclopes among the gods.

6 The ancient interpretation of μέροπες (I. 250 and elsewhere) in this sense is significant, although due to a false derivation.

7 II. 488–91. This seems to be the best interpretation of ἐπάρουρος, but others translate it by 'attached to the soil', 'as a serf'.

8 *Works and Days*, 225–37. Cf. *Od.* 19. 109–14.

9 *Barbarians in Greek Tragedy* (Yale University Press, 1961), p. 170.

10 *P.V.* 807–15, trans. Rex Warner (Bodley Head, 1947).

11 Frs. 169, 215 Bergk. Cf. fr. 43.

12 Alcman: fr. 13 Diehl. Sappho: fr. 96 Lobel and Page. Alcaeus: fr. 69 Lobel and Page.

13 Fr. 41. On the problem of the text and interpretation of this fragment, see Kirk and Raven, *The Presocratic Philosophers* (Cambridge, 1957), p. 204. The general sense is not affected.

14 Fr. 114. The translation does not reproduce the pun between ξυνόν and ξὺν νῷ. Cf. also fr. 113.

15 Fr. 53. Cf. frs. 51 and 80.

16 Man and animals: fr. 21b. Mind in all living things: frs. 11 and 12; cf. Kirk and Raven, pp. 376 and 393. Hands: A 102.

17 442–61, trans. G. Thomson (Cambridge, 1932).

18 332–64, trans. E. F. Watling (Penguin Books, 1947). Cf. Eurip. *Suppl.* 196–218.

19 Teucer's further words αὐτὸς δὲ μητρὸς ἐξέφυς Κρήσσης show that Sophocles thought the Cretans were barbarians, at any rate in prehistoric times. On later attributions of cosmopolitanism to Teucer, cf. Haarhoff, *The Stranger at the Gate* (Blackwell, 1938), p. 52.

20 V. Ehrenberg, *The People of Aristophanes* (2nd ed., Blackwell, 1951), p. 363.

21 *Ion*, 239–40. 'The look of them' seems a better translation of σχῆμα than 'manner' or 'bearing'.

22 *I.A.* 1400–1. Cf. *ibid.* 1273–5, 1380; fr. 719. On Euripides' attitude, cf. Bacon, *op. cit.* pp. 151 ff.

23 *Andromache*, 173, 243–4.

24 *Ion*, 854–6. Cf. fr. 511.

25 I presume here that πάντων μέτρον ἄνθρωπος (fr. 1) refers to the individual, not to man as a type. Speech in Plato's *Protagoras*: 320 c–8 d.

26 Cf. *Rep.* 493 a.

27 Fr. 3. On the point discussed in this paragraph I have followed W. K. C. Guthrie, *In the Beginning* (Methuen, 1957), pp. 88–93, rather than G. B. Kerferd, *J.H.S.* (1953), pp. 42–5.

28 Περὶ ὁμονοίας: cf. fr. 44 a. Surviving fragments: 45–8, 63, 65, 67–71.

29 *Paideia*, Eng. trans. (Blackwell, 1947), vol. III, p. 6.

30 Loeb edition of Hippocrates, vol. I, p. 143.

31 There might seem to be an exception in Περὶ διαίτης III. 68–9, where a distinction is made between the majority and those who are well enough off to concentrate on their health. But there is no suggestion of any difference in basic nature between them.

32 *On Ancient Medicine*, 20. Cf. *ibid.* 1.

CHAPTER III

1 *Gorgias*, 485 d–e. Cf. *Apol.* 31 d–2 a, 32 e.

2 *Cambridge Ancient History*, vol. VII, p. 39.

3 Iamblichus, *Vita Pythagorae*, 237 (DK 58 D 7).

4 The Δημοκράτους γνῶμαι (frs. 35–115) and those from Stobaeus (frs. 169–297). Most scholars accept the latter as genuine.

5 Frs. 98, 99, 100, 106.

6 Frs. 110, 111, 214, 273, 274.

7 Quoted by Aristotle, *Rhet.* 1373 b 18.

8 Fr. 4 Edmonds. For date, cf. Edmonds *ad loc.*

9 Lysias, XXXI. 6. πᾶσα γῆ πατρίς looks like a reminiscence of Euripides, e.g. fr. 1047. Cf. also Aristoph. *Plutus*, 1151: πατρὶς γάρ ἐστι πᾶσ', ἵν' ἂν πράττῃ τις εὖ.

10 Fr. 39 Edmonds. He suggests 377 B.C. as the date of the play.
11 Cf. V. Martin, *Mus. Helvet.* (1944), pp. 13–30.
12 *Cyrop.* VIII. 1. 43–4. Some editors regard the last clause as a later addition.
13 *Panegyricus*, 3 and 15.
14 *Panegyricus*, 159. Cf. *Helen*, 67–9: Helen first united the Greeks against the barbarians!
15 *Paideia*, Eng. trans., vol. III, p. 153.
16 *Panegyricus*, 50. J. Jüthner, *Hellenen und Barbaren* (Leipzig, 1923), p. 36, claims that Isocrates is here limiting the name 'Hellenes' to Greeks with Attic culture, rather than extending it to foreigners who share Greek culture; but his view has not been widely accepted.
17 Cf. *Antidosis*, 209–14; *To Nicocles*, 12.
18 Diod. XIII. 20–7. On derivation from Ephorus, cf. Kroll in Pauly–Wissowa *s.v.*; Mühl, *Die antike Menschenheitsidee in ihrer gesch. Entwicklung* (Leipzig, 1928), pp. 36–8.
19 27. 6, reading ἐν ἀσχήμονι χιτῶνι (Capps) and εὐημερίαν (Madvig).
20 Cf. p. 54 above.
21 469c–e. Cf. 487d–9b.
22 Cf. *Gorgias*, 521d; *Rep.* 517c–d, 519c–d, 520c.
23 *Rep.* 473c–4a. Cf. *Epist.* VII. 326b, *Statesman*, 293c–e.
24 *Gorgias*, 507e–8a. Cf. Dodds *ad loc.*
25 *Rep.* 373a. Cf. 467 ff.
26 507e–8a. Cf. p. 77 above. Geometrical equality: cf. Dodds *ad loc.*
27 781a–b, reading διπλάσιον with the MSS. See Taylor *ad loc.*
28 Cf. *Rep.* 454a–e; *Laws*, 804e–6c.
29 Cf. p. 169 below.
30 Early Greeks like barbarians: *Rep.* 452c, *Cratylus*, 397c, 421d. Ancestors: *Theaet.* 175a. Character due to climate, etc.: *Rep.* 435e; *Tim.* 24c; *Crit.* 109c, 111a; *Laws*, 747d–e. Pausanias: *Symp.* 182b.
31 262c–d. Cf. Skemp *ad loc.* and Andreotti, *Historia* (1956), p. 262. A different estimate: Badian, *Historia* (1958), p. 444, n. 81.
32 626a. Cf. p. 77 above.
33 Cf. Morrow, *Mind* (1939), pp. 187–8.
34 *Laws*, 930d, 915a. Cf. Morrow, *op. cit.* pp. 198–9.
35 Cf. *H.A.* 490b16–19.
36 Distinctive physical characteristics: *P.A.* 662b20–3, 673a7–9, 658a15–16; *G.A.* 780b4–5; *H.A.* 497b32, 492a31–2.
37 Speech: *Pol.* 1253a9. Tongue: *P.A.* 660a17–28.
38 Ability to acquire knowledge: *Top.* 133a20–3. Value judgments: *Pol.* 1253a10–18.
39 Cf. W.W. Jaeger, *Aristotle*, Eng. trans. (2nd ed., Oxford, 1955), pp. 395–7, 437 ff. On relation of *Protrepticus* to the *Nicomachean Ethics*, see also I. Düring, *Aristotle's Protrepticus* (Göteborg, 1961), pp. 277 ff.

40 ἀνθρωπεύεσθαι: *E.N.* 1178b7.
41 On the distinction between φρόνησις and σοφία, cf. *E.N.* 1141b2–23. Can achieve εὐδαιμονία: *E.N.* 1099a31–b8.
42 *E.N.* 1179b11–16. Cf. *E.N.* 1167b2–16.
43 *Met.* 1058a29 ff. *Timaeus*: cf. p. 79 above.
44 *E.E.* 1242a23–8, omitting the corrupt words ἀλλ' αἱ διὰ δύμον αὐλικόν.
45 Subordination of female to male: *Pol.* 1254b13–15, 1259b2–10. Wife's authority: *E.N.* 1160b33–5. Woman's virtues: *Pol.* 1260a29–31.
46 No deliberation: *Pol.* 1260a13. No power to follow own choice: *Pol.* 1280a34; but contrast *Poet.* 1454a19.
47 *Pol.* 1254b23, 1260b5–8.
48 No happiness: *E.N.* 1177a6–9. Enslavement beneficial: *Pol.* 1255b6–13; but only κατὰ συμβεβηκός, *Pol.* 1278b36.
49 *Pol.* 1252b8. Cf. p. 36 above.
50 More slavish than Greeks: *Pol.* 1285a20–3. Greeks could rule: *Pol.* 1327b 32–3.
51 *Pol.* 1256b25–7, 1334a3.
52 *De Alex. Magni Fortuna aut Virtute*, 329b. See p. 119 below.
53 Differences: *Pol.* 1285a20–3, 1327b20 ff. Carthage: *Pol.* 1272b24 ff. Whether these passages represent a later view depends on the difficult problem of the order of composition of the *Politics*. Cf. Badian, *Historia* (1958), pp. 440–2.
54 Diog.L. v. 14–15.
55 Type rare: *E.N.* 1145a30–2. Among barbarians: *E.N.* 1148b19–9a20. Burnet *ad loc.* cites as an example the completely fearless Celts of *E.N.* 1115b28.
56 Zeller, Eng. trans. (1868), *Socrates and the Socratic Schools*, p. 275; Kärst, *Gesch. d. Hellenismus* (2nd ed., 1926), vol. II, pp. 108–10; Wilcken, *Alex. d. Grosse* (1931), pp. 10–11.
57 Cf. Philodemus, Περὶ Στωϊκῶν (Crönert), cols. 13–14 and 7. Antipater is cited as mentioning 'Diogenes' opinion, which he recorded in the *Politeia*'.
58 *Quellen-Untersuchungen zu Leben u. Philosophie d. Diogenes v. Sinope* (Philol. Suppl. XVIII, 11, Leipzig, 1926), pp. 55–7. Von Fritz regards the doxography in Diog.L. VI. 72 as derived from Diogenes' *Politeia*.
59 *Alexander the Great* (Cambridge, 1948), vol. II, pp. 407–9.
60 *A History of Cynicism* (Methuen, 1937), p. 29.
61 VI. 72. Cf. von Fritz, *op. cit.* pp. 59 ff.; Dudley, *op. cit.* p. 36; Hoïstad, *Cynic Hero and Cynic King* (Uppsala, 1948), pp. 113 and 139 ff.
62 Diog.L. VI. 29 and 74. Cf. von Fritz, *op. cit.* pp. 22–7.
63 Cf. Philod. *op. cit.* col. 10.
64 Weapons: Philod. *op. cit.* col. 14 (ἀχρηστία τῶν ὅπλων). Currency: Athenaeus, IV. 159c; Philod. *ibid.* (from the *Politeia*).
65 Diog.L. VI. 38—a quotation from a now unknown tragedy.

66 Cicero, *Tusc. Quaest.* v. 37. 108; Plutarch, *De Exilio*, 5; Epictetus, *Diss.* i. 9.1.
67 Diog.L. vi. 85, reading περίρρυπος in the second line with Stephanus. The play of words on θύμος, 'thyme', and θυμός, 'strength', in the fifth line can hardly be reproduced in English: 'heartsease' is Dudley's suggestion. Hoïstad (*op. cit.* pp. 129–30, cf. 138–9) seems to miss the point of these lines.
68 *Lycurgus*, 31. 2. See p. 154 below on this passage.
69 Diog.L. vi. 35. But on this cf. von Fritz, *op. cit.* pp. 15–18.
70 Cf. Dudley, *op. cit.* p. 43.
71 I cannot agree with Hoïstad in placing this development much earlier.
72 Lucian: *Vit. Auct.* 8. Cf. Diog.L. vi. 4, 6; Stob. *Ecl.* iii. p. 462; Dio Chrys. viii. 7.
73 But according to Strabo (xv. 1. 54) Onesicritus expressed approval of the absence of slaves among the Indians.

CHAPTER IV

1 E. Schwartz, *Rhein. Mus.* (1885), pp. 223 ff. For criticism of Schwartz's view, cf. Badian, *Historia* (1958), pp. 433 ff.; Baldry, *J.H.S.* (1959), p. 13.
2 *Amer. J. Philol.* (1939), pp. 41–70; *Alexander the Great*, vol. ii, app. 25.
3 Questioned by Badian, *op. cit.* p. 426.
4 Arrian, *Anab.* vii. 8 ff. Other sources are Plutarch, *Alex.* 71; Curt. x. 2–3; Diod. xvii. 109; Just. xii. 11 ff.
5 vii. 11. 8–9. Trans. from Barker, *From Alexander to Constantine* (Oxford, 1956), pp. 5–6.
6 *Die Weltreichsidee Alexanders d. Grossen* (Freiburg, 1935), p. 18.
7 *Historia* (1953–4), p. 431.
8 *Die letzten Pläne Alexanders d. Grossen* (Berlin, 1937), p. 10, n. 6.
9 Εὔχετο δὲ τά τε ἄλλα ἀγαθὰ καὶ ὁμόνοιάν τε καὶ κοινωνίαν τῆς ἀρχῆς τοῖς τε Μακεδόσι καὶ Πέρσαις. On the interpretation of the Greek, cf. Badian, *op. cit.* pp. 430–1.
10 Strabo, i. 4. 9. Cf. Ehrenberg, *Alexander and the Greeks* (Blackwell, 1938), pp. 85 ff. See also pp. 169–71 below.
11 P. 99 above.
12 *Op. cit.* p. 435.
13 Rejection in practice, but not, apparently, rejection publicly announced, as Plutarch asserts (330c). If any statement on the subject by Alexander had been known to Strabo, he could not have speculated as he does about Alexander's intention.
14 Diod. xviii. 4. 4, finishing with the words: ὅπως τὰς μεγίστας ἠπείρους ταῖς ἐπιγαμίαις καὶ ταῖς οἰκειώσεσιν εἰς κοινὴν ὁμόνοιαν καὶ συγγενικὴν φιλίαν καταστήσῃ. Improbability: Tarn, *Alexander the Great*, vol. ii, pp. 383, 429. Authenticity supported: e.g. Berve, *Klio* (1938), pp. 163–6.

15 *Alexander the Great*, vol. II, p. 399. Cf. the beginning of *Alexander the Great and the Unity of Mankind* (1933).

16 *E.N.* 1155a16–22. Cf. p. 90 above.

17 50. Cf. p. 69 above.

18 *Yale Classical Studies* (1928), pp. 52–102.

19 Delatte, *Les Traités de la royauté d'Ecphante, Diotogène et Sthénidas* (Liège, 1942), reviewed by Goodenough in *Class. Philol.* (1949), pp. 129–31. Cf. also Skemp, *Plato's Statesman* (Routledge, 1952), p. 62; Sinclair, *History of Greek Political Thought* (Routledge, 1951), p. 301.

20 Cf. Athenaeus, III. 98 d–f; Strabo, VII, fr. 35; Clem. Alex. *Protr.* IV. 54. Tarn's reconstruction: *Alexander the Great and the Unity of Mankind*, pp. 21–4; *Alexander the Great*, vol. II, pp. 429–34. Here, as in most of his views of Alexander, Tarn is followed by Festugière: cf. *Le Dieu Cosmique* (Paris, 1949), pp. 191–2.

21 Cf. B. V. Head, *Historia Numorum* (2nd ed., Oxford, 1911), p. 206.

22 Athenaeus, III. 98e: ὁμάρμων πρόμοις γαθεῖν. Wilamowitz emended to ὁμαιμέων, Usener to ὁμαίμων, which Tarn adopts. Gulick's trans.: Loeb ed. *ad loc.*

23 *A History of Greece to 322 B.C.* (Oxford, 1959), p. 639.

24 *Social and Economic History of the Hellenistic World* (Oxford, 1941), vol. II, p. 1035.

25 *Op. cit.* p. 1053. Bactria seems to have been at any rate a partial exception to this general picture.

26 Within the vast area where Greeks settled; but there was, of course, still a sharp antithesis with the 'barbarians' who threatened parts of this area from without, especially the Gauls.

27 *A History of Greece to 322 B.C.*, p. 645.

28 *Hellenistic Civilisation* (3rd ed., Arnold, 1952), p. 79.

29 *Le Dieu Cosmique*, p. 176.

30 6: ἀπάνθρωπός τις ἄνθρωπος. For the meaning, cf. Jebb on Sophocles, fr. 1020.

31 Women: 932. Crowds: 7, 932. The mass: 484–5.

32 Cf. pp. 99 and 119 above and p. 169 below.

CHAPTER V

1 *Alexander and the Greeks*, pp. 92–5.

2 The word translated 'akin' in these quotations from Theophrastus is οἰκεῖος, here, though not always, close in meaning to συγγενής, with which it is combined three times in the second passage. I follow Pohlenz (*Grundfragen der stoischen Philosophie*, p. 47; *Die Stoa*, vol. II, pp. 65–6) and Brink (*Phronesis*, 1956, pp. 140–1) in believing that the doctrine of οἰκειότης here is to be distinguished from the doctrine of οἰκείωσις which developed

within the Stoic school: the latter was primarily psychological, related πρὸς ἑαυτόν, although Chrysippus applies it to relation to offspring (*Stoicorum Veterum Fragmenta*, III. 179). At a later stage the Peripatetic οἰκειότης was combined with the Stoic οἰκείωσις, thus extended to relationship to all mankind; and this combination could be represented as either Peripatetic or Stoic. To this phase belong Cicero, *De Fin.* v. 65–8 and Stobaeus, *Ecl.* II, pp. 116ff. Wachsmuth, too often treated as evidence for Theophrastus; and these will therefore be discussed later. Cf. below, pp. 191–4.

3 *Alexander the Great*, vol. II, p. 428.

4 *E.N.* 1155 a 16–22. Cf. p. 90 above. On Tarn's misinterpretation of this passage, cf. p. 123 above. Aristotle's words are φίλος and φιλία, but these are not far removed in meaning from οἰκεῖος and οἰκειότης.

5 *Pol.* 1256 b 23–7; *H.A.* 487 a 11 ff.; *E.N.* 1141 a 26.

6 Title: cf. Diog.L. v. 49. On Theophrastus' view of animals, cf. Brink, *Phronesis* (1956), pp. 128–31 and references there given.

7 Cf. Cicero, *ad Att.* II. 16. On the *Magna Moralia* as evidence for such a view among Peripatetics at this time, cf. Jaeger, *Aristotle*, 2nd ed., app. II.

8 *De Offic.* II. 5. 16. Fr. 24 Wehrli.

9 *De Abstinentia*, IV. 2. Fr. 49 Wehrli.

10 Geography: γῆς περίοδος, frs. 104–15 Wehrli. Chaldaeans and Egyptians: frs. 55–8.

11 *Divin. Instit.* III. 17. 42. In the second century A.D. Diogenes of Oenoanda expresses a different view (fr. 24 William), but this shows how the idea of one human family eventually became current in all the schools, rather than that it was accepted by Epicurus or his early followers. Cf. Festugière, *Epicurus and his Gods* (Blackwell, 1955), p. 92.

12 Cf. Plutarch, *Contr. Epicur. Beat.* 1098 c; *Adv. Colot.* 1125 d.

13 Cf. maxims 31 and 32; fr. 530 Usener. I agree with Bailey (*The Greek Atomists and Epicurus*, p. 512) that Bignone and Philippson are wrong in supposing that Epicurus believed in a 'natural justice'.

14 As Mr F. H. Sandbach points out to me, Epicurus is the only likely common source for Lucretius, v, and Diogenes of Oenoanda, cols. 10–11.

15 I. 8. 1–2. For the difference between this and Lucretius' version, see Guthrie, *In the Beginning*, pp. 77–8.

16 Fr. 107. Cf. p. 58 above.

17 *Op. cit.* p. 42.

18 *Sent. Vat.* 52, retaining ἡ φιλία with MSS.

19 Lines 12–13, trans. J. Adam. Cf. Heraclitus, fr. 64.

20 *De Nat. Deor.* II. 154. Cf. p. 189 below.

21 Diog.L. VII. 4. I have discussed Zeno's *Politeia* in more detail in *J.H.S.* (1959), pp. 3–15.

22 Περὶ Στωϊκῶν (Crönert), col. 15.

23 Plutarch, *Lycurgus*, 31. On the misinterpretation of this passage by von Arnim, Tarn and others, cf. *J.H.S.* (1959), p. 8. *Erōs* a god: Athenaeus, XIII 561 c.

24 Cf. Philod. Περὶ Στωϊκῶν (Crönert), col. 14: both Chrysippus and Diogenes wrote περὶ ἀχρηστίας τῶν ὅπλων. In Menander's *Dyskolos* (743–5), where the repentant Cnemon talks like a Cynic (or like Zeno), war is coupled with law-courts and prisons as due for abolition, if all followed his example of goodwill. Cf. p. 135 above.

25 Diog.L. VII. 124. Cf. Arist. *E.N.* 1159 b 29 ff.

26 Cf. *SVF*, III. 253.

27 329 a–b. For further discussion of this passage, including Tarn's contention that it does not refer to Zeno's book, see *J.H.S.* (1959), pp. 12–13. Cf. also p. 114 above on the alleged derivation of this passage from Eratosthenes. I have not attempted to reproduce in translation the pun between νομός and νόμος involved in the words ἀγέλης συννόμου νόμῳ κοινῷ συντρεφομένης.

28 That δήμους means 'peoples' and δημότας 'fellow-countrymen', rather than 'demes' and 'fellow-demesmen', is indicated by the use of δῆμον at I. 8 (330 d): ἕνα δῆμον ἀνθρώπους ἅπαντας ἀποφῆναι βουλόμενος.

29 Athenaeus, XIII. 561 c; Diog.L. VII. 33. Cf. *SVF*, I. 266.

30 274 e, cf. *Laws* 680 e. Cf. p. 77 above.

31 On Pohlenz's view that Zeno's ideal state was set in the distant past, cf. *J.H.S.* (1959), p. 7.

32 For more detailed discussion of the form of Zeno's book, cf. *J.H.S.* (1959), pp. 5–6.

33 *Op. cit.* col. 18.

34 *SVF*, II. 1153–4; III. 367, 371, 390, 462.

35 *SVF*, III. 627. As with many of the passages attributed to Chrysippus by von Arnim, there can be no certainty that this comes from him.

36 *Chrysippe et l'ancien Stoïcisme* (Paris, 1951), p. 266. Possibly one sequel to Zeno's *Politeia* is to be found in the story of Iambulus (Diod. II. 55–60), which contains so many parallels to it that one is tempted to regard the whole as a distorted and exaggerated version of the same ideal, recalling Zeno's picture in outline and general principles, though augmented with a fantastic medley of detail from many sources. Diodorus implies throughout, although he does not state, that all the inhabitants are σπουδαῖοι. Their ὁμοιότης is carried to the extreme by making them all physically alike (56. 2), and all wear clothes made from the same downy stuff (cotton?) and coloured with the same purple dye (59. 4). There is no rivalry among them, and they remain free from strife and always place the highest value on ὁμόνοια; and one means whereby they achieve this is the possession of women and children in common (58. 1). There is no reference to πόλεις among them: they live κατὰ συγγενείας καὶ συστήματα, not more than

400 in each (57. 1). There is no mention of temples, law-courts, or gymnasia. Other features might speculatively be used to fill some of the many gaps in our information about Zeno's Utopia. Whether the original author's intention was serious or satirical can hardly be judged from Diodorus' summary, and does not affect the possibility of a relationship to Zeno.

CHAPTER VI

1 Romulus: fr. 45 Jacoby. Endurance of pain: fr. 20. Plutarch, *De Alex. M. Fortuna aut Virtute* 330a, may also come from the *Geographica*, perhaps from the passage to which Strabo, I. 4. 9, refers. Cf. Badian, *Historia* (1958), p. 437.

2 v. 33. Cf. Walbank, *A Historical Commentary on Polybius* (Oxford, 1957), vol. I, p. 9.

3 VI. 56. Cf. x. 2.

4 VI. 56. Cf. Livy, XXVI. 22. 14: *si qua sit sapientium civitas quam docti fingunt magis quam norunt.*

5 *Aristotle*, Eng. trans., 2nd ed., p. 461.

6 Cf. pp. 142-4 above.

7 Geographical works: fr. 51 van Straaten. Attention to Plato, etc.: frs. 55, 57. Eruditissimus: *Pro Murena*, 66.

8 Cf. I. 107 ff. I cannot agree with Pohlenz (*Die Stoa*, vol. I, p. 201) that because of this attention to individual differences Panaetius goes further than the early Stoics in dividing mankind.

9 I. 34-5. Cf. *ibid.* 74-8.

10 *Stoics and Sceptics* (Oxford, 1913), p. 94.

11 *Op. cit.* p. 88.

12 I. 1. 3. Cf. I. 3. 6 and 6. 2.

13 Cf. Seneca, *Epist. Mor.* 90. 5.

14 On the relation of Piso's account to Antiochus, cf. Pohlenz, *Grundfragen der stoischen Philosophie* (Göttingen, 1940), pp. 47-81.

15 *De Fin.* v. 65. Cf. II. 45, probably also from Antiochus.

16 *Ecl.* II, pp. 116 ff. Wachsmuth. The two passages quoted are from pp. 120-1. On sources, cf. Wachsmuth *ad loc.*; Pohlenz, *Die Stoa*, vol. II, pp. 65-6; Brink, *Phronesis* (1956), p. 141.

17 E.g. p. 118, l. 12: φύσει γὰρ ᾠκειῶσθαι πρὸς ἑαυτόν.

18 Pindar, *Nem.* VI. 1. Cf. p. 30 above.

19 E.g. *De Offic.* III. 31 and 69.

20 Cf. p. 185 above.

21 *Ad Quint. Fratr.* I. 1. 27.

INDEX OF PASSAGES QUOTED
OR REFERRED TO

Fragments of the Pre-Socratics are numbered as in Diels–Kranz, *Die Fragmente der Vorsokratiker* (6th ed., 1951); other references are to the A sections of Diels–Kranz.

Fragments of the early Stoics are listed under *Stoicorum Veterum Fragmenta* (von Arnim).

Fragments of tragedy are numbered as in the second edition of Nauck, *Tragicorum Graecorum Fragmenta*.

GENERAL INDEX

Titles of works are given under their authors, but only where no particular passage from the work is cited.
Bold figures denote a main entry.

219

Menippus, 107, 108
μέροπες, 204 n. 6
Metrodorus, 147
Monimus, 105, 107
Morrow, G. R., 206 nn. 33, 34
Mühl, M., 206 n. 18
Mys, 151

Naucratis, 17
Nicolaus, 71
nomos, 19, 26, 37, 42–4, 51, 106
nous, 29, 91

oikeiōsis, 178–9, 182–3, 190, 209 n. 2
oikeiotēs, 143, 178–9, 182–3, 190, 209
n. 2, 210 n. 4
oikoumenē, 128, 130, 150, 153, 168, 169,
173, 175, 187
'Old Oligarch', 35, 56, 87
Olympic Games, 22, 54
Onesicritus, 208 n. 73
Opis, banquet at, 116, 117–21, 128
Ouranopolis, 124

Panaetius, 6, 166, 179–86, 190, 192, 194,
195
Panchaea, 125
Panhellenism, 22, 33, 43, 63, 66, 71
Pascal, 54
pax Romana, 201
Peloponnesian War, 28, 33, 62, 176
Pera, 109–11
Peripatetics, 103, 141–7, 149, 151, 168,
177–9, 180, 193
Persia and Persians, 18, 19, 20, 22–4,
33, 43, 64, 65, 66, 69, 70, 83, 117–19,
126–7
Persian Wars, 22, 27, 46, 83
philanthrōpia, 2, 71, 111
Philip of Macedon, 66, 87, 127, 133
Philippson, R., 210 n. 13
Philo, 5
philobarbaros, 47
Philodemus, 103, 106, 162
Phoenicians, 9, 10, 107, 151
phronēsis, 67, 92, 145
Phrygians, 32, 83
physis, 50, 106

Pindar, 19, 20, 30, 75
Plato, 2, 47, 53, 59, 60, 72–87, 88, 93,
96, 98, 105, 107, 108, 122, 147, 151,
154, 155, 156, 160, 162, 184, 190,
201; Apology, 55, 74, 105; Crito, 74;
Epistle VII, 74; Gorgias, 75, 81; Laws,
77, 80, 84, 122; Menexenus, 81, 122;
Phaedo, 55, 74; Protagoras, 39–43, 44;
Republic, 59, 64, 73, 76–8, 81, 91, 98,
122, 124, 153, 155, 161, 184; States-
man, 73, 79, 122, 146; Symposium,
155; Timaeus, 77
Plutarch, 99, 119–21, 127; Alexander
115; De Alexandri Magni Fortuna aut
Virtute, 113–14, 116, 126, 154, 155,
159–63
Pohlenz, M., 209 n. 2, 211 n. 31, 212
nn. 8, 14, 16
Polybius, 171–6, 177, 180, 181, 186–8
Porphyry, 142–4, 146
Posidonius, 6, 186–90, 194; Histories,
187; The Ocean, 187
Prometheus, 19, 30, 31, 40, 105
Protagoras, 39–42, 52, 55, 73, 110, 122,
144, 202
psychē, 53, 69, 73, 89
Punic Wars, 171, 174
Pythagoras, 28
Pythagoreans, 54, 56, 58, 73, 75, 77,
124
Pytheas, 128

racial divisions, 9, 21, 23, 62, 66, 69, 81,
84, 107, 127, 128, 131, 138, 140, 172;
see also barbarians
reason as characteristic of mankind, 12,
26–32, 40–1, 53–5, 73, 95, 111, 137,
151–3, 158, 164, 181, 183, 185, 196–8;
see also logos
Romulus, 171, 172
Rostovtzeff, M., 130, 132

Sandbach, F. H., 210 n. 14
Sappho, 21
Satyrus, 102, 103
scala naturae, 89
Sceptics, 164, 178, 195, 198

222